The Making of Monolingual Japan

MULTILINGUAL MATTERS
Series Editor: John Edwards, *St. Francis Xavier University, Canada*

Multilingual Matters series publishes books on bilingualism, bilingual education, immersion education, second language learning, language policy, multiculturalism. The editor is particularly interested in 'macro' level studies of language policies, language maintenance, language shift, language revival and language planning. Books in the series discuss the relationship between language in a broad sense and larger cultural issues, particularly identity related ones.

Full details of all the books in this series and of all our other publications can be found on http://www.multilingual-matters.com, or by writing to Multilingual Matters, St Nicholas House, 31–34 High Street, Bristol BS1 2AW, UK.

MULTILINGUAL MATTERS
Series Editor: John Edwards, *St. Francis Xavier University, Canada*

The Making of Monolingual Japan

Language Ideology and Japanese Modernity

Patrick Heinrich

MULTILINGUAL MATTERS
Bristol • Buffalo • Toronto

For Rossella

Library of Congress Cataloging in Publication Data
A catalog record for this book is available from the Library of Congress.
Heinrich, Patrick.
The Making of Monolingual Japan/Patrick Heinrich.
Multilingual Matters: 146
Includes bibliographical references and index.
1. Language and languages—Study and teaching—Japan. 2. Second language acquisition–Japan. 3. Language and languages—Variation—Japan. 4. Linguistics—Study and teaching—Japan. 5. English language—Japan. 6. Language and culture—Japan. 7. Japan—Languages.
I. Title.
P57.J3H45 2012
306.44'952–dc23 2011048971

British Library Cataloguing in Publication Data
A catalogue entry for this book is available from the British Library.

ISBN-13: 978-1-84769-657-1 (hbk)
ISBN-13: 978-1-84769-656-4 (pbk)

Multilingual Matters
UK: St Nicholas House, 31–34 High Street, Bristol BS1 2AW, UK.
USA: UTP, 2250 Military Road, Tonawanda, NY 14150, USA.
Canada: UTP, 5201 Dufferin Street, North York, Ontario M3H 5T8, Canada.

Copyright © 2012 Patrick Heinrich.

All rights reserved. No part of this work may be reproduced in any form or by any means without permission in writing from the publisher.

The policy of Multilingual Matters/Channel View Publications is to use papers that are natural, renewable and recyclable products, made from wood grown in sustainable forests. In the manufacturing process of our books, and to further support our policy, preference is given to printers that have FSC and PEFC Chain of Custody certification. The FSC and/or PEFC logos will appear on those books where full certification has been granted to the printer concerned.

Typeset by Techset Composition Ltd., Salisbury, UK.
Printed and bound in Great Britain by the MPG Books Group.

Contents

Preface		vii
1	Language Ideology as a Field of Enquiry	1
	Overcome by Modernity	3
	The Study of Ideology	9
	The Study of Language Ideology	12
2	The Call of Mori Arinori to Replace Japanese	21
	Mori's Proposal	22
	Reactions	31
3	The Creation of a Modern Voice	42
	The *genbun itchi* Movement	43
	The *Bun* Debate	48
4	The Unification of Japanese	59
	Ueda Kazutoshi: Japan's First Modern Linguist	60
	The National Language Research Council	70
5	The Linguistic Assimilation of Ryukyuans and Ainu	83
	Japanese Language Spread in the Ryukyu Islands between 1868 and 1945	84
	Japanese Language Spread in Ainu Mosir between 1868 and 1945	93
	Japanese Language Spread in the Ryukyu Islands under US Occupation	99
	Japanese Language Spread from Within	103
6	The Most Beautiful Language in the World	107
	Kokugo Mondai: The National Language Problem	108
	Language Ideology in Shiga's Proposal	114

7	Language Ideology as Self-Fulfilling Prophecy	122
	The Great Dialect Debate	124
	The Progressive Erasure of Ryukyuan Languages	132
	Language Shifts among Indigenous Linguistic Minorities in Japan	138
8	Current Challenges to Modernist Language Ideology	150
	The Case of Autochthonous Minorities	151
	The Case of Allochthonous Minorities	161
9	Language Ideology in 21st-century Japan	172
	The Fundamental Ideological Entities of *Kokugo*	172
	How Language Ideological Entities Evolved	173
	The Impact of Modernist Language Ideology	174
	Examining the Linguistic Consequences of Modernity	177
	The Difference between Claiming and Practising Equality	179
	References	183
	Index	202

Preface

This book is the result of several years of research into the languages of Japan as part of Japan's history of thought. My interest in this topic began with a study of the reception of western linguistics in modern Japan for my PhD thesis, through which I came to understand that linguistics did not evolve in a vacuum but sought to provide solutions to problems exceeding those of language *tout court*. In Japan, there is a small branch of linguistics dedicated to what is called *kokugo mondai* (problems of national language). Having dealt with the very broad topic of the reception of western linguistics, I decided to restrict my research to *kokugo mondai* for a while. I can still remember the first time I came across the small section on *kokugo mondai* at the library of the National Institute for Japanese Language in Tokyo. At the time, I was due to take a position at Duisburg University as an assistant to Florian Coulmas, and so I quickly wrote down the titles of all the books on *kokugo mondai* on the shelves there, with the intention of writing something on this issue during my time at Duisburg. I have long since left Duisburg, and so I can safely say that the topic demanded far more attention than the few books on the shelves at the National Institute for Japanese Language suggested. For this is more than just a book about the problems of a national language in Japan – it is about the problems caused by the idea of a national language too. In writing this book, it was not finding material that proved difficult, but deciding on how best to present what material. Undoing ideology demands the conscious questioning of ontological knowledge, but it is not easy to produce academic work on such shaky ground.

Many people have helped me in forming the ideas behind this book. Above all, I am most indebted to my teachers Florian Coulmas, J.V. Neustupný and Josef Kreiner, and their influence is written all over the book. Inoue Fumio, Takaesu Yoriko, Miyara Shinsho and Ishihara Masahide were my hosts during prolonged research visits to Japan, during which times I studied matters that found their way into this book. In Duisburg, Sugita Yuko and Imai Jun discussed many of the issues presented here with me, and in Uchinaa (Okinawa), Fija Byron was an important source of support and friendship. Michael Cresswell helped me to finish the manuscript and provided much needed encouragement while it was being written, and Scott Saft generously supported me while making revisions. Peter Backhaus remembered me saying that I wanted to write a book on ideology, and took the picture that appears on the front cover while studying Tokyo's linguistic landscape. I have given dozens of talks at various conferences on matters relating to language ideology, and so it would be impossible to list all those who have contributed in one form or another to the present study, but all contributions were gratefully received. My research into language ideology was supported by scholarships from the Japanese Society for the Promotion of Science, the German Science Foundation (DFG), the German Academic Exchange Program (DAAD), the Japan Foundation and the Humboldt Foundation. Their kind support, too, was very much appreciated. I am also grateful to the anonymous reviewers for their helpful comments, to John Edwards for having this book be part of his series, and at Multilingual Matters to Anna Roderick for overseeing the process that turned a manuscript into a book.

A brief word on conventions. Japanese words are transcribed in the modified Hepburn system, while Japanese names are given in the traditional manner of family name first. Okinawa is termed as 'Uchinaa' here, as in the local language, because many of my friends and colleagues there were uncomfortable with the Japanese term 'Okinawa'. It remains in place, of course, for designations such as Okinawa Prefecture. All translations into English are mine unless otherwise accredited. Tradition also dictates that I hereby declare all remaining errors and inadequacies mine.

Finally, let me acknowledge that taking so many years to write one book does not come without its share of problems. I had to move several times to take up new positions, and while that was fine with me, it was a burden on my family. That they never wavered in their support for me has truly humbled me. My son Stephen is cool enough to still tease me for taking such a long time to write such a short book, but I know my wife Rossella will be more proud of this work than I will ever be. I shall dedicate it to her.

Patrick Heinrich
Sicily, Summer 2011

1 Language Ideology as a Field of Enquiry

Language ideology is an ever-present component of our communicative behaviour, for it regulates the way we talk. Yet this is something of which most of us are unaware, and so we assume our linguistic choices and attitudes to be entirely natural. The term 'ideology' is therefore a fitting one, and while language ideology escapes the attention of many of us most of the time, once one purposefully starts looking for it one encounters it everywhere. Consider the following examples of language ideology at work in Japan.

On 18 January 2000, a consultation body organized by the late Prime Minister Obuchi Keizō published a booklet which proposed the establishment of English as a second official language in Japan. In the resultant discussion on the appropriateness of such a proposal, linguist Tanaka Katsuhiko (2000) drew attention to the fact that Japan does not actually have a first official language.

On 20 February 2009, the evening edition of the daily newspaper *Asahi shinbun* led with the headline, 'Hachijo Language'?, followed by the statements, 'UNESCO: 2,500 languages world-wide threatened by extinction', 'Eight languages in Japan endangered' and 'Also [Japanese] dialects are independent languages'. Such was the response of Japan's most influential newspaper to the publication of the latest UNESCO *Atlas of the World's Languages in Danger*, which identified eight endangered languages in Japan (UNESCO, 2009).

On 26 May 2009, colleagues and friends of mine met at my office at the University of the Ryukyus. Frustrated by the lack of a language policy supportive of Ryukyuan languages, radio presenter Fija Byron commented, 'if we had a governor who said, all of a sudden, 'From now on, I will speak only Uchinaaguchi' (Okinawan)...Someone with that kind of faith...That would be it'!

In February 2009, Florian Coulmas handed me a copy of Tomasz Kamusella's *The Politics of Language and Nationalism in Modern Central Europe* and asked me for a review. On the plane from Tokyo back to Naha, I read Kamusella's words:

> The most ethno-linguistically homogenous nation-states (that is, almost without any native speakers of other languages than the national) are Iceland, Japan, and Poland. In the cases of Iceland and Japan, this unusual homogeneity was achieved by the long lasting maritime isolation of both parties. (Kamusella, 2009: 60)

It is easy to find such conflicting attitudes and opinions when dealing with the issue of language in Japan, yet few people take the time to consider the reasons for this incongruity, where it originated and how it might be resolved. Here, the issue of language ideology is crucial. As will be demonstrated in the course of this book, incongruity arises from the fact that the dominant language ideology in Japan is far removed from the country's sociolinguistic situation. To understand this disparity, we must trace the social and historical genealogy of dominant ideas about language in Japan, for by doing so we will find that there is a single ideology present in all the vignettes above which was proliferated towards the end of the 19th century. The idea is that of language nationalism. Of course, language nationalism is in no way unique to Japan, nor is it exceptional that the creation of a modern nation-state following the Meiji restoration of 1868 necessitated the establishment of a national language for Japan. That said, however, the events recounted in this book are in many ways unique. The implementation of language nationalism, its adaption to the Japanese socio-political and linguistic context, and the impact on the linguistic situation of present-day Japan will be dealt with in the chapters that follow.

The significance of studying language ideology encompasses the field of history of thought, to which this topic might be most closely related. Three reasons will be shown to be relevant for a consideration of language ideology for all orientations of linguistics. Firstly, all ideologies emerge in specific socio-cultural conditions and thus do not form an appropriate base for a general linguistics worthy of that name. Secondly, these conditions grow quickly obsolete due to the normalization of ideological claims. Hence, ideologies pass as fact and appear to be common-sensical and natural, and they are usually also shared by linguists. Thirdly, language ideology influences the sociolinguistic realities on the ground in making them more similar to ideological claims. In brief, linguistics is involved in changing sociolinguistic situations due to its negligence of the socio-cultural conditions under which ideologies are created. This results in confusing ideological claims for fact, and hence, in further support for ideology. Since the basis of dominating ideology is power, linguistics will be shown in this book to assist in changing the sociolinguistic situation in ways which are beneficial to powerful actors. This book will also make clear that non-idelogical linguistics is not possible, and it will be argued that power-based ideologies should be replaced by ideologies based on cultural liberty and solidarity.

In considering the importance of language ideology to the creation and spread of a 'national language', we will look in this book at (1) the fundamental ideological entities of *kokugo* (national language) in Japan; (2) their evolution; and (3) their impact. We will thus attempt both to trace the ideological genesis of the ontology of *kokugo*, and to reveal the impact of *kokugo* ideology on Japanese society. Chapters 2–4 deal with language ideology and the creation of *kokugo*. In Chapters 5–7, we will turn our attention to the ways language ideology functions. Chapter 8 highlights contemporary attitudes and challenges to the legacy of *kokugo* ideology in late-modern Japan. In Chapter 9, we will return to the three central considerations outlined above, and discuss language ideology as a generative principle which constantly creates new meaning as contexts evolve. Given the scope of this book, it is perhaps appropriate to begin with a brief review of modernization as it occurred in Japan, and also to introduce some of the fundamentals of language ideology study, by way of preparing the ground for a more detailed discussion which will follow.

Overcome by Modernity

Following the reopening of Japan to contact with the outside world as enforced by Commodore Matthew Perry (1794–1858), Japan was suddenly and involuntarily faced with a need to define its place in the modern world. Japan's transformation into a modernized state required the formation of a new cultural and linguistic consciousness, something for which its feudal society was quite ill prepared. Identity and loyalty were shifted from pre-modern feudal domains to the emerging state, the modernization of Japan thus redefining the inhabitants of old Japanese provinces as Japanese nationals. A common notion of Japanese identity had quite simply not existed before the Meiji restoration of 1868 (Gluck, 1985). Writing in 1875, enlightenment scholar Fukuzawa Yukichi (1835–1901) wrote (quoted from Craig, 1968: 118–119), 'I would say that though there is a government in Japan, there is no nation.' As in every other part of the modern world, internal differences were suppressed whilst difference from the outside world was highlighted in order to define, and thereby create, the idea of a Japanese nation.

At the outset, the internal linguistic situation was one of great variety. Nanette Twine ascertains that prior to the modernization of Japan, local dialects served as linguistic standards within

> each feudal domain [...], fulfilling the primary function of language, that is communication. Farmers, fishermen, and forestry workers had no need of any other medium of communication, since restrictions on travel made it unlikely that they would have much occasion to converse with speakers of other dialects. (Twine, 1988: 435)

In other words, a unitary national language had not existed prior to Japanese modernization precisely because there was no need for one. This is crucial because, in contrast to Benedict Anderson's (1991) view that national languages were a resource for nation building which had previously lain dormant, in fact, such national languages did not come into existence by themselves. National languages are – like nations – ideological constructs. The idea of Japanese as a national language was thus actively and purposefully created in response to the very specific requirements of Japanese modernization.

As the first non-western country to join the modern world, Japan's situation was always going to be different from that experienced elsewhere. Due to the enforced opening of the country to the outside world, Japan had both to establish unity within its own borders and to restore the self-esteem of its own people vis-à-vis the outside. The struggle of Japan to gain both autonomy and respect from the west was not limited to fields such as economy, politics and culture, but included language as well. In order to be seen as a legitimate power by the western world – and thereby avoid colonization – the young Meiji government sought to demonstrate that Japan's society, culture, education and language was just as developed as that of countries in the west. Japanese modernization thus required the creation and proliferation of a unitary Japanese language, one comparable to the standardized national languages of the western world. This was no easy task. Hirai Masao's (1998: 477–497) *History of Problems of the National Language and Script* (*Kokugo kokuji mondai no rekishi*) details no less than 343 language planning schemes proposed in the Meiji period (1868–1912) alone.

The Idea of a Unitary Language

Let us consider the idea of a unitary national language in Japan in more detail. In Japanese 'national language' is called *kokugo*, a term generated from the two Chinese characters denoting 'country' and 'language'. According to the *Comprehensive Dictionary of the National Language* (*Kokugo daijiten*), *kokugo* refers to the following four concepts: (1) the official language or common language of a country; (2) Japanese as the language of Japan; (3) a Japanese word or a word not borrowed; and (4) a subject taught at school. It is important to note here that the second and fourth definitions emerged only during the course of Japanese modernization (Yasuda, 1997b: 29–30). The entry 'national language' in the *Comprehensive Dictionary of National Linguistics* (*Kokugogaku daijiten*) confirms the semantic expansion of this term. It states:

> [Following the Meiji restoration], the perception of Japanese shifted from the idea that one's language is the index of one's native province (*kotoba wa kuni no tegata*), that is to say, from different languages in each feudal domain, to the idea that Japanese is the language of the state, and what is called national language (*kokugo*) came into existence. (Kokugo Gakkai, 1980: 861)

The term *kokugo* as national language thus designates something that had not existed in pre-modern Japan. National languages are modernist ideological constructs, and the case of Japan does not constitute a deviation from this definition.

The idea of national language as we know it today was not developed in Japan, however. Its origin is historically tied to the emergence of the European nation-states and to their efforts to establish a common identity through one national language by one specific name. Examples of this are German, French, Russian or Italian. Johann Gottfried Herder (1744–1803) was the first to use the term national language (*Nationalsprache*), and was influential in the popularization of the idea of an isomorphism of language and nation (Ising, 1987: 335). Herder and other German philologists such as Wilhelm von Humboldt (1767–1835) argued that language was one of the conditions that formed a nation, in the same way as climate, religion or political systems do (Coulmas, 1997). By relating language to the world-view and collective identity of a nation, an ideological construct was established in which variation of language within a nation was downplayed, if not forcibly suppressed. It is for this reason that national languages are represented by – if not equated with – their standard varieties. As an effect, the term national language should not be taken at face value, nor too should that of standard language. Standardization, in the sense of creating a homogenous speech community, is an impossible undertaking as variation in spoken language is irrepressible (Joseph & Taylor, 1990; Milroy & Milroy, 1985).

The fact that national language and standard language are ideological constructs does not mean that they bear no relation to the sociolinguistic field they claim to represent. The establishment of standardized national languages has far-reaching effects on the sociolinguistic field. James Milroy writes the following on this issue:

> The establishment of the idea of a standard variety, the diffusion of knowledge of this variety, its codification in widely used grammar books and dictionaries, and its promotion in a wide range of functions – all lead to the devaluing of other varieties. The standard form becomes the legitimate form, and other forms become, in the popular mind, illegitimate, because, of course, it is important that a standard language, being the language of the state and, sometimes, a great empire, should share the (glorious) history of that nation state. (Milroy, 2001: 547)

With regard to Japanese, Yasuda Toshiaki (1999a: 34–35) comes to similar conclusions, drawing attention to the fact that local varieties of Japanese became representative of backwardness after the Meiji restoration.

Standardized national languages have to provide for what Paul Kroskrity (2000: 28) calls 'the horizontal camaraderie of citizenship in a nation state'. As powerful symbols of nationhood, national languages take their particular shape as a result of discursive solutions to the historical, social and political contexts from which they emerge. Grammarians, lexicographers, teachers and so on need to respond to the broader socio-political contexts in which they pursue the task of standardizing and codifying language (Jernudd & Neustupný, 1987). Let us therefore turn our attention next to some of the problems faced by Japan, which will be discussed in more detail in Chapters 2–4.

Problems and Tasks of Japanese Language Modernization

Even the most basic grasp of mathematics will support the claim that linguistic nationalism is ideology, for whilst there are more than 6000 languages in the world, there are only 200 states. That is to say, the proportion of languages to nation-states is roughly 30 to 1, which means that the vast majority of states are multilingual. Japan is no exception. In order to join the modern world and create 'the Japanese' as an imagined community, Japan invented itself as monolingual, a process which required suppression of linguistic diversity. However, the problem posed to the state by linguistic minorities was not seen as important until the early 20th century, by which time the modernization of Japanese had largely been achieved and national language been spread to all but the peripheries of the Meiji state. Thus, the issue of linguistic diversity was left alone, whilst other, more pressing issues of linguistic modernization, were dealt with. One such issue was diglossia, whilst another was the widely held view that only western languages could be developed into standardized modern languages. Let us therefore briefly review these two issues.

As in many other countries, one of the most important undertakings of linguistic modernization in Japan was the dissolution of diglossia. In diglossic situations, the high variety (H) cannot be exchanged for the low variety (L) in order to signal social distance or proximity. According to Charles Ferguson (1959: 338), three developments contribute to a decline of diglossia: (1) increasingly widespread literacy; (2) increasing communication over geographical distances; and (3) the desire to establish a standard language. Most important, however, is that the dissolution of diglossia requires that those proficient in the H-variety take part in the establishment of the L-variety for all uses, including writing. Although proficiency of the H-variety corresponded to the group of the educated elite in Japan, the H-variety was used exclusively for the written form of the language. The various written styles (*bungo-tai*) with Sino-Japanese (*kanbun*) at the apex were never used in any other context but writing by anyone at any time, nor did they constitute a native language to anyone. The only way to acquire the H-variety was through formal education. The complementary distribution between H and L had been very stable; neither were written forms ever intended to be used as spoken language, nor were spoken forms considered suitable for serious writing before the 1870s, with very few exceptions (see Carroll, 2001; Seeley, 1991; Twine, 1991 for details).

In its attempts at language modernization, Japan was also forced to confront the western perception of Indo-European languages as constituting the top of a linguistic hierarchy, one in which Japanese was placed far below. Edward Said's (1978: 40) dictum that the west saw the Orient as 'irrational, depraved (fallen), childlike, "different"; thus that European is rational, virtuous, mature, "normal"' was manifested in western perceptions of oriental languages too. Paul Garvin stresses this point in stating that:

> Traditionally linguistics used to distinguish languages such as those of Europe from primitive languages such as those of the native populations of the different regions of the world that were colonized by Europeans. According to this tradition, only civilized languages are capable of a standardization process, while the so-called primitive languages are destined to remain underdeveloped since they do not have the inherent potential for the development of the attributes required for modernization. (Garvin, 1993: 45)

In addition to the existence of that ideology in which the character of a nation is seen as being embodied in its national language, and that in which the Orient is seen as in every way in opposition to the west, representations of the Japanese language as childlike, immature, primitive, peculiar, undeveloped and lacking grammatical rules may be found in various western accounts of the 19th century (see Mühlhäusler, 1996 for a discussion of the Pacific context). An essay by the German missionary Carl Munzinger (1894) on the psychology of the Japanese language illustrates this clearly. Consider the following extracts from Munzinger's work:

> How often can one hear people sighting about the insurmountable difficulties of the Japanese grammar, its constant deviation of all grammatical rules of the west! However, those who lament in this way are mistaken and fail to recognize the quintessence of the matter. In reality, we are not dealing with particular or unnumbered deviations from our grammar – we are not dealing with grammatical forms and formulas. More accurately, the Japanese grammar is very simple because the Japanese language is not very developed with regard to grammar. What we are dealing with is the thought, the spirit, the completely different way of expression of an antipode people, a foreign race. (Munzinger, 1894: 105)

> It suffices to remark here that the Japanese idiom is more illustrative and vivid, whereas the Indogermanic [...] is deeper and more concise. (Munzinger, 1894: 114)

In seeking to explain why European children are able to learn Japanese so quickly, Munzinger claims that:

> The true reason however [other than the simple pronunciation of Japanese words P.H.], which is at least as important, is the fact that the Japanese idiom is on a par with the idiom of a child. It conforms much more to a child's capacity and point of view than it does with our matured and developed languages. (Munzinger, 1894: 127)

> The educated German or Englishman hardly perceives a difference whether he expresses himself by using the active or the passive. The German peasant on the other hand perceives it and will always prefer the active, 'It has been decided in the Imperial Diet' sounds too inconvenient – 'They have decided in the Imperial Diet' [...] is more familiar to him. Such is the case in Japanese for the language across the entire population. (Munzinger, 1894: 132)

> In its present form, the Japanese language is incapable of becoming the bearer of modern Japanese culture. (Munzinger, 1894: 141)

Thus, one of the most important undertakings of the Meiji Japanese language planners was to liberate Japanese from such prejudice. Scholars of the Japanese enlightenment set out to prove that Japanese could be developed in the same way as western languages. This required the forging of an empowering language ideology, and a reframing of the perception whether the Japanese language was suited to the requirements of modern age. So let us now turn our attention to the study of ideology, and the relationship between ideology and empowerment.

The Study of Ideology

The brief summary of the study of ideology below will centre on those approaches and developments which serve the present study best. We will follow this with an investigation of existing approaches to the study of language ideology, before deciding which of the many perspectives is most suited to this book. For more detailed accounts of the study of ideology see Boudon (1988), Eagleton (1991), Geuss (1981) and Thompson (1984, 1990).

Historical Development of Ideology Studies

Attempts to study the way in which thoughts are structured and connected with epistemology, ontology and social practices predates the coining, in 1796, of the term 'ideology' by Destutt de Tracy (1754–1836). Precursors to the discipline of ideology studies were such intellectual key figures as Francis Bacon (1561–1626), John Locke (1632–1704), David Hume (1711–1776) or Étienne de Condillac (1715–1780). Not until de Tracy, however, did the study of ideology attain a critical tone, for it was he who first gave voice to the notion that such groups as the clergy were deliberately engaged in the distortion of truth for their own benefit. In so doing, this new direction of study dismissed contradictory ideas as unscientific or non-sensical. Such ideas, de Tracy argued, should be discredited, overcome and replaced, and he argued strongly in favour of secular mass education towards achieving this end, which he believed would prevent the intentional distortion of facts by members of the elite seeking to sustain their own privilege. Unsurprisingly, his ideas were not entirely popular. Furthermore, de Tracy's atheism and laic beliefs, as well as his affiliation to republicans, presented a latent threat to the autocratic ambitions of Napoleon Bonaparte (1769–1821). Following the re-establishment of the Catholic Church in France in 1801 (French Concordat), Napoleon started deriding ideologues as day-dreamers and visionaries – in fact, it was through Napoleon that the term ideology first attained its pejorative denotation, that is referring to ideas perceived to be unrealistic, abstract, impractical and elitist.

In Germany, Ludwig Feuerbach (1804–1872) drew on French criticism of religion and religious institutions. His aim, similar to that of de Tracy, was to expose what he perceived to be religion's oppressive influence over mankind. Feuerbach argued that reason should liberate mankind from the restrictions imposed by religion. In so doing, he provided an important impetus for subsequent studies of ideology in Germany, most notably for the work of Karl Marx (1818–1883) and Friedrich Engels (1820–1895). In *German Ideology*, Marx and Engels famously contested Feuerbach's idea of autonomy of reason. They claimed that consciousness is materially conditioned, and therefore that it is impossible for classes subjugated through ideology to successfully contest oppressive ideology and achieve emancipation. Marx and Engels' materialistic notion of history and society thus contradicted the beliefs articulated by Feuerbach. In their opinion, directly confronting the circumstances which had given rise to ideology were the only means to rid oneself of oppression, for they believed ideological thought to be socially determined, while hiding – at the same time – the interests that ideology serves. In a sense, Marx and Engels developed the pejorative Napoleonic view of ideology into a theoretical framework, and from there into a critical political programme.

Karl Mannheim (1893–1947) further shifted the emphasis away from the influence of ideology on thought to the social structures which give rise to ideology. He attempted to expand the study of ideology into a non-partisan investigation of the social and historic determination of knowledge, and to liberate ideology from political struggles over the distribution of authority and power which were so prominent a feature of the work of Marx and Engels. To this end, Mannheim differentiated between particular ideology and total ideology, the former referring to ideas not shared among political opponents (e.g. bourgeois ideology to Marxists), the latter being the total structure of consciousness of a specific social group at a particular period of time. According to the concept of total ideology, all thought is interested, and, as a consequence, all thought is ideological. Mannheim thus asserted that everyone responds to ideological pressures all the time, and thus, that ideology penetrates every aspect of human life. Accordingly, the study of ideology should aim at a conscious dissociation from established, initialized world-views and thought patterns, in order that these may be connected to the social structures in which they originated.

Another approach worth considering is that of Vladimir Ilyich Lenin (1870–1924), who saw ideology as a potent tool for self-empowerment. Departing from the belief that the prevailing ideologies were not appropriate to the interests of the working class, Lenin asserted that more appropriate ideologies must be purposefully crafted, the ultimate aim being to satisfy the particular wants, needs and interests of the working class. A similar view of ideology as an effective tool for self-empowerment may be found in the work of Georg Lukács (1885–1971), who emphasized the need for the proletariat to develop their own ideology. Lenin and Lukács thus extended the reach of ideology, giving it the power to promote the interests of any group or class engaged in social conflict.

Classifying Approaches to the Study of Ideology

In order to determine which approach is most appropriate to the study of language ideology, it is important to take those studies into account which classify existing approaches. In an important work on the subject, French sociologist Raymond Boudon (1988: 75–95) identifies four differing approaches. He first draws a line between what he calls 'traditional conceptions', that is to say, approaches where ideology is subjected to the criteria of truth, and 'modern conceptions', those in which ideology is defined by its aptitude to create meaningful interpretations. Boudon then makes a distinction between 'rational' and 'irrational' explanations of ideology. Approaches classified as irrational basically account for the emergence of ideology by considering psychological and physiological aspects. Rational approaches, on the other hand, explain ideology by recurrence on the social context from which they emerge. Boudon (1988: 76) characterizes these four approaches as follows:

(1) Ideologies are neither true, nor the result of (psychological or physiological) forces which cannot be controlled.
(2) Ideologies are not true, but their creation and acceptance is understandable.
(3) Ideologies are sense-making, and the result of forces which cannot be controlled.
(4) Ideologies are sense-making and their creation and acceptance is traceable.

In his discussion of the above, Boudon (1988: 23) argues in support of the fourth approach, and identifies Karl Mannheim's work as its best example.

Another classification of ideology, by US philosopher Raymond Geuss (1981: 4–26), sheds further light on the issue of ordering the many possible directions of ideology study. Geuss identifies three categories: (1) descriptive approaches to the study of ideology; (2) pejorative approaches to the study of ideology; and (3) positive approaches to the study of ideology.

According to Geuss, descriptive approaches (1) are those often labelled as neutral, non-evaluative or total, for example, the study of ideology in anthropology. Descriptive approaches to ideology are mainly concerned with cultural systems of ideology, in which concepts, attitudes and social dispositions are studied in a non-evaluative way. Such descriptions may be concerned with values, religion, works of art, or with language. Pejorative approaches (2) are those otherwise labelled as critical, particular or negative, those which characterize ideology as delusional rationalizations and false beliefs, as in the Marxist tradition. From such a standpoint (Geuss, 1981: 21), 'the term "ideology" is used [...] to criticise a form of consciousness because it incorporates beliefs which are false, or because it functions in a reprehensible way, or because it has a tainted origin'. Following such a line of thought, ideology is always conceived of as 'the thought of the other', and describing ideas as ideological implies criticism. Pejorative approaches focus on the ways in which ideologies distort and confuse, invariably at the expense of truth, and of the less privileged. Finally, positive approaches to the study of ideology (3) highlight the capacity of ideology to inspire specific groups to pursue their interests, a direction of study exemplified by Georg Lukács. Positive ideology is aware of the desire to create meaningful and positive collective identities. This kind of ideology results from attempts to structure beliefs, society and language in a profitable way. Ideology in this sense is, as Raymond Geuss (1981: 23) puts it, une *'verité à faire'* – a truth to be crafted. Studying ideology in this way is not pejorative. Where it differs from the descriptive approach, however, is that it emphasizes the usefulness of ideology in the realization of desirable goals. Accordingly, this approach will be termed as 'empowering' henceforth.

Before turning to an inspection of language ideology, however, let us first summarize our findings so far. In reviewing the most important developments in the study of ideology, we have seen that ideas are neither neutral nor unbiased. Furthermore, the study of ideology has, from the outset, attempted to come closer to the end of either assessing the world more objectively, or of purposefully making use of ideology to instigate social and political change. Let us now consider some seminal works of the study of language ideology next.

The Study of Language Ideology

Despite increased usage of the term 'language ideology' in publications from the 1990s onwards (Koerner, 2001: 254), there exists no consensus on how to best pursue its study. As a reaction to this, some prominent scholars in the field have sought to provide comprehensive overviews.

Of these, one of the most important was compiled by Kathryn Woolard. Woolard (1998: 4) identifies three main approaches to the study of language ideology and gives specific examples for each: (1) Language ideology as being concerned with different cultures of language ideologies and their mutual interrelation to language structure. The most notable example of this pragmatic approach is the work of Michael Silverstein (1976, 1979, 1993). (2) Language ideology as a field of study in which the role of language ideology in language contact, or contact between language varieties, is investigated. Several prominent sociolinguists have contributed to research along these lines, for example, Heath (1989, 1991), Hill and Hill (1986) and Milroy and Milroy (1985). (3) Language ideology as a field of study devoted to exposing the role of language ideology in historical investigations into public or academic discourses. Such works are either located within the context of historical sociolinguistics, or else in the historiography of linguistics. Important contributions include those made by Joseph and Taylor (1990), Hutton (2001) and Koerner (1993, 2001).

Paul Kroskrity (2000: 8–23) has provided another influential overview of the field. He identifies four approaches and their representatives: (1) The study of language ideologies pursued in connection to specific interests of social and cultural groups. Works include Briggs (1998), Errington (1998), Irvine and Gal (2000) or Woolard (1985); (2) Language ideology studies involved in investigations of multiple language ideologies within socio-cultural groups, for example, those of Errington (2000), Gal (1992) and Hill (1998); (3) Language ideology engaged in differing degrees of awareness to language ideologies between individual members of a speech community, at specific sites, or with regard to specific aspects of language. This approach is usually associated with the works of Silverstein (1979), Phillips (2000) and Kroskrity (1998); and (4) Finally, a study of language ideology that looks at how inconsistencies arising from different social structures and forms of talk are mediated or bridged, such as the work of Irvine and Gal (2000), and Silverstein (1985).

In Japan, the study of language ideology is both less prominent, and also less well developed. It has largely been focused on two specific issues so far: (1) historical investigations into language ideology, in particular Japanese language imperialism, and (2) the language of Japanese women. While contributions to the historical investigation of language – for example, Tanaka (1978, 1989, 1997), Lee (1996), Yasuda (1999a, 2000a) and Masiko (1997) – and language imperialism – Kawamura (1994), Lee (1996), Lee (2002), Matsunaga (2002), Osa (1998), Shi (1993), Tani (2000), Yasuda (1997a, 1997b, 1999b) – are mostly written in Japanese, work on the language of women has more often been published in English; see Abe (2000), Fair (1996), Ide (1999), Inoue (1996, 2003, 2006), Kondo (1990), Ohara (1999) or

Okamoto (1995). Under the classification proposed by Kathryn Woolard, Japanese works of historical investigations fall into the category of historiography of linguistics. They are harder to place within Paul Kroskrity's framework, which is more concerned with approaches of linguistic anthropology. In the works focused on women's language, we can see two different perspectives on the Japanese context, the first being linguistic anthropology (e.g. Inoue, 1996), the second, critical linguistics (e.g. Ohara, 1999). The Japanese tradition of women's language studies cannot be easily assigned to any of Woolard's categories, but within Kroskrity's system, either approach aligns, at least partly, within either the tradition of multiple language ideologies within socio-cultural groups, or else within that which studies specific interests of social and cultural groups.

In attempting to fit works on language ideology in the Japanese context into the frameworks proposed by Kathryn Woolard and Paul Kroskrity, we come to understand two important things. Firstly, that several types of language ideology study either do not exist or are little developed in the case of Japan. Secondly, the classifications proposed by Kathryn Woolard and Paul Kroskrity are merely descriptive attempts to catalogue, group and label works of language ideology which have been published in English. Thus, in the Japanese context, their proposals are of limited application. More importantly, such systems and categories do not allow for analytical insight, as do the classifications of ideology studies by Raymond Geuss and Raymond Boudon. Before setting out to remedy such analytical shortcomings, let us briefly review existing definitions of language ideology and see what can be adapted for use when dealing with the issues discussed in this book.

Definitions of Language Ideology

Several definitions of language ideology have been proposed so far. Probably the most widely cited is that of Michael Silverstein (1979: 193) who defines language ideology as 'sets of belief about language articulated by users as a rationalization or justification of perceived language structure and use'. In defining language ideology in this way, Silverstein stresses the importance of taking the speaker's own rationalization and justification of their language into account.

A second well-known definition of language ideology is Judith Irvine's. Irvine identifies language ideology as 'the cultural system of ideas about social and linguistic relationships, together with their loading of moral and political interests' (Irvine, 1989: 255). This offers a similarly broad definition of language ideology to Silverstein's, but adds a further dimension by emphasizing the political and moral loading of language ideologies. In Irvine's view, ideologies are not simply concerned with language alone.

Rather, discourse attains its ideological loading through the connection of particular linguistic phenomena to non-referential or non-linguistic phenomena. It is this act of connecting language with other issues which renders language an ideological entity.

A final important definition of language ideology is that of Paul Kroskrity, who writes that language ideologies 'are profitably conceived as multiple because of the multiplicity of meaningful social divisions (class, gender, clan, elites, generations, and so on) within socio-cultural groups that have the potential to produce divergent perspectives expressed as indices of group membership' (Kroskrity, 2000: 12). Emphasizing the multiplicity of language ideologies takes into consideration their range by trying to locate the boundaries of specific ideologies. Kroskrity's definition accounts for the fact that erasing or discrediting ideas and phenomena contradictory to dominant ideas is an important feature of successful ideologies, and that the study of language ideology must be careful not to simply reproduce vicarious ideology. This definition allows for the study of why and how one particular ideology emerges as dominant, why opposing systems of belief are dismissed, and how unsuccessful ideologies are rendered either non-sensical or invisible.

Apart from the traditions of linguistic anthropology summarized above, further information on ways of studying language ideology may be obtained from the field of critical linguistics. In contrast to linguistic anthropology, critical linguistics is predominantly concerned with the ways in which ideologies are manifested, disseminated and reproduced through language, thereby focussing more on the effects of language ideologies on society. Another essential difference to linguistic anthropology is that a critical stance towards dominant ideology is taken. Critical linguistics examines how ideological notions emerge. It examines the ways in which common sense is discursively (re)created, and how social relations and power inequalities are thereby legitimized. A good example of this may be found in the work of Norman Fairclough, who writes:

> Institutional practices which people draw upon without thinking often embody assumptions which directly or indirectly legitimize existing power relations. Practices which appear to be universal and commonsensical can often be shown to originate in the dominant class or the dominant bloc and to have become *naturalized*. Where types of practice, and in many cases types of discourse, function in this way to sustain unequal power relations, I shall say that they are functioning *ideologically*. (Fairclough, 2001: 27, emphasis in the original)

Critical linguists like Norman Fairclough are thus less concerned with the socio-historical background which gave rise to certain beliefs, preferring instead to actively confront and undo those ideologies which sustain inequalities of power.

Gaps in Approaches to Language Ideology

When reviewing definitions of language ideology within the frameworks of ideology study proposed by Raymond Geuss (1981) and Raymond Boudon (1988), we find that the definitions by Michael Silverstein, Judith Irvine, Kathrin Woolard and Paul Kroskrity share an outlook which Geuss terms as descriptive and Boudon terms as modern (capacity to 'make sense'). In other words, we find few differences between the proposals of Silverstein, Irvine, Woolard and Kroskrity. Meanwhile, critical linguistics falls within the boundaries of what Geuss defines as pejorative and Boudon as traditional, that is to say, as defined by the criteria of truth rather than by the criteria of the creation of meaning. Thus, we come to understand that several positions in the orientation of the study of ideology are not covered by language ideology, while some other ideas, like the pejorative ('untrue') direction, have already largely disappeared from sociological approaches.

The existing works on language ideology in the Japanese context which take a historical perspective deal with the study of language ideology in a descriptive and 'modern' way. The same applies for those works dealing with the language of Japanese women which fall within the tradition of linguistic anthropology, while other studies of Japanese women's language may be seen as belonging to the tradition of critical linguistics. These fall neatly within Geuss and Boudon's pejorative and traditional definitions. Let us now briefly consider the advantages and disadvantages of existing approaches to the study of language ideology, before attempting to reach a definition of language ideology best suited to the aims of this book.

We shall consider the critical approach first. Its obvious benefit is that it renders the inequalities of power behind ideology visible, thus focusing on the effects of ideology, and identifying the proponents and practices which sustain and reproduce those inequalities. The disadvantage of this approach, however, is the narrow focus on what Mannheim calls particular ideology, where being ideological is tantamount to being wrong. Such methodology severely limits insight into why specific groups are ideological in the first place. In other words, the sense-making aspect of any ideology, the motive behind its very creation, is sidestepped. Moreover, by actively siding with those who lack power and are oppressed, critical studies take an ideological stance, and themselves form part of ongoing ideological struggles over power. It goes without saying that such approaches compromise their own effectiveness and the credibility of any insight they produce.

On the other hand, descriptive approaches to ideology avoid such methodological pitfalls. After all, being descriptive is first and foremost about avoiding exercising any kind of influence over the object of one's research – that is effectively the first commandment of anthropological research. Compared to critical linguistics, the focus on ideology is broader and extends beyond those with which one does not agree on ideological grounds. However, such a wide-reaching approach to ideology has a major drawback, in that the concept of ideology loses much of its analytical edge. What is more, ideology risks being expanded beyond an analytical application. When all thought is seen as ideological, a non-ideological perspective on ideology is rendered as a paradox. In this way, a descriptive approach to the study of ideology inevitably falls foul of its own relativism.

In short, the dilemma of studying language ideology is that pejorative approaches are too narrow, while descriptive approaches are too wide – the former approach is overly critical, the latter not critical enough. The best solution, then, is to combine the positive aspects of each approach. Accordingly, the task becomes one of expanding ideology while maintaining a critical edge. In order to remedy this methodological dilemma, the British literary theorist Terry Eagleton (1991: 29, emphasis in the original) suggests that ideology should best be studied in ways 'which attend to the *promotion* and *legitimation* of the interests of [...] social groups in the face of opposing interest'. Eagleton's take on ideology is thus narrower than that of the concept of total ideology (every thought is ideological), as advocated by Karl Mannheim, but wider than the particular ideology of Karl Marx. Eagleton proposes that ideology be expanded beyond the limitations of particular ideology, whilst simultaneously being limited to those cases in which total ideology is interrelated with power issues.

A similar proposal to Eagleton's is that of the historian E.P. Thompson (1984: 4), who argued for an approach by which 'ideology [...] is to study the ways in which meaning (or signification) serves to sustain relations of domination'. Thompson (1984, 1990) thus promotes a study of ideology which focuses on two central ideas: firstly, that power is required in order to disseminate ideologies successfully; secondly, that successful ideologies sustain and reproduce existing power relations. Following Eagleton and Thompson's respective proposals does not imply that only powerful actors create and disseminate ideology, however. Rather, it is only powerful social actors and social groups who are able to spread ideologies successfully beyond those groups whose interests are directly served by those ideologies. In other words, Terry Eagleton and E.P. Thompson both argue for a descriptive approach to ideology which pays attention to power relations and can therefore remain critical. In this sense, being critical does not explicitly demand taking sides with any of the parties involved in any ideological struggle.

Departing from such conceptual propositions, the following definition of language ideology is offered for the present study: 'The study of language ideology investigates the origin and effect of beliefs about language structure and use, as well as the ways in which those beliefs are promoted and spread beyond the social groups whose interests they serve.' This definition of language ideology forces us to differentiate between those for whom language ideology is beneficial and those for whom it is not, but who nevertheless, and to their own detriment, subscribe to dominant ideology. We will consider this in more detail below.

Language Ideology Brokers and the Linguistic Margin

A work such as this cannot depart from the assumptions it aims to deconstruct. We cannot advance our arguments from the view that a homogenous speech community has ever existed outside ideology. Thus, what the French sociologist and ethnographer Pierre Bourdieu (1991) aptly terms as 'linguistic communism' must be purposefully deconstructed, and the ideological mechanism which give rise to such ideological imagination of unitary language be moved to the fore. Drawing largely on the work of Bourdieu (1977, 1991), the difference between 'language ideology brokers' and the 'linguistic margin' will be highlighted throughout the book. Underlying this distinction is Bourdieu's view of language use as constituting a social proficiency. Bourdieu (1991: 62) stresses that the existence of homogenous national speech communities can only be assumed because the recognition of legitimate language is more widely accepted than it is possessed. This, in turn, results in the silencing of those who do not possess the registers or styles deemed necessary for specific situations (Bourdieu, 1991: 90–104), and this is why the so-called 'popular speech' is actually less popular than its name implies, for popular speech translates into silence in most contexts. It is this which is hidden by the fact that the shared recognition of language as legitimate hides the unequal distribution of legitimate language proficiency within a speech community – a recognition frequently evidenced by silence or linguistic hypercorrection. Silence and hypercorrection must be understood for what they are, that is, manifestations of unequal distribution of linguistic resources.

Language as social proficiency gives rise to linguistic domination over those who do not possess these varieties by those who do. Such dominance, Bourdieu maintains, 'can only be exercised by the person who exercises it, and endured by the person who endures it, in a form which results in its misrecognition as such, in other words, which results in its recognition as legitimate' (Bourdieu, 1991: 140). This is an important observation. The acceptance of a particular language variety by speakers who do not control the said variety is an implicit acknowledgement that it constitutes legitimate language. In other words, while there exists an unequal social distribution of skills in legitimate language, the system of attitudes and evaluations behind legitimate language is shared among all members of a speech community, including those not fully proficient therein. The acceptance of language ideologies which regulate the use and acceptance of legitimate language – and silences those who do not possess complete proficiency – means that a large part of the speech community ends up participating in their own linguistic subjugation on language ideological grounds.

In so doing, Bourdieu defines the difference between language authorities, and those who recognize that authority. The relation between the two is regulated by shared ideological views of language. Henceforth, these two sides of the speech community will be referred to as 'language ideology brokers' and the 'linguistic margin', respectively. Highlighting the important role of language ideology brokers is by no means exclusive to this book. In existing sociolinguistic literature, we find various means of designating those who are seen to have linguistic authority over others. Roy Harris (1980) calls these speakers 'language makers', Pierre Bourdieu (1991) 'language experts', Claude Hagège (1993) 'language builders', Ulrich Ammon (1995) 'language norm authorities' and Jan Blommaert (1999) 'ideology brokers'. For the sake of convention, I will use the term 'language ideology brokers', since I believe it to be the most appropriate definition. The term language ideology broker implies that their central activity is the dissemination and reproduction – rather than the creation – of language ideologies.

Of equal importance to gaining a clear understanding of the spread and effects of modernist language ideology, though far less prominent in sociolinguistic literature, is a consideration of 'the other side of the speech community', the recipients of language ideology, as it were, and how their views and experiences relate to those of the language ideology brokers. Because ideologies influence everyone's life all of the time, their study should include consideration of everyone's situation, at least as far as possible. Responding to such demands, Inoue Miyako (1996) has spoken in favour of those at the margin. According to Inoue, the margin covers those whose language is given little prestige, for example, dialect speakers, linguistic minorities, language learners, speakers with little formal education and so on. By studying such speakers, the linguist can hopefully avoid reproduction, confirmation and rationalization of dominant language ideologies. The view from the margin is particularly helpful when attempting to explain existing conventions of language use and the distribution of power within a speech community. Margins confuse the boundaries between ideologically mediated common-sense and ideologically erased alternatives, hinting at the arbitrary nature and active formation of language ideology as common-sense knowledge. The linguistic deviance of the margin from ideologically proclaimed norms is helpful in identifying the range and validity of ideological claims. Taking the margin into consideration also foregrounds alternative views which deviate from dominant ideologies.

Based on these preliminaries, let us now examine the language ideologies of Japan prior to the creation and implementation of Japanese national language, or *kokugo*. Discussing this specific period in the linguistic modernization of Japan is a useful exercise. It reveals the groundbreaking efforts of Meiji period Japanese language planners in modernizing, for the first time, a non-western language, a process crucially driven by the establishment of an empowering ideology of what Japanese should be under modernity. Initially, many doubted that Japanese could actually be developed into a standardized national language. And in the decades following the Meiji restoration of 1868, the idea of national language was not yet widely known, much less understood. Let us now consider, then, the case of Mori Arinori (1847–1889), the most famous of the Japanese language sceptics, who proposed in 1873 the replacement of Japanese with English.

2 The Call of Mori Arinori to Replace Japanese

The events analysed in this chapter took place in the early 1870s, a time of sudden and massive change for Japan and its people. Examples of this change include: all Japanese were required to take family names; women were prohibited to blacken their teeth; the first post offices were established; the practice of issuing licences for domestic travel was ended; restrictions on marriages between feudal ranks were abolished; feudal domains were reorganized into modern prefectures; commoners were granted permission to ride horses; the first daily newspapers appeared; compulsory school education was established; and the western calendar was adopted.

Modernization also required the creation of a new elite. With the old elite and its institutions discredited by its inability to withstand the western military challenge, young graduates of western universities or of the newly founded western schools and academies in Japan moved quickly to usurp it. They filled the power-vacuum that had emerged as a consequence of the enforced opening of Japan (Pyle, 1969: 12). This new elite was not a counter-elite, however, rather a development of that which preceded it. The young men who formed it were determined that Japan be on a par with western nation-states. Thus, modernization initially translated into westernization, since the western model provided the blueprint for such a project. The emergence of the new elite and its ideas did not go unchallenged, however. Change brought with it power struggles, of which the struggle over language was one of the most intense. One debate which arose from this particular struggle was focused on whether or not Japanese should be replaced by a foreign language. In 1872, Mori Arinori (1847–1889), at that time Japan's ambassador in Washington and later Japan's first Minister of Education, proposed that Japanese be replaced by English.

Mori's Proposal

Mori was one of the first Japanese students to enrol at a western university. After his return to Japan in 1867, he joined the Meiji government where he became known as an ardent promoter of western ideas and culture. In January 1871, Mori was sent as ambassador to the United States. His political ideas are recorded in the three books he published during his time in the United States: *Life and Resources in America* (1871), *Religious Freedom in Japan* (1872) and *Education in Japan* (1873). Although Mori was broadly interested in a variety of subjects, he devoted most of his time to educational matters (Hall, 1973: 188).

The exact details of Mori's proposal on language remain controversial, but the general consensus is that he was in favour of the adoption of a simplified form of English for use in Japan. Mori made his proposal to replace Japanese with English in May 1872, at the same time that the Iwakura Mission – a Japanese diplomatic world tour which took place from 1871 to 1873 – was staying in Washington (Hall, 1973: 155–156). Arguably one of the most ambitious missions ever organized, the Iwakura Mission had about 50 members. Many of them were leading Japanese statesmen at the time, such as Iwakura Tomomi (1825–1883), Ōkubo Toshimichi (1830–1878), Kido Takayoshi (1833–1877) and Itō Hirobumi (1841–1909), while others were scholars from various fields of learning. Amongst other things, one of the mission's aims was to convince the west that Japan was unlike other Asian nations and that it was ready and willing to join the modern world. It sought to redress the inequality of established treaties which granted western powers extraterritorial rights and low trading tariffs and had dealt a major blow to Japanese self-esteem (Ōkubo, 1972: 57).

Mori proved indispensable to the mission during its time in Washington, serving as chief interpreter and making substantive contributions to the negotiations as well as to the agenda. Swale points out that Mori 'played a major role in persuading the Iwakura Mission to [...] renegotiate the ill-balanced trade agreements that had been established two decades earlier' (Swale, 2000: 59). US President Ulysses Grant (1822–1885) signalled his readiness to engage in consultations, though negotiation never went much beyond polite discussion as the United States had little interest in granting Japan the recognition it desired. The failure to negotiate new treaties disillusioned the members of the mission, and it was made clear to them that such negotiation would not occur without considerable internal reform on the part of Japan. It was within this context that Mori Arinori proposed the replacement of Japanese with English.

A month before the Iwakura Mission met with President Grant, Mori had sent an open letter to a number of American educators seeking advice on education in Japan, in particular with regard to 'the material prosperity [...], commerce [...], agricultural and industrial interests [...], social, moral and physical condition of the people [...] and its influences upon the laws and government' (Hall, 1973: 181). It is worth noting that Mori did not explicitly seek advice on matters of language in his letter. Mori later printed the 13 replies he received in his 1873 book *Education in Japan*. In one reply, Joseph Henry (1797–1878), a physicist of world-wide recognition and president of the National Academy of Science at the time, brought up the issue of language, urging discussion on the merits of introducing English as a medium for writing and use in selected domains such as learning, trade and diplomacy. Henry wrote the following:

> [P]rior to the elaboration of your system of education, an essential question will arise as what written language you shall adopt as the vehicle of thought, your own, as we are informed, being too cumbrous and difficult of acquisition to suit for the wants of higher education of your own people, or to be adapted for communication with foreign nations. As Americans, we would naturally give the preference to our own tongue; but, on other grounds than national prejudice, we think from the power of language itself and the enterprising character and increasing influence of the people who speak it, the English language would be best for you as a commercial nation. (Quoted from Ōkubo, 1972: 352–353)

Henry presents here three arguments against the use of Japanese: (1) that written Japanese is (too) complicated; (2) that education cannot be conducted in Japanese; and (3) that Japanese is unsuitable for international communication. On the other hand, Henry believed English to be suitably developed and internationally recognized enough to provide the alternative. Mori Arinori would later use these same arguments to support his own proposal to abandon Japanese in favour of English. In commenting on Henry's letter, Ivan Hall (1973: 172) states that Mori had introduced Henry to his ideas about language reform on an earlier occasion, the two men having often written to each other. Hall (1973: 190) is in no doubt that the idea of replacing Japanese with English was in fact Mori's idea, rather that Henry's. Nevertheless, it was not until receiving Henry's reply that Mori chose to pursue the idea further, initially by writing to Dwight Whitney (1827–1894), a linguistics professor of international acclaim, to consult him about his ideas for language reform.

Letter from Mori to Whitney (3 May 1872)

Mori's letter to Whitney is one of three important documents concerning the language replacement proposal, the second being Whitney's reply, the third Mori's introduction to his 1873 book *Education in Japan*. In all three documents, ideological statements about language abound, repeatedly and systematically linking language to non-linguistic issues.

Mori's decision to write to Whitney was based on the latter's 'high rank [...] in the fields of Science and Literature' (all citations of the letter taken from Ōkubo, 1972: 305–310). Japan, Mori asserted, was determined to 'keep pace with the age' and aspired 'to attain the highest degree of civilisation'. Japanese ambition was hindered, however, by the fact that it was 'unprovided with that great essential to [...] individual and national progress, – a good language'. In Mori's opinion, Japanese was 'inadequate to the growing necessities of the people of that Empire', which is why he advocated adopting 'a copious and expanding European language'.

According to Mori, the Japanese language was not even adequate for communication among Japanese, let alone for communication about international issues or in international contexts. He stated: 'It having been found that the Japanese language is insufficient even for the wants of the Japanese themselves, the demand for the new language is irresistibly imperative, in view of our rapidly increasing intercourse with the world at large'. He portrayed written Japanese as beset by all kind of problems. Japanese was in his opinion 'too poor to be made, by phonetic alphabet, sufficiently useful as a written language'. Furthermore, 'the written language now in use in Japan [...] has little or no relation to the spoken language'. Thus, according to Mori, two issues stood in the way of Japanese language modernization, diglossia and the excessive number of homophones in written Japanese. Mori appears to be undecided as to the feasibility of writing Japanese in the Latin alphabet, however, contradicting the statement above by suggesting that

> the only course to be taken, to secure the desired end [of conducting school education in Japanese P.H.] is to start anew, by first turning the spoken language into a properly written form, based on a pure phonetic principle. It is contemplated that Roman letters should be adopted. (Ōkubo, 1972: 309)

This contradiction has been the subject of much discussion, by such writers as Hall (1973), Kobayashi (2001, 2002), Lee (1990, 1996) and Nakamura (2000), as it invites the inference that what Mori was actually proposing was the introduction of English as an additional language to Japanese, not a replacement. My understanding, however, is that Mori initially supported the romanization movement, but grew increasingly pessimistic about this project. Mori is known to have been an early advocate of romanization, but by the end of 1872 he had given up on this attempt at language reform

(Hall, 1973: 191). Even in the quotation above, Mori can be seen to distance himself from the romanization movement by using the passive construction 'it is contemplated' (see below for further discussion).

It was concern about Japanese rather than admiration of English, which led Mori to his radical proposal for language reform. In addition to his criticism of Japanese, however, Mori also pointed out several weaknesses of English, such as its complicated orthography, and the irregular verb and noun inflexions which were to be found 'among the most frequently occurring words in the language, which make the matter worse'. He even went so far as to say that English was so complicated that even 'by far the larger proportion of persons, with whom it is the vernacular, speak and write it incorrectly'. Mori, therefore, proposed to reform English first. He suggested, for example, the substitution of 'saw' by 'seed', 'spoke' by 'speaked' and 'bit' by 'bited' with regard to irregular verb inflexion, and 'phantom' by 'fantom', and 'inveigh' by 'invey' with regard to orthography.

On the basis of his views on written and spoken Japanese, and on English as a foreign language, Mori proposed the following means of solving Japan's language problems:

> I propose to banish from the English language, for the use of the Japanese nation, all or most of the exceptions which render English so difficult of acquisition even by English-speaking people, and which discourage most foreigners who have the hardihood to attempt to master it, from persevering to success. (Ōkubo, 1972: 308)

Mori was certain that it would be 'quite impossible to force upon [the Japanese] the language in its present form'. At the same time, however, he did not imagine that the simplifications he proposed would in any way be problematic:

> [M]any of the reasons which make Americans and Englishmen hesitate to attempt radical changes in their language for their own people, do *not* apply to the case under consideration, which is the adaptation of the English language to the necessities of a foreign nation of forty million souls, separated by thousands of miles from the English-speaking nations, and which affords an entirely free field, for the introduction of a new language; there are no obstacles whatsoever in the Empire itself. (Ōkubo, 1972: 306, emphasis in the original)

Mori thus suggested that simplified English might be used first for school education, and later for general use by the entire population. He wrote that there would be 'little or no difficulty in introducing into all schools of the Empire, and gradually into general use, a "simplified English"' and emphasized that this was an idea supported by many of his contemporaries with whom he had discussed the matter. A month later, Whitney sent his reply. This letter, too, was included in *Education in Japan*.

Letter from Whitney to Mori (29 June 1872)

Whitney did not explicitly disapprove of Mori's proposal for language reform. He did express certain reservations about his methods, however. He agreed with Mori that English orthography was problematic and could well be reformed for the benefit 'of the English and Americans, as well as the Japanese' (all citations of the letter taken from Ōkubo, 1972: 414–423). However, Whitney flatly rejected Mori's call to simplify English verb and noun inflexion, stating: 'You cannot join the community of English speakers without frankly accepting English speech as they have made it, and now use it'. Furthermore, 'any community acquiring English had better take them [irregularities in inflexion P.H.] as they are, and be thankful that the case is no worse'. Whitney emphasized that the simplifications Mori proposed would give 'the whole language a new and strange aspect, offensive to those to whom it now belongs'. The new English created by Mori 'would seem laughable and absurd to the speakers of the old [English], and those who used it would be visited with the contempt of the latter'.

Dwight Whitney's own recommendations for Japanese language reform demonstrate clearly his prejudices towards Japanese and Chinese, and a corresponding bias towards English. That said, he also recommended that more than just the 'inherent superiority of the English language' be taken into consideration. Japanese language and culture should also be respected, he maintained, making it clear that a wholesale abandoning of Japanese seemed wrong to him:

> I feel very unwilling to take a depreciatory view, or to accept any plan for the advancement of culture in Japan which does not include the ennobling and enriching of the native speech so that itself shall become a means for the increase of culture. (Ōkubo, 1972: 420)

Rather, Whitney proposed, Japanese should be developed into a medium suitable for modern use, and advocated romanization of written Japanese as one means of achieving this. Since he agreed with Mori that 'nothing of value can any longer be hoped for Japan's advancement from the side of China', he proposed that English should take over the status that Chinese had enjoyed for so many years in Japan:

> Let the English language be studied as much as possible; let it take in Japan the place so long occupied by the Chinese; let it become the learned tongue, the classical language; let its treasures of expression be drawn upon as freely as circumstances shall admit and favour – but let the beneficial effect of all this be felt in the Japanese tongue itself; let the experiment be fairly and fully tried whether this is not capable of being raised and perfected, so as to be the worthy instrument of an advanced civilization. (Ōkubo, 1972: 421)

Whitney warned Mori that attempting to establish English as the dominant language in Japan would not be without its problems. In concrete terms, he highlighted two specific problems: firstly, that the introduction of English would widen the gap between the elite and the rest of the population; secondly, that it would result in subjugation of the Japanese people by English-speaking nations. Thus, in contrast to Mori Arinori, Dwight Whitney believed that Japanese nationals ought to have equal access to a common language of their own. The alternative, the introduction of a foreign language, would swing the balance of power in favour of those of higher education. Consequently, he did not consider the introduction of English a suitable means of modernizing language in Japan, believing as he did that language reform should do 'justice to the masses of the Japanese population [which] requires their vernacular to be made for them a means of higher culture', and that if 'the masses are to be reached it must be mainly through their own native speech'.

Whitney's argumentation to provide all nationals with one uniform language can be read as a summary of the linguistic and social problems language modernization has to overcome:

> To carry on the process [of replacing Japanese by English P.H.] in this way would be likely to rest in the formation of a learned class, of limited number, in whose hands would be all the knowledge and culture, with a wholly ignorant lower class, separated from the other in nearly all its sympathies – such a state of things as prevailed in Europe in the middle ages, when Latin was the common speech of the learned, and the popular dialects were perfectly rude and poverty stricken. Now, as you know, every European language is filled with (Greek and) Latin words, but in every country the speech of all classes is (with certain limitations) the same. (Ōkubo, 1972: 420–421)

In the preceding extract, Whitney is essentially outlining modernist language ideology: all nationals, regardless of class or status, should have access to an adequate, elaborate and cultivated language. Equal access to one elaborate and learned language creates the idea of belonging to one nation. Thus, the development of language was only one half of the work to be accomplished by language modernization, the other half being to make that language accessible to everyone. Whitney was well aware that English could not fulfil the second criteria in the case of Japan because the educated elite would inevitably have better access to it. Accordingly, he saw no alternative to the development of a modern language based on Japanese.

Whitney pointed out further obstacles. While the introduction of English might allow the Japanese to make progress along the lines of that made by English-speaking nations, language history proved that nations usually only abandoned their languages 'under the influence of the superiority in culture of the speakers of the other language [...] aided also by political supremacy or social preponderance'. Whitney thus asserted that the adoption of English by Japan would be seen in the west as an indication of submission to English-speaking nations. Regardless of the position on language, he added, language reform in Japan would take generations to complete, and so the best that could be hoped for at the present time was the initiation of 'a movement which shall be carried out by those who come after us'. Clearly, Whitney underestimated the pressure to reform felt by the Japanese modernizers. In their eyes, reform – including that of language – had to be achieved as quickly as possible in order to re-establish national sovereignty and restore Japanese pride. Mori himself never commented directly on Whitney's suggestions, and continued to propose the replacement of Japanese with English. In January 1873, he published *Education in Japan*, which not only contained Whitney's letter, but also the details of his proposal for language reform in Japan.

Education in Japan (January 1873)

Mori's proposal became widely known after *Education in Japan* was published in January 1873. Given the attention his book attracted at the time, it is worth quoting the passage which deals with language reform in its entirety:

> A allusion [*sic*] to the subject of the Japanese language bears a most direct relation to the contents of this book. In the style of expression, the spoken language of Japan differs considerably from the written, though in their structure they are both mainly the same. [...] The words in common use are very few in number, and most of them are of Chinese origin. There are some efforts being made to do away with the use of Chinese characters by reducing them to simple phonetics, but the words

familiar through the organ of the eye are so many, that to change them into those of the ear would cause too great an inconvenience, and be impracticable. Without the aid of Chinese our language has never been taught or used for any purpose of communication. This shows its poverty. The march of modern civilization in Japan has already reached the heart of the nation – the English language following it suppresses the use of both Japanese and Chinese. The commercial power of the English speaking race which now rules the world drives our people into some knowledge of their commercial ways and habits. The absolute necessity of mastering the English language is thus forced upon us. It is a requisite of the maintenance of our independence in the community of nations. Under the circumstance, our meagre language, which can never be of any use outside our islands, is doomed to yield to the domination of the English tongue, especially when the power of steam and electricity shall have pervaded the land. Our intelligent race, eager in the pursuit of knowledge, cannot depend upon a weak and uncertain medium of communication in its endeavour to grasp the principal truths from the precious treasury of western science and art and religion. The laws of the state can never be preserved in the language of Japan. All reasons suggest its disuse. (Ōkubo, 1972: 265–266)

As in his letter to Whitney, Mori perceives diglossia to be at the heart of Japan's language problems. In his opinion, spoken Japanese (*kōgotai*) could never be satisfactorily used for writing (see also Chapter 3). Furthermore, no spoken standard had been established at the time. Nor could written Japanese be romanized effectively, as the large numbers of homonyms in the Sino-Japanese lexicon of written Japanese would inevitably lead to ambiguity once the reader no longer had access to the semantic information provided by Chinese characters. All of this led Mori to conclude that Japanese was unfit for modernization and should be abandoned. As an alternative, English seemed to him to be the obvious choice, owing to its status as an international *lingua franca* of science and international commerce. Unlike Whitney, Mori did not believe that Japanese could be developed satisfactorily. To him, there were 'good languages' and 'meagre languages', and Japanese clearly belonged to the latter category.

Mori Arinori is known to have been influenced by the work of Herbert Spencer (1820–1903) (Swale, 2000: 188–198). Spencer's views on society and progress were widely embraced by Japanese intellectuals at the time, who sought to raise Japan to a level comparable to that of western nations. The idea of 'survival of the fittest' provided the basis on which modernization efforts would be developed, judged and coordinated. During his stay in

Washington, Mori studied Spencer's works intensively. In an analogy to the evolution of biological species, Spencer believed that human cultures, social systems and type of states evolved towards more heterogeneous, complex and better forms. Instead of relativity between cultures, Spencer stressed differences which could be evaluated with regard to their state of development or quality. In Spencer's view, languages, too, could be graded with regard to complexity, development and quality. The fact that Mori perceived Japanese to be inadequate in the modern context further confirmed his opinion that Japanese should be left abandoned. Accordingly, Mori even conducted all written communication within the Japanese embassy in Washington in English. At times, he even sent dispatches to Tokyo in English (Hall, 1972: 93, 1973: 171).

Mori's proposal attracted much attention at the time, and continues to do so today. See Kobayashi (2001, 2002) for a comprehensive discussion of literature related to this issue. He was ridiculed by many of his contemporaries, and continued to come under attack in the 20th century. More recently, discussion on Mori's scheme centred on the question of the role Mori had in mind for Japanese after the introduction of English (Kobayashi, 2001, 2002; Lee, 1990, 1996; Nakamura, 2000). Speculations about the proposal tend to focus on three issues in particular. Firstly, Mori was an early supporter of romanization efforts, but his feelings about romanization are unclear in his proposal. Secondly he never indicted what he believed should happen to Japanese after the introduction of English. Finally, he avoided further public comment on language problems after the publication of *Education in Japan*, though it is known that he abandoned the idea of introducing English in favour of development of Japanese after his return to Japan (Swale, 2000: 81).

Ōno Susumu (1983) and Kobayashi Toshihiro (2001, 2002) interpret the proposal as suggesting replacement of Chinese elements of Japanese by elements of simplified English. Kobayashi supports this interpretation by pointing out that Mori's scheme would otherwise be inconsistent with his call for romanization. According to Kobayshi, Mori sought to enrich Japanese through the addition of English elements, thereby creating a new language to be written in the Latin alphabet. Dankwart Rustow (1968: 89), on the other hand, is of the opinion that Mori wanted only to introduce English as the written language of Japan, while Lee Yeounsuk (1996) argues that Mori's use of the word 'disuse' rather than 'abolish' suggests that he aimed only at a restriction of Japanese to the private domain. Lee points out that Mori never explicitly stated that he believed in the abolition of Japanese (Lee, 1996: 7–9). This argument is taken up by Nakamura Kei (2000: 17), who draws attention to the fact that a policy of 'introducing' and 'adopting'

English does not necessarily infer the 'abolishing' of Japanese. To Nakamura (2000), it is unclear as to whether Mori believed simplified English ought to be used only in Japan, or throughout the world. Such speculation is based on Mori's remark that 'not only English speaking people, but the world at large, would be greatly benefited through a re-cast of English orthography' (Ōkubo, 1972: 306). It seems likely, however, that this remark was more rhetorical than indicative of any global language policy scheming on Mori's part. In fact, this passage is in indirect speech – quoting the opinion of 'eminent men who have made language a life study'.

In discussing the various interpretations of Mori's proposal, we will focus on what Mori actually wrote and refrain from postulation as far as possible. While it is true that Mori never explicitly stated that Japanese should be abolished, neither did he ever suggest its continued use in the private domain. In addition, speculation about the creation of a bilingual Japanese–English language regime runs counter to the monolingual western model Mori was familiar with. If he had such a situation in mind, we may reasonably expect him to have commented to that effect. Replacing Chinese lexical elements of Japanese with simplified English, on the other hand, is such an intricate and complicated undertaking that one would expect Mori to have given more detailed ideas about how such a scheme might be achieved had he actually intended such a strategy of reform. Finally, there is little to support the view that Mori believed in the adoption of simplified English on a global scale. Thus, one can be fairly certain that Mori Arinori's proposal was indeed a call to replace Japanese with a simplified version of English. Certainly, this was the way his contemporaries interpreted it, and the reason he came in for so much criticism. This view is further supported by the fact that Mori never defended his proposal against such an interpretation.

Reactions

Mori Arinori's beliefs are not entirely concurrent with modernist ideas about language. His suggestion to simplify English indicates that he did not believe that English speakers alone had the right to call for such reform. To Mori, English did not belong exclusively to its speech community. Nakamura (2000: 19) points out that this is the issue for which Whitney criticized Mori most severely. Nor did Mori support the use of language in order to create a sense unity and a Japanese nation. The adoption of simplified English by Japan is in fact counter to the idea of taking pride in one's native tongue. Apparently, Mori did not perceive this to be important. It was Whitney who pointed out that speakers of simplified English would be ridiculed by native speakers. Lee (1996: 3), too, comments on Mori's apparent lack of affinity with the Japanese language. Mori, Lee (1990: 51) writes, appears to have acted like a 'linguistic traitor to his country'. Mori was similarly berated by his contemporaries, who, by way of attacking Mori, defended Japanese and thus started creating modernist and empowering Japanese language ideology.

The reactions to Mori's proposal were overwhelmingly unfavourable, in Japan as well as in the west (Hall, 1973: 194). Mori was attacked for being elitist and unpatriotic (Yasuda, 1997b: 32). The first and most detailed criticism was made by fellow enlightenment scholar Baba Tatsui (1850–1888) in 1873. At the time, Baba was studying in England where he was, according to Eugene Soviak (1963: 163) 'a self-confident, self-appointed expositor and defender of Japanese culture and self-impelled educator of the English public'. Where many chose to attack Mori Arinori's character and to make fun of him, Baba Tatsui took Mori's proposal seriously and made great efforts to counter his pessimistic view of Japanese (Lee, 1996: 14).

Baba Tatsui

Motivated by Mori Arinori's proposal to replace Japanese, Baba Tatsui went on to compile the first grammar of spoken Japanese and the first Japanese-as-a-foreign-language textbook ever. In the foreword to his *An Elementary Grammar of the Japanese Language* (1873), Baba espouses the view that Japanese language problems were far less serious than Mori and other Japanese scholars had claimed. Baba's opinion of Japanese was the very antithesis to Mori's pessimism. Baba's optimism owes greatly to the fact that his principal concern was with spoken Japanese, whereas Mori had primarily the written language in mind. Baba never mentioned written language, or the significant gap between written and spoken Japanese. Mori's main argument, of course, was that a language that could not be written stood in the way of progress, an opinion Baba clearly did not share.

Baba's grammar was a direct reaction to Mori's book. On the first page he stated the purpose of his grammar to be two-fold (all citations from Ōkubo, 1972: 9–15). The first being 'to give a general idea of the Japanese language as it is spoken; and the second to protest against a prevalent opinion entertained by many of our countrymen, as well as foreigners who take some interest in our country'. The very fact that spoken Japanese 'has grammar' at all was intended to counter Mori's argument.

Refuting Mori's argument that laws could never be written in Japanese, Baba wrote: 'In the translation of Roman laws into the English language [...] many words or phrases [...] are retained; yet this does not show the poverty of the English language, but only their difference in the ideas and customs'. Unlike Mori, Baba did not differentiate between 'poor' and 'good' languages but rather between developed and developing languages. He diverted attention towards the fact that English, too, had required development before laws could be written in it. He also believed that English is a difficult language to master, especially for Japanese, being so different from their native tongue. It would therefore 'require a very long time [for English] to be mastered by so many people, so that precious time is thrown away'. Although he agreed with Mori that English was, in certain aspects, superior to Japanese, he highlighted exceptions to this. In comparison with English, Japanese excelled in 'regular orthography and more uniform pronunciation [...], while it is generally admitted that the English language in both these respects is very defective'. Baba was in no doubt that Japanese could continue to be used satisfactorily in all domains and that existing language problems could be solved, and sought to defend Japanese from unfavourable views borne out of Japan's sudden and enforced exposure to the outside world.

According to Baba, Japanese was as good as any other (western) language and he backed this up by basing his *An Elementary Grammar of the Japanese Language* on western grammars, despite the fact that pre-modernist Japanese models in the framework of national philology (*kokugaku*) already existed and would arguable have been easier to copy (see Bedell, 1968; Heinrich, 2002: 17–30; Miller, 1975 for an overview of the linguistic studies of *kokugaku*). To Baba, however, models of the national philology with word classes such as 'dresses' for verbs and adjectives, 'hairpins' for adverbials and pronouns and 'shoelaces' for suffixes and postpositions were inadequate in the modern age. Accordingly, Baba presented to his readers a language in which 'rules are observed throughout [...] [all] eight parts of speech [...] [with] tense, moods, or voices of verbs, rules of syntax, and so on'. Baba's attempt to create a grammar of Japanese by strictly applying western conceptions at times resulted in long-winded descriptions of features not existing in Japanese. For instance, Baba had the following to say about number and gender:

> There are two numbers, the Singular and the Plural. In Japanese, nouns change their forms in a few cases; generally they have the same forms, both the plural and the singular. [...] Nouns have three genders – the Masculine, Feminine, and Neuter. The masculine denotes the male sex; as, *otoko*, man. The female denotes the females sex; as *onna*, woman. The neuter denotes whatever is without sex; as, *yama*, mountain. (Baba, 1873: 4, italics in the original)

Baba thus confused natural and grammatical gender and suffixation as a means to express plurality with plurality expressed in the predicate. His method was perhaps based on a belief that a language lacking gender and plurality would have appeared incomplete and inferior to westerners. In order to 'have grammar' and to be at par with the modernized western languages, Baba attempted to give Japanese such gender and plurality.

Baba Tatsui made frequent references to western scholars in order to lend his views more authority, asserting that the linguistic opinions of such eminent figures as John Locke, John Austin, Francis Wayland and Dwight Whitney were just as applicable to Japanese as to any western language. Baba quoted Locke as stating that the functions of language would be 'first, to make known one man's thought or ideas to another; secondly, to do so with as much ease and quickness as possible; thirdly, thereby to convey the knowledge of things' and concluded that Japanese was 'sufficiently systematic to accomplish these ends with certain exceptions'. Thus, on the basis of Locke's ideological outlook on language, the replacement of Japanese by English could not be justified. Quoting Dwight Whitney, Baba asserted that the adoption of a new language was usually indicative of a nation's subordination to a superior power. He added that nations forced to adopt a new language often retained their native one(s). Bilingualism, however, was undesirable to Baba. Its unwanted effects could be observed 'amongst the Welsh, Irish, and Scotch, who, in fact, are learning two languages at present, and throwing away the time which is precious to us all'. He referred too, to the effects of what might today be called linguistic imperialism, using the example of India, where 'a deep gulf [...] separates the higher and educated from the lower portion of society' due to the introduction of English. Such a schism in society, Baba warned, would be created in Japan too, were English to be introduced in line with Mori's proposal:

> If affairs of state, and all affairs of social intercourse are to be transacted through the English language, the lower classes will be shut out from important questions which concern the whole nation [...]; the consequences being that there will be an entire separation between the higher class and the lower, and no common sympathies between them. (Ōkubo, 1972: 14)

To Baba, that Japanese should be retained by all means and in all domains of use was indisputable. Education, for example, could only be conducted in Japanese as it was an issue of national concern. The best option, therefore, appeared to him to be 'to try to enrich and complete that which we have already [...], than to discard it and substitute, at great risk, that which is entirely different and necessarily strange to us'. Baba did not conceive of language merely as a tool for the acquisition of knowledge, for writing laws and educating people, but also as being an important element in the creation of a united Japanese identity. Baba wrote on this issue: 'We must try to educate the whole mass of the people and unite them into one, in order to promote the common happiness of the community.' (Ōkubo, 1972: 9–15) According to Baba, only Japanese could provide for the promotion of a sense of unity, and thereby contribute to the 'common happiness' of the people.

Baba's criticism of Mori's proposal proved to be seminal. Kobayashi (2002: 43–45) asserts that it was in fact Baba, not Mori, who provided the keywords of the discussion of the latter's proposal. Baba wrote that Mori intended to 'exterminate the Japanese language' and to 'substitute the English language for it', though Mori's actual words were 'disuse' and 'replacement' respectively (see above). What became known in Japan as *kokugo haishi eigo saiyō-ron* (proposal for the abolition of the national language and adoption of the English language) owed more to Baba's interpretation of *Education in Japan* than to the work itself, and further criticism of Mori was also inspired more by Baba's reaction than the actual contents of Mori's proposal.

Further Japanese Reactions

Mori's critics included other enlightenment scholars, as well as scholars of the pre-modern *kokugaku* (national philology) and its modern successor *kokugogaku* (national linguistics). Nishi Amane (1829–1897), who had studied in the Netherlands between 1862 and 1865, and became one of the key intellectuals during the period of Japan's modernization, charged Mori with disseminating unproven statements about Japanese. Like Baba, Nishi also believed that the introduction of English would lead to a schism in Japanese society. Reacting to the idea of adopting a modern European language for use in Japan, he wrote in 1874 (quoted from Braisted, 1976: 7): 'I do not believe this to be true. After all, the language of a people is innate. It arises inalterably from the mutual association of the basic factors race, climate, and environment.' As can be seen here, Nishi was already familiar with the Herder–Humboldtian ideology by which language is seen as one of elements key to the formation of a national character and identity (see Chapter 1).

Further criticism of Mori's proposal was based largely on pre-modern language ideologies. Kurokawa Mayori (1828–1906), a scholar of national philology, wrote in 1885:

> A view exists according to which it would be good and useful to change the language of our empire when changing our script, but if language

connects heaven and earth and builds and resuscitates the spirit created by the emperor and the spirit that creates the emperor, it surely also has its affect on the state of the people. (Quoted from Hirai, 1998: 175)

In Kurokawa's comments exists a view of Japanese as a language with a spirit. This contrasts strikingly not only with the utilitarianism of Mori, but also with the ideology of Baba, who stressed that languages can actively be developed and expanded. It differs, too, from Nishi's assertions that a language forms a nation in the same way as race, climate and environment do. To Kurokawa, language was spiritual, and as nation and language are linked in a spiritual way they cannot be divided. The abandonment of Japanese would thus lead to spiritual turmoil. The origin of the ideology of such a language spirit (*kotodama*) dates back to the eighth century, where it appears in beliefs connected to word taboo. Later, this ideology was expanded to the effect that sounds were believed to be directly meaningful. The national philologists of the Edo period (1602–1868) claimed that a direct and natural correspondence between sound and meaning existed only in Japanese, and that Japan was thereby 'the country of words' (see Lewin, 1982; Miller, 1975 for details). Like the national philologists, Mori saw the contemporary Japanese language as defective. However, Mori looked towards the west for the solution, whereas pre-modernist ideologies preferred to look back in time.

Though Mori's scheme appears 'absurd' (Coulmas, 1985: 252) today – a 'strange episode from Meiji history' (Miller, 1982: 109) – it continued to be considered seriously during the 20th century, and scholars of national linguistics (*kokugogaku*) made frequent reference to it. Lee Yeounsuk (1996: 4–5) compiled a collection of such references, worth quoting in their entirety:

> When Mori Arinori was serving as ambassador in the United States of America [...], he stated that our national language (*waga kokugo*) had many shortcomings which made it inefficacious for education. He made public his idea that the national language (*kokugo*) should be totally abolished and that English ought to be made the national language (*kokugo*). In this context, he sought advice from American scholars. (Yamada, 1935: 285)

> In the same way as the national philologists of the Edo period, who looked down on the spoken language as the language of the common people and for being slang, yearning for the language of the Japanese classics instead, the people of the Meiji period held at first a pessimistic view about the extreme confusion in their spoken and written language. [...] Certain persons in earnest longed for the spoken and written language of the west, perceiving the idea of abolishing the national language (*kokugo*) and using a language from the west as an ideal. (Tokieda, 1940: 157)

Although the story of Mori Arinori being reproved by the American linguist Whitney for his proposal to abolish Japanese and to adopt English is a famous anecdote, he was not the only person entertaining such views in the early Meiji period. (Tokieda, 1962: 40)

Mori Arinori [...] held the view that Japanese (*nihongo*) was awfully complicated and without rules so that he worried whether it would not be rather difficult to obtain adequate results if national education was conducted in it. He therefore considered whether it would not be an advantageous policy to conduct education in English. (Hoshina, 1936: 11)

Our intellectuals, who had come into contact with the superior western civilization, admired the west so much that they considered a proposal to reform the national language by substituting it with English as the national language (*kokugo*). Following the Meiji restoration, the same phenomenon took place as after [the first contact with] Chinese civilization, when Chinese characters and texts were introduced to our country and immediately attained official status [...]. In this way, the proposal to adopt English, announced in 1872 by Mori Arinori [...] is representative of this attitude. (Hirai, 1998: 173)

Many of our thinkers and intellectuals believed at that time that the western civilization was the only civilization and that assimilation [to the west] was the only way of opening up Japan. As a result, they were fascinated by the European phonetic letters. This fascination went later as far as to propose a reform of the national language by trying to adopt a European language as national language (*kokugo*). In June 1872, [...] Mori Arinori [...] sent Yale University linguistics professor Whitney his ideas about creating a Japanese language by using English in place of Sino-Japanese. (Ōno, 1983: 19)

These quotations serve to highlight a number of issues. Yamada Yoshio (1873–1958), Tokieda Motoki (1900–1967) and Hirai Masao (born 1908) all use the term *kokugo* (national language), and Ōno Susumu (1919–2008) both *kokugo* and *nihongo* (Japanese). It goes without saying that the use of this terminology is rather problematic. Mori himself never used the term national language, but referred instead to the Japanese language as 'Japanese', 'the language of Japan', 'our language' and so forth. The reason for this is that at the time of his proposal the very concept of a national language of Japan did not yet exist. Only with the work of Ueda Kazutoshi (1867–1937) in the mid-1890s (see Chapter 4) did the idea of *kokugo* come into being. The above comments are thus somewhat anachronistic, having been made under the influence of what Lee Yeounsuk (1996) terms an ideology called *kokugo* (*kokugo to iu shisō*). Lee infers that by judging Mori from a modernist perspective, the scholars quoted above fail to take into account the historical context in which his proposal was created. However, Lee (1996: 5) believes that such readings of the proposal provide 'a key to unlock the Japanese language awareness'. She argues that the ideology of *kokugo*, that is, of Japanese as a national language, is so all-consuming that its very existence, and its entirely man-made origins, are all too often overlooked by those who came after Mori, who dealt himself with '[Japanese prior to [its becoming the] national language' (Lee, 1990: 51).

In the light of this fact, Jiří Neustupný (1995) and Kobayashi Toshihiro (2001) have forcefully argued that Mori's proposal must be understood within its historical context. The scholars quoted above, however, see Japanese as a unitary, monolithic language, in line with *kokugo* ideology, and apply this modernist view of Japanese to the pre-modernist linguistic situation of 1872. Mori's repeated use of the expression 'the language of Japan' is significant. Clearly, he did not consider it self-evident that Japanese (*nihongo*) be the language of Japan. Thus, what he proposed was neither abandoning Japanese as 'the national language' of Japan nor the adoption of English as a new 'national language', because the very notion of a national language was not part of his ideology. His proposal to introduce a simplified form of English was an attempt to provide Japan with a unified and modernized language, rather than a national language.

Western Reactions

The *Japan Weekly Mail* of 1 May 1873 reported the proposal of Mori Arinori. The article was highly critical, viewing the proposal as 'a flagrant instance of this dangerous superficiality' with which the process of modernization was treated in Japan (*Japan Weekly Mail*, 1873a). The report included an excerpt of Mori's letter to Dwight Whitney different from the one we find in the *Collected Works of Mori Arinori* (1972) as edited by Ōkubo. The letter as published in the *Japan Weekly Mail* on 1 May 1873 is reprinted in the journal *Eigo seinen – The Rising Generation* of October 1934. Ivan Parker Hall (1973) refers to the original letter at Yale University Library since the *Collected Works* of Mori Arinori were not printed when he wrote his monograph on Mori. Being a contributor to the collected works himself, Hall advises his readers to rely on Ōkubo's work in the future. We must therefore assume that the letter printed therein is the original. The punctuation, spelling, grammar, style and even content of the letter printed in *Japan Weekly Mail* have been significantly edited. Several passages are omitted or reformulated, while others have been added. The most important difference is in the first paragraph. Italics indicate the passages which were added.

The spoken language of Japan being inadequate to the growing necessities for the people of that Empire, and too poor to be made, by a phonetic alphabet, sufficiently useful as a written language, the idea prevails *among many of our best educated men and most profound thinkers*, that, if we would keep pace with the age, we must adopt a copious, *expandable* and expanding European language,

print our laws and transact all public businesses in it, as soon as possible, and have it taught in our schools as the future language of the country, to the gradual exclusion of our present language, spoken and written. (Japan Weekly Mail, 1873a)

The first of the insertions is taken from a later part of Mori's letter, while the second and third are presumably 'creative' editorial additions. Though inaccurate, they are of interest in so much as they give some insight into the contemporary interpretation of Mori's proposal, at least that of the anonymous editor. The interpretation here is that English should gradually replace Japanese in all domains. This certainly deals neatly with the apparent contradiction between Mori's support of both romanization and replacing Japanese with English, indicating that what was being proposed was initially to romanize Japanese, and later to replace it entirely.

The *Japan Weekly Mail* reported on three further occasions on Mori's proposal, on 7 July, 19 July and 2 August 1873. Mori's ideas for language reform were dealt with in the context of higher education in Japan. The proposal was considered inadequate, and Mori was ridiculed for considering the introduction of simplified English as a solution to the challenges Japan faced with regard to the modernization of its language:

Mr. Mori has proved himself so unpractical and reckless a visionary in his educational views, that little apology need to be offered for our having paid no attention in England to his vagaries. When a man has seriously made a proposition to carry over the English language bodily to Japan, and there tinker it for easy adaptation to the wants of the people, there is no further necessity for arguing with him. (*Japan Weekly Mail*, 1873b)

The same article included a discussion on possible alternatives to Mori's proposal. However, the possibility of western knowledge being transmitted in Japanese by western teachers was ruled out for the following reasons:

The difficulties it involves are enormous on account of the intractable nature of the Japanese language, the length of time required for its mastery in any sufficient measure to enable the students to lecture in it, and the entire absence from it, at least at present, of a scientific terminology adequate to the accurate definition indispensable for the pursuit of science. (*Japan Weekly Mail*, 1873b)

One of the *Japan Weekly Mail* articles also included a response to an article published in the *Springfield Weekly Republican* on 13 June 1873, titled 'Humbugs of Education in Japan' (*Japan Weekly Mail*, 1873c). The *Japan Weekly Mail* commented: 'The writer sets out by referring to Mr. Mori's much and properly ridiculed scheme for the displacement of Japanese by the English language.'

Oxford linguistics professor Archibald H. Sayce (1846–1933) also expressed scepticism about Mori's scheme, stating:

A paternal government may compel the acceptance of a foreign speech, in place of the familiar mother-tongue, like the rulers of Japan, who were said, a short time ago, to be mediating the substitution of English for the native language under pain of death. But even a government of this kind cannot invent a new grammar and a new dictionary; it can only borrow from others. (Sayce, 1880: 100)

From Mori's proposal, and the reactions which followed it, emerge different ideological views about language which illuminate the importance of their respective historical contexts. Mori's views on Japanese never achieved much popularity, his proposal constituting a peculiar blend of pre-modern and modernist ideologies (Neustupný, 1995). His ideas about language were rooted in pre-modern views on language in the sense that he did not view language as constituting any common bond of identity or marker of ethnicity, while being modernist in the sense that he strove for a unified and developed language. Much of the criticism Mori thus attracted came from either those of pre-modern or modernist ideological dispositions in particular.

Mori's proposal and its repercussions are an example of one ideology forming as a response to another. The prevalent modernist Japanese language ideology emerged from a particular historical context in which Japanese was under attack from other ideologies, both from within Japan and from outside. That is to say, the language ideology created during Japan's modernization was a response aimed both at Japanese and at westerners. To Mori, enlightened culture was western culture, and modern languages were western languages. The idea of an enlightened non-western culture, and of a modern non-western language were yet to be developed, and were novel not only in Japan, but also in the west. The modernization of Japanese thus required building confidence in a non-western language sufficient to serve the demands of modernity. This, in turn, required the creation of an empowering ideology linked to language. While Mori's proposal itself was ultimately discarded, his ideas about what functions a modern language for Japan should perform persisted. In contrast to what he had proposed, however, it was in fact Japanese which would fulfil those functions. The creation of a unified language began with a confrontation of the issues of diglossia related to Meiji period Japanese, thereby giving rise to a new and modern voice for Japan. It is to this topic that we shall now turn.

3 The Creation of a Modern Voice

In 1889, 16 years after Mori Arinori's proposal to replace Japanese with English and 21 years after the end of the Meiji restoration, and despite endless debating of the issue (see Hirai, 1998), a modernized and standardized version of Japanese was yet to be realized. This notwithstanding, the idea that Japanese must be adapted to the needs of modernity had firmly taken root, and many viewed the creation of a common language to unite all Japanese nationals as essential to the successful modernization of Japan.

The imagining of a unified language was initially largely focused on the written form. This demanded stylistic reform, the most important contribution towards which came from the Movement to Unify Spoken and Written Language (*genbun itchi undō*). Needless to say, such unification struggled to be more than idealistic. Tanaka Akio comments that,

> rapprochement to the spoken language called unification of spoken and written language was, strictly speaking, not a unification of 'the spoken language' and 'the written language'. Rather, it must be seen as a shift from the written language towards the spoken language of that time. In that sense, a considerable gap continues to exist [between spoken language and *genbun itchi* writing P.H.]. (Tanaka, 1999: 211)

Moulding language to an ideology, which claimed that spoken and written language were the same, resulted in mixtures of spoken and written language, both for spoken and for written language (Hagenauer, 1952: 447–448).

Written styles are emblems of authenticity and learning, and any attempted prescription of written style demands a rational underpinning. In this chapter, we will consider how the prevalent tradition of perceiving and conceptualizing written Japanese was exposed as an ideology, and subsequently replaced by another. Under normal circumstances, ideological concepts are hidden under almost impenetrable layers of common-sense, their appropriateness and legitimacy remaining unquestioned. It is usually only in times of crisis, confrontation or reform that ideology visibly surfaces (Blommaert, 1999). For this very reason, such debates deserve the attention of all those who study language ideology.

Through the course of the modernization of Japanese, the idea of what Pierre Bourdieu (1991) calls cultural capital – language being a part thereof – was altered across all strata of Japanese society. This required a redefining of who could be trusted as an authority on language. It is hardly surprising then, that the debate surrounding the *genbun itchi* movement became increasingly emotionally charged. Indeed, Nanette Twine (1978: 333) characterizes it as 'one of the most significant and bitterly contested reforms of the Meiji period'.

The *genbun itchi* Movement

In the final three decades of the 19th century, Japan found itself forced into deciding which parts of western culture to adopt, and which parts of its own to uphold. With regard to language, the sudden exposure to the west initially forced only a review of script reform, the focus of attention expanding only slowly from writing systems to written styles. This expansion was brought about by a mounting belief that script reform was pointless without prior reform of written style. At the time, written Japanese was subject to a greater degree of influence from Chinese than is Japanese today, and was accordingly less intelligible when read aloud. The term *genbun itchi* was itself coined in 1885, by Kanda Takahira (1830–1898), a scholar of western learning who was later to become an influential statesman. The debate over the need to unify spoken and written Japanese reached its climax in 1889, during a discussion that evolved in the journal *Bun* (*Letters*) (Takamatsu, 1900: 39). We shall study this in detail further below.

The perception of a need to reform written Japanese was not simply a construct of modernist imaginings, however. Consider the situation at the start of the Meiji period. The written language had a great many distinct forms, the most prestigious of these being so difficult to master that they demanded many years of diligent study. The main forms of the written language were *kanbun* (Sino-Japanese), *wabun* (classical Japanese, *sōrōbun* (epistolary style) and *wakan konkōbun* (Japanese–Chinese mixed style), each of these themselves comprising several sub-styles. The prevailing variety of Japanese–Chinese mixed style, for example, consisted of sub-variants such as *gazoku setchū-tai* (refined–colloquial mixed style), a combination of *gabun-tai* (elegant style), *zokubun-tai* (colloquial style) and *futsūbun* (general-purpose style). What the *genbun itchi* movement proposed, however, was a single, national standard of writing, and with this came the call to abolish all other styles. This idea was quite revolutionary since, as we will see in the following subchapter, written styles served to identify the social status of the writer in what was linguistically a rigidly stratified society.

Development of the *genbun itchi* Movement

The *genbun itchi* movement was actually more amorphous than the term itself implies. It involved three distinct groups, (1) the supporters of enlightenment; (2) novelists and literary critics and, latterly; (3) western-trained Japanese linguists. The development of the argument in favour of the new written style, *genbun itchi*, can be seen as having two distinct stages (Twine, 1978: 339), the first being driven largely by utilitarian motives and lasting for just a decade from the mid-1870s onwards. The second, literary phase lasted from the mid-1880s until 1910, during which the influence of western-trained linguists in rationalizing and legitimizing of the *genbun itchi* style can be seen.

In its first decade, the *genbun itchi* movement was little more than an offshoot of the various language reform movements that called for the abolishment of Chinese characters. It gathered further momentum in 1874 when the enlightenment *Meiji Six Journal* (*Meiroku zasshi*) was launched. In the year Meiji 6, stylistically simplified writing was often recommended and occasionally put into practice. The practitioners of the unification of spoken and written Japanese *avant la lettre* reads like a Who is Who of Meiji period intellectual life. It includes such scholars and academics as Nishi Amane (1829–1897), Fukuzawa Yukichi (1835–1901), Katō Hiroyuki (1836–1919), Maejima Hisoka (1835–1919), Taguchi Ukichi (1855–1905), Mozume Takami (1847–1928) and Baba Tatsui (1850–1888), journalists like Fukuchi Gen'ichirō (1841–1906), and high-ranking officials from the Ministry of Education such as Nishimura Shigeki (1828–1902) or Ōki Takatō (1832–1899).

The second stage of the *genbun itchi* movement began with the publication in 1886 of a book titled *The Essence of the Novel* (*Shōsetsu shinzui*) by literary critic, translator and writer Tsubouchi Shōyō (1859–1935). In this influential monograph, Tsubouchi advocates that the conventions of western realism be adopted for the nascent modern Japanese novel, urging Japanese authors to write as they would speak. The most prominent authors to uphold Tsubouchi's proposal were Futabatei Shimei (1864–1909) and his friend Yamada Bimyō (1868–1910) (Yamamoto, 1981: 69–71). Futabatei is generally hailed as having written the first modern Japanese novel, *Drifting Clouds* (*Ukigumo*), published in 1887 and written entirely in the new *genbun itchi* style. Although less well known as a writer than Futabatei, Yamada was more vocal in defending the causes of *genbun itchi* in various essays and speeches (see below for more details on him).

The second phase of the movement reached its peak at the turn of the century, losing much of its momentum by 1910, by which time *genbun itchi* was already established in various domains, subsequently becoming the norm for written language. In the closing stages of the movement, two more groups of advocates formed, one the Genbun Itchi Club (*Genbun Itchi-kai*), the other the National Language Research Council (*Kokugo Chōsa I'inkai*). Both groups comprised western-trained Japanese linguists, and their role in shaping modernist language ideology in Japan will be discussed in more detail in Chapter 4.

The individuals and institutions mentioned above subsequently engaged in language reform activities with regard to the corpus, status and prestige planning of Japanese. Corpus planning was centred on grammar, selection of a copula, sentence final particles and auxiliary verb inflection. They also included syntactical simplification, which found expression in more transparent sentence construction and in increased use of conjunctions and punctuation. Status planning was concentrated on proscription and spread of the new *genbun itchi* style. Owing to the involvement of the National Language Research Council, founded in 1902, *genbun itchi* was promoted as the only style adequate for cultural and professional domains at the national level. The effect of this was that by 1903 all schoolbooks were written in *genbun itchi* style. By 1908, all novels – and by 1926, all newspaper editorials – had followed suit. The last traces of the old written standard in public life were removed in 1946, when the new, post-war constitution was composed in the *genbun itchi* style (Inoue, 1991).

Aims of the *genbun itchi* Movement

Whereas the early advocates of *genbun itchi* and the members of the National Language Research Council endeavoured to spread the new written style throughout society, novelists writing in *genbun itchi* style did not actively propagate their favoured style of writing for any particular group, fellow writers of the modern novel aside. The literary *avant-garde* simply strove for a description of reality without exaggerated stylistic device or ornament. According to literary critic Tsubouchi, modern literature had to start paying attention to ordinary life, and the modern novel to accept the protagonist as its narrator. Beyond these demands, in Tsubouchi's view the narrator–protagonist could reasonably take any form – be they a child, a fool or a thief, for example – and the novel any subject, from landscape to disease to the events of daily life (Karatani, 1993: 178). A faithful and authentic approach to the depiction of the protagonist's centred psychological experience presupposed, in turn, a plain form of expression that had also to be aesthetically pleasing.

Lack of political ambitions notwithstanding, the novelists thus played a pivotal role with regard to the acceptance of *genbun itchi* and the nation building process. It was they who created a 'We' in the sense of Benedict Anderson (1991), that is to say, the books of the *genbun itchi* novelists broke new ground in addressing a readership inclusive of all Japanese, and only 'all Japanese'. In so doing, these works were of critical importance in the establishment of 'the Japanese' as an imagined community. Even more importantly, perhaps, these novelists also created a body of works representative of 'good' *genbun itchi* writing. The contributions of the *genbun itchi* novelists were much appreciated by those who aimed to raise national pride and national identity through the promotion of civilization and enlightenment (*bunmei kaika*). According to supporters of Japanese enlightenment, its success demanded the establishment of mass education, which itself necessitated the simplification of writing. Those advocating *genbun itchi* for utilitarian rather than for aesthetic reasons, sought, and quickly found, support in the Ministry of Education, which was faced with the task of developing curricula for compulsory education at the time. They also found support among the newly established popular newspapers, which sought to expand their readership.

It is important to keep in mind that, at the time, a formal, state-sanctioned language policy was yet to even be proposed, let alone implemented. As such, there existed no institutional political support for the creation of a uniform written style. In fact, tight control of domestic authority had resulted in the government repressing the Movement for Freedom and People's Rights (*Jiyū minken undō*). Because the civil rights movement in Japan had adopted *genbun itchi* style in order to better reach out the masses, government repression of the movement also temporarily halted further expansion of *genbun itchi*, and the style was not revived until novelists once again turned their attention to reforming the written language in the late 1880s. Initially, little support could reasonably be expected from scholars either, and it was not until 1902, with western linguistics now firmly established in Japan, that the first western-trained linguist at Tokyo University, Ueda Kazutoshi (1867–1937), would successfully call for the establishment of a National Language Research Council and the launch of a state-supported language policy (see Chapter 4).

In seeking inspiration from the west, and through their imitation of western models, the enlighteners and the novelists took a similar line in their search for a new written style. In order to reach the masses through written language, the more utilitarian factions argued for a reduction in the usage of Chinese characters, something that could only reasonably be achieved by taking written Japanese closer to the spoken language. Following the methods of the French playwright Molière (1622–1673), enlightenment writer Fukuzawa Yukichi asked his housekeeper to read and comment on his work, in order to verify its intelligibility to the masses. Fukuzawa was also the first to consciously restrict, in a purposeful and organized fashion, the number of the Chinese characters he used in his published works. It is worth noting that many of Fukuzawa's works, such as *Conditions of the West* (*Seiyō jijō*) and *An Encouragement of Learning* (*Gakumon no susume*) were bestsellers at the time, and even today remain unparalleled in terms of their reception by the Japanese public.

Whereas works produced by this utilitarian faction contain many stylistic idiosyncrasies, the literates attempted to form a cohesive, uniform *genbun itchi* style. Futabatei Shimei turned his attention to the spoken language of pre-enlightenment Tokyo (Edo). In his search for a colloquial style, Futabatei was aided by the development, in 1882, of a Japanese shorthand system that facilitated the transcription of spoken language for study purposes. This system was devised by Takusari Tsunaki (1854–1938). That said, it should be noted that Futabatei believed contemporary Tokyo speech to contain too much variation to serve as a model for a unifying and uniform language (Ryan, 1965: 91).

Generally speaking, all *genbun itchi* writers drew on established styles of both spoken and written language. One such influential source for writing was the language employed in the traditional storytelling performances known as *rakugo* (comic storytelling) or *gesaku* (playful-literature) of the Edo period (1602–1868). In order to reduce the gap between written and spoken language, advocates of *genbun itchi* searched for spoken styles that could most easily be transcribed as written language. Rather than casual speech or conversation, the advocates of *genbun itchi* favoured public speeches (Morioka, 1985), comic storytelling (*rakugo*), lectures and lay sermons (*shigaku dōwa*) as models of spoken language suitable for use in the creation of *genbun itchi* writing (Tanaka, 2001: 769). Japanese translations of the naturalistic novels of western writers also provided important material. Futabatei Shimei himself translated the work of Ivan Turgenev (1818–1883), something that forced him to experiment much with styles of writing in order to communicate effectively Turgenev's straightforward language. Having mastered the translation of naturalistic Russian literature into Japanese, Futabatei went on to write much of his groundbreaking novel *Drifting Clouds* first in Russian, and then translated these passages into his own language.

In view of the contemporary social and political context, much of these ideological decisions were the result of debate between intellectuals, academics, politicians and novelists. Few outside these circles were convinced of the demand for, and aesthetic appeal of, the *genbun itchi* style. What we call prestige planning in language planning theory today remained the preserve of those involved in these debates. The issue of writing served as a battleground to settle conflicts between traditionalists and the newly emerging, westernized intellectual elite, both sides believing that only one could be victorious. Of course, ideological debate about language is never about language alone (Cameron, 1995). Rather, such debate serves a vehicle for deciding issues of power and legitimacy (Duchêne & Heller, 2007), and the debate on *genbun itchi* in the journal *Bun* was no exception.

The *Bun* Debate

It is worth analysing this debate in some detail, particularly with respect to the linguistic commentary manifested within it. We will focus first on the abundance of meta-pragmatics, both explicit and implicit, before turning to issues pertaining to ideology and power.

The *Bun* debate took place between March and July 1889, the year of the proclamation of Japan's first constitution. In the ongoing struggle between westernization and adherence to its own traditions, Japan experienced a period in which the traditionalists regained the upper hand in the Japanese modernization process. After 1877, the tendency was to take direction from traditions of Japanese culture, and the practice of *genbun itchi* writing almost completely disappeared from journals and newspapers (Twine, 1978: 342). It was in such a climate that Miyake Yonekichi (1860–1929), editor of *Bun* and a staunch supporter of *genbun itchi*, opened a column to its discussion. In a lecture to the Roman Letter Club (*Rōmaji-kai*) in early 1887, Basil Hall Chamberlain (1850–1935), the first professor of linguistics at Tokyo University, had argued in favour of writing Japanese with the Latin alphabet (Twine, 1978: 344). Such reform would require that writing be based on contemporary spoken Japanese (Matsushita, 1960a: 48), and it was from these comments that the *Bun* debate originated.

The debate comprised 25 articles by 12 authors: Anezaki Shōji, Aoki Yoshimasa, Fujiyama Yutaka, Hekikai Rōjin, Hyōtan Sei, Kizaki Aikichi, Kojima Kenkichi, Komai Chikafusa, Matsumoto Inkyō, Nishi Moroi, Yamada Bimyō and Yoshimi Keirin. Among them, Yamada Bimyō, the foremost advocate of *genbun itchi*, and Kojima Kenkichi, his principal opponent, were central. Vicarious ideology clearly played a role in who would be remembered and who would not, for among these authors the only who remains well-known today is Yamada Bimyō, heralded in modern-day Japan as one of the great men of the Meiji period (1869–1912).

At the time of the debate, Yamada was working as an editor of the literary journal *Metropolitan Flower* (*Miyako no hana*). Having failed to be accepted to Tokyo University in 1887, Yamada took up professional writing, establishing himself with a collection of short stories published in the same year. In later essays such as 'The Infancy of Meiji Period Literature' (*Meiji bungaku no yōran jidai*, 1906) and '*Genbun itchi* Sacrifices' (*Genbun itchi no gisei*, 1907), Yamada looked back at reasons behind his conversion to *genbun itchi* (Yamamoto, 1981: 72). These were, principally, an awareness that *genbun itchi* was practised as an ideal in the west, Geoffrey Chaucer's (1343–1400) use of vernacular language and the impression this made upon him, Chamberlain's speech about the possibilities of romanizing Japanese, and an essay titled *Genbun itchi* written by the lexicographer and Tokyo University professor Mozume Takami (1847–1928). A year before the *Bun* debate, Yamada had already published an essay titled 'Outline of *genbun itchi*' (*Genbun itchi gairyaku*) in which he set out his arguments in favour of the unification of spoken and written Japanese (see Matsushita, 1960b).

In all, the debate contained 11 contributions in favour of *genbun itchi*, and 11 against. A further three took a centralist position on the issue, but for the sake of brevity these will not be discussed further here. Of those articles in favour of *genbun itchi*, Yamada's accounted for 74%, while Kojima Kenkichi was responsible for 66% of those contributions in opposition.

Textlinguistic Characterization of the Contributions

Before examining explicit meta-pragmatic comments made in the debate, let us quickly review textlinguistic characterizations, by way of illustrating the considerable stylistic differences between the writing of the advocates and critics of *genbun itchi*. We may reasonably view this variation in style as an example of what Michael Silverstein (1993) calls implicit meta-pragmatics. Implicit meta-pragmatics refers to an attempt to attach prestige to a text not only by commenting on the superior quality of one's written style but by putting such style into practice. Throughout the articles of the *Bun* debate, the authors' stance regarding *genbun itchi* is evidenced as much by the stylistic choices those authors make as by their words.

The most striking stylistic difference between the texts of the two sides is in the length of sentences. Whereas those articles opposing *genbun itchi* contain sentences with an average of 369 characters, those in support average just 104. Pro-*genbun itchi* contributors Nishi and Anezaki, however, deviate from this, with sentences averaging 319 and 454 characters, respectively.

Exclude their material from this calculation and the difference between the two sides is even more marked, the average sentence length of the remaining essays being now only 42 characters. Comparing Kojima (anti-*genbun itchi*) and Yamada (pro-*genbun itchi*) further illustrates this difference, Kojima averaging 407 characters per sentence, Yamada just 31. The longest sentence Kojima uses throughout the debate contains no less than 1139 characters, while Yamada's longest is just 118 characters long. Kojima's shortest sentence, conversely, totals 56 characters, but Yamada's is just two characters in length! Even such an elementary comparison as this illustrates quite clearly that the written work of those in favour of the *genbun itchi* style are more accessible to the average reader.

It goes without saying that such pronounced differences in sentence length have an effect on the complexity of both morphology and syntax, though these lend themselves less easily to quantitative analysis than sentence length. It will suffice, however, to comment on the most significant differences between the two sides, again setting the contributions of Nishi and Anezaki aside. As has been widely commented upon (e.g. Inoue, 2006; Tanaka, 2001) in the literature on the *genbun itchi* movement, stylistic innovations were centred on the choice of the copula and on the use of clause final particles. Clause final particles are almost completely absent from contributions by those authors arguing against *genbun itchi*. The most frequent copula verbs are *naru* and *taru*, both exclusively part of literary language today, as are the negative suffixes -*zu* and -*nu*, which also occur frequently. The same is true with regard to auxiliary inflection, neither -*beshi* (shall), -*bekarazu* (shall not), nor -*gotoku* (as) featuring in modern-day spoken Japanese.

The near-total absence of conjunctions in the contributions of those opposed to *genbun itchi* is another feature worth noting. The long sentences constructions are either accomplished by using gerunds, which express a sequence of actions or simultaneous actions, or through the continuative verb-base (*renyōkei*) which functions as a coordination conjunction similar to 'and' in English. A predilection for the use of literary language is also evident in lexical terms. Expressions such as *chitose* (a thousand years), *hippu hippu* (humble men and women), *raidō* (follow blindly) or *gojin* (we), all used by Kojima, are absent from colloquial Japanese today, and Kojima is not alone making frequent use of such literary expressions. Komai (1889a), for instance, uses metaphors of classical Chinese such as *enkōgetsu*, which refers to a monkey trying to catch the moon's reflection in water, and meaning 'to bring ruin upon oneself by attempting to do something beyond one's power'.

Nishi and Anezaki aside, the language used by those contributors who support *genbun itchi* differs on each and all of the aforementioned lexical and syntactical areas. In particular, they contain extensive use of clause final particles, a feature of spoken language at the time. The biggest difference, however, is in the choice of copula verbs. Advocates of *genbun itchi* made almost exclusive use of *desu* and *da* in their essays. These verbs signify the T–V distinction; that is to say, they express difference in levels of politeness and social proximity. Yamada (1889c) even uses the assertive construction *no desu*, which is a marker of informality in written language. This extends also to negative constructions, *-nai* and *-masen* prevailing (again, T–V distinction). Whilst their sentences are much shorter, the pro-*genbun itchi* writers also make far greater use of conjunctions like *moshi* (if) or *kara* (because). With regard to lexis, an abundance of everyday words is evident in the work of these advocates, of whom Yamada is by far the most innovative writer, using interjections such as *yoshi* (alright) and even, unusual at the time, loan words from European languages such as *idiomu* (idiom).

Another crucial difference is in the organization of the respective contributions. In contrast to the advocates of *genbun itchi*, the critics make little effort to organize their writing into paragraphs. Yamada, on the other hand, makes frequent use of enumerations, as well as briefly juxtaposing his own views against Kojima's before discussing them in detail. All of this makes for much easier reading of the contributions of the pro-*genbun itchi* writers, and that one of their essays, that of Kizaki (1889), deals exclusively with matters of layout and font is a further indicator of the novelty of such changes in the organization of written texts at the time.

Meta-Pragmatic Comments

Explicit meta-pragmatic commentary, that is, the expression of feelings and ideas about what language ought to be, abound in the debate. We may divide these broadly into (1) general comments about the Japanese language; (2) commentary on the language use of those opposed to *genbun itchi*; and (3) comments made about the critics themselves and relating to their use of language. Throughout the debate, these critics of *genbun itchi* are on the defensive, protective of ideals of Japanese spirit and tradition. The advocates of *genbun itchi*, on the other hand, attack these positions, which they perceive as backward, old-fashioned and inappropriate for modern life.

Turning our attention firstly to those meta-pragmatic comments relating to language – rather than their users – we see that in the eyes of the critics of *genbun itchi*, language is first and foremost a means of writing. Written language, in turn, signifies elegant writing (*gabun*), itself defined as an art (Kojima, 1889a). Kojima (1889a) claims that elegant writing 'elevates the soul' and 'captures a spirit of Japaneseness unknown to western languages', and is something 'beautiful and pure' (Kojima, 1889c), while to Yoshimi

(1889), writing is 'the embellishment of the spoken language'. Conversely, colloquial language, whether spoken or written, was portrayed as 'ordinary', 'primitive' and 'without rules'. As such, these critics viewed writing based on spoken language was as 'primitive', 'artless' (Matsumoto, 1889b) and 'coarse' (Kojima, 1889d). They deemed contemporary spoken language to be lacking in quality, and used this to justify their reliance on ancient forms of language. As Kojima (1889d) put it, if *genbun itchi* writing was of high quality, 'it would arise by itself' to become the standard for writing. Kojima (1889d) warns that it is 'hazardous' to 'mix ordinary and refined language', as the former will inevitably ruin the latter. Thus, as far as the critics were concerned, spoken and written language were to be kept separate at all costs.

That the language used by advocates of *genbun itchi* was viewed with disdain by their detractors is, then, hardly surprising. Of Hyōtan Sei it is said that he 'writes like a schoolboy', while the written style of Yamada is described as 'verbose' and 'tiresome' (Kojima, 1889b), and Fujiyama's essay is labelled 'boring', 'presumptuous in tone' and altogether 'lacking skill' (Kojima, 1889e). Authors who spoke in support of unifying spoken and written language were considered unqualified to engage in debates over language (Kojima, 1889b), and prone to 'oversimplification' (Matsumoto, 1889b). Yamada, in particular, is characterized as being attracted by 'odd things' (Kojima, 1889c), and derided for apparently 'considering himself learned' (Kojima, 1889d). Indeed, the entire debate surrounding *genbun itchi* was seen by those opposed to it as nothing more than a means of 'concealing the ignorance in writing' of those who argued in its favour (Kojima, 1889a).

Of course, these were the very beliefs and opinions the advocates sought to counter, and they did so by foregrounding the instrumental function of writing. To them, contemporary language was a means of advancing society. To that end, *genbun itchi* was presented as a 'more powerful' alternative than elegant writing (Yamada, 1889a). They believed elegant writing to be 'inadequate' for 'the age of enlightenment' (Yamada, 1889d), and unsuitable for the expression of modern concepts and ideas (Yamada, 1889b). Hyōtan (1889a) argued that, because writing is 'a matter of everyday concern', *genbun itchi* should be 'used exclusively'. Moreover, *genbun itchi* was portrayed as a 'precondition of the development of the sciences' in the west, thus, by analogy, the 'contemporary spoken language of Tokyo' should be 'appropriated for the modern age' (Yamada, 1889e). Any notion of refinement, therefore, was seen as nothing more than 'a question of taste', of aesthetics, and perfectly achievable with any 'language material' (Yamada, 1889a).

Just as the critics of *genbun itchi* criticized the language used by its supporters, so was the reverse true, the latter attacking Kojima, in particular, as being too wordy. Yamada (1889c) summarized two pages of Kojima's work in nine lines in order to demonstrate the superiority of his own writing, undermining Kojima's efforts to lend authority to refined writing by rendering it in *genbun itchi* style. In a later contribution, Yamada (1889f) goes as far as to point out flaws in Kojima's writing, suggesting that his use of language is less refined than he would have his readers believe. Such passages are an attempt to expose the implicit meta-pragmatics practiced throughout the debate by every author but Nishi and Anezaki. Yamada's aim in doing so is to discredit Kojima both as a writer and as an authority on language, thus making a connection between one's use of, and knowledge about, language with one's personality in the minds of his readers.

The critics themselves, as well as their use of language, came under criticism as well. The view espoused by Anezaki (1889) was that the critics were reluctant to use spoken language as a model for writing on account of their learnedness. Fujiyama (1889), too, criticizes Kojima for appearing to equate one's level of knowledge with one's aptitude in the 'memorizing of written characters'. Kojima is repeatedly characterized as lacking sufficient knowledge about matters of contemporary spoken language, mocked, for example, by Yamada (1889f) for proclaiming himself to be knowledgeable, and a staunch defender of the Japanese language, while at the same time stating that contemporary spoken language lacked rules. Kojima's classification of *genbun itchi* writing as low-minded language served only to further doubts about his credentials as an authority on language (Yamada, 1889e). Scepticism surrounding the linguistic expertise of the critics did not end with spoken language, either. Yamada (1889a) points out that his critics seem unaware that elegant writing has its basis in the spoken language, too, in the spoken language of an ancient time, and continues this argument in later contributions to the debate. Yamada (1889e) is here giving his adversaries a taste of their own medicine, using notions of tradition to lend *genbun itchi* more prestige. The question of whether the *genbun itchi* style lacks quality seems superfluous to him, for as far as Yamada is concerned, elegant writing is itself an 'ancient form of *genbun itchi*'.

Language, Ideology and Power

Of course, the idea that standardized, codified and institutionalized language varieties are superior is far from exclusive to Japan. The same is true of the view that 'good language use' may generally be defined as that language inherited from previous generations. What was more uniquely Japanese was how the field of written language continued to be affected by pre-modern class distinctions, despite their nominal abolition by the Meiji government in 1871. These class differences remained firmly entrenched through stylistic choices, and so what we called, in the introduction to this book, the linguistic margin was not 'explained away', as it was later to be under the influence of modernist ideology in the 20th century. Rather, in 1889, the margin both existed and was openly acknowledged, and its status as marginal was seen as justified. In other words, the idea of 'linguistic communism', that is, of equal distribution of linguistic skill between all Japanese, had not been established yet.

Those claiming to be educated were supposed to have mastered the standards of both written and spoken language, while those not having mastered these legitimized language skills were expected to remain silent and to accept their participatory exclusion on linguistic grounds. Violating this convention was the very affront that the *genbun itchi* advocates committed in the course of the debate. Kojima (1889a) had explicitly voiced the opinion that people with little formal education 'do not matter' in affairs related to the 'advancement of civilization', and it is for this reason that the debate centred on both the question of the (alleged) quality of *genbun itchi* writing and, more importantly still, on the legitimacy of those using *genbun itchi* to debate matters of Japanese culture and tradition.

The *genbun itchi* style was characterized by its detractors as devoid of meaning, ordinary, odd and artless, and its advocates as ignorant and uneducated, dilettantes and lunatics who produced texts which were essentially worthless, unconvincing, boring, presumptuous and as useless as the whole endeavour to unify spoken and written language. Of course, any such assessment rests on the assumption that those voicing such opinions themselves represent exactly the opposite. In any case, the advocates of *genbun itchi* were branded as lacking the necessary intellectual prowess to engage in such intellectual debates: to borrow from Bourdieu (1991: 55, emphasis in the original), they were seen as lacking the competence 'to produce sentences that are likely to be *listened to*, likely to be recognized as *acceptable*'. It was on these grounds that Kojima (1889d) urged Yamada to give up his debating, seeming to take pity on him for making a 'fool of himself'.

The advocates of *genbun itchi*, however, saw language as a means of advancing society, and it is in this clash of opinions that we are able to see how social structures give rise to ideologies. In a time of massive social, cultural and economic change, a new ideology of language arose, and the ensuing confrontation was inevitable. Based on their idea of language as social proficiency, the critics were destined to view the acceptance of spoken language patterns in writing as evidence of language decline. Moreover, they believed the spoken language of the day to be in a state of confusion, and this prompted the critics of *genbun itchi* to rush to the defence of what they saw as appropriate linguistic behaviour.

The advocates of *genbun itchi* had quite different ideas about language and society, for they sought to empower the people by simplifying written style. Writing, they argued, should not be the sole preserve of those of 'privileged descent' (Hyōtan, 1889b) or to the 'tone of alleyway houses' (Yamada, 1889b). Nishi Moroi and Yamada Bimyō went further still, stressing the integrating role that language had to fulfil if Japan was ever to be modernized. Nishi (1889), in particular, believed that, in order for Japan to successfully modernize, the educated had to take responsibility for the rest of the population. Thus, being of the opinion that *genbun itchi* represented a means of uniting the Japanese people, the existence of a difficult written style constituted a barrier to modernization. Consequently, in his first contribution to the *Bun* debate, Yamada (1889a: 396) asks 'is the taste on which the high esteem of elegant writing rests still appropriate for the people and the present time'?

Just as with Mori Arinori's proposal to replace Japanese with English, the present discussion features multiple language ideologies. Debate alone, however, could not settle the resultant ideological conflict, for ideology was rooted in social discord. Here, one ideology, that of the advocates of *genbun itchi*, attempts to empower the masses, while on the other side, the ideological aim is to defend a stratified social order that now found itself under threat. The latter view traced its origins back to feudal Japan, and had so much become the accepted status quo that the opponents of *genbun itchi* saw it as nothing less than common sense. Attempts by the advocates to debate the validity of such a position were therefore destined to meet with derision. Fujiyama (1889) explicitly challenged the critics to make the arguments for their assertion that elegant writing was more appropriate than *genbun itchi*, but the critics believed so completely in their language ideology, which had been enforced and reinforced by authority and power for centuries, as to deem its defence entirely unnecessary. In this way, the *Bun* debate illustrates a manifestation of power shifts and the struggle for power which accompanied the wider social upheavals of the Meiji period (1868–1912).

The argument about *genbun itchi* was therefore only possible because its advocates themselves believed, indefatigably so, that they were better able to debate matters related to the coming of the modern age. Indeed, those elements of the debate concerned with the western experience of modernization were all introduced by the advocates, who vigorously asserted that they, and not their opponents, were best placed to discuss such things as western literature, the development of modern science and the emergence of the western national languages. From this came the advocates' belief that it was they who, under modernity, were now the legitimate experts in linguistic matters, and this was the basis of their subsequent efforts to wrestle power from those seeking to perpetuate an ideology and associated practices rooted in pre-modern times. For their part, the critics largely resorted to making disparaging remarks about the advocates and their use of language, as well as to branding the entire debate as futile and of little consequence. This was an attempt to avoid a full-blown challenge to the *status quo* by breaking the will of the advocates early on, but its failure as a strategy allowed the advocates to make visible the former's now outdated ideology, to portray it as an artefact, and by so doing, to clear the way for a new ideology and new linguistic practices.

The very fact that *genbun itchi* became a topic worthy of discussion in the journal *Bun* reveals the weakening grip of the old ideology of writing as craft, which had long served to legitimize the existing social order. Ideology, once perceived of as an artefact, becomes vulnerable. As Fairclough puts it:

> Ideology is most effective when its workings are least visible. If one becomes aware that a particular aspect of common-sense is sustaining power inequalities at one's own expense, it ceases to *be* common-sense, and may cease to have the capacity to sustain power inequalities, i.e. to function ideologically. (Fairclough, 2001: 71, emphasis in the original)

When Yamada defines elegant writing as merely a matter of taste, a psychological phenomenon, he exposes standing common sense as something actively created, and as something which serves one group better than others. In so doing, he breaks through naturalized concepts, deviating from what Bourdieu (1977) has defined as the recognition of legitimacy through misrecognition of the arbitrary grounds on which legitimacy rests. That is to say, the recognition of the arbitrary grounds upon which the appreciation of written language rested came to be recognized and, as an effect, its consequences on society were reflected upon, and alternatives to it were envisioned. In short, ideology no longer functioned ideologically.

Acceptance of *genbun itchi*

In one brief summary of the debate, Matsushita (1960a: 53–55) portrays Kojima as the victor, asserting that Yamada had failed to put forward a convincing argument for the implementation of *genbun itchi*. One could equally well argue, however, that neither side came out the winner, for the advocates of *genbun itchi* could not be convinced of the appropriateness of elegant writing. For students of language ideology, however, the idea of the debate having winners and losers is rather irrelevant. After all, not language itself, but legitimacy and expertise relative to matters of language and society were the focus of the debate, and, ultimately, its outcome was not decided by arguments but by the shifting distribution of power.

The debate about *genbun itchi* did not stay within the pages of the journal *Bun*. The following year, in 1890, several articles in the journal *Imperial Literature* (*Teikoku bungaku*) were strongly critical of the use of *genbun itchi*. In fact, the early 1890s witnessed a return to the *gazoku setchū-tai* (refined–colloquial mixed style), a written style that had first emerged in the Edo period (1602–1868). The most prominent practitioner of *genbun itchi* writing, Futabatei Shimei stopped writing novels in the 1890s, and Yamada Bimyō turned his attention to poetry. This return to the refined–colloquial mixed style was finally halted in 1895, however, with the Japanese defeat of China in the Sino-Japanese War. The resultant increase in the nation's self-esteem led to an abandonment of those written styles modelled closely on Chinese, paving the way for the wholesale adoption of *genbun itchi* (Clark, 2002: 235–236; Twine, 1988: 444; Yamamoto, 1981: 261).

By the turn of the century, *genbun itchi* had grown into the dominant written style and the voice of modern Japan. Around 1910, use of the term *genbun itchi* outside academic circles ceased, and the ideological notions accompanying this once-novel style became so normalized as to be considered common sense. *Genbun itchi* became the new normative model of 'correct' written Japanese, and the arbitrary grounds on which its conventions rested became invisible. A mixture of spoken and written styles that was continuously refined and polished, it was dissimilar to any spoken language form that had existed at any time previously. The rules of its grammar were discovered, and where they did not exist they were created (see Chapter 4), forming and perpetuating ideological views shaped over the course of countless debates about language and society under modernity, of which the *Bun* debate of 1889 was just one, albeit an important contribution.

In Chapter 1, we considered how the modernization of Japan entailed a certain redistribution of power, accomplished through the social upheavals of the Meiji period (1868–1912). The debate in the journal *Bun* is one manifestation of such a power struggle, and a reminder that ideologies are not inherently common sense but must be made that way. Once established as common sense, ideologies become invisible. Following the *Bun* debate, written language modelling itself on spoken language was not only not perceived to be ugly, unrefined or crude, in the minds of the Japanese, it could not be imagined to not be modelled on spoken language any longer.

As a result of debate about written style, and the canonization and institutionalization of the *genbun itchi* style in the Meiji period, the idea of writing as craft fell from grace. *Genbun itchi* became the *status quo*, carrying with it the idea that writing belonged to all Japanese people, regardless of region, class or milieu. The displacement of existing writing conventions also affected the spoken language, for writing always acts as a blueprint for speech, rather than a representation thereof (Coulmas, 2003: 9). The newly formed *genbun itchi* style thus came to serve as the model for both written and spoken Japanese. What is more, the *genbun itchi* movement was seminal in envisioning a homogenous Japanese speech community, a speech community in which all could be equal. What remained absent was a comprehensive ideology to account for and rationalize such views about language and society, which would later be devised and introduced by the 'founding father' of Japanese national language linguistics, Ueda Kazutoshi. The development of modern Japanese was completed by the creation of the National Language Research Council, in which Ueda's influence could also be seen. In the next chapter, we will examine this in greater detail.

4 The Unification of Japanese

This chapter covers events that took place, for the most part, in the last 20 years of the Meiji period (1868–1912). As a result of seemingly endless debate and a significant body of published work, the common use of contemporary spoken language by the educated classes in Tokyo had gained substantial recognition by that time. Accordingly, an idea of what modern Japanese might eventually look like had begun to take shape. The next crucial step in the process of language modernization was to gather the support of the Japanese people for language unification. This first required the existence of a common, shared understanding of what language ought to be, for it demanded that all Japanese nationals change their use of, and behaviour towards, language in a co-ordinated way. This chapter details the emergence and materialization of a language ideology suited to overcoming what resistance to a unified national language spoken by all Japanese remained. We will examine the means by which Ueda Kazutoshi (1867–1937) provided the central idea of Japanese as the national language of Japan (see section on 'Ueda Kazutoshi'), and how the National Language Research Council (1902–1916) codified Standard Japanese in accordance with the ideological framework laid down by Ueda (see section on 'The National Language Research Council'). In the following discussion, we will focus on language ideology (for more comprehensive accounts of language planning activities in the Meiji period, see Carroll, 2001; Coyaud, 1983; Hirai, 1998; Twine, 1991).

Ueda was the first to insist that language problems had a political (creating a sense of unity within the emerging Japanese nation, using Japanese as a symbol of nationality, and so on) as well as a linguistic dimension (for example, script reform, stylistic reform, expansion of the lexicon). Implicit within this assertion was the need to establish and spread new notions of language ideology. Essentially, modernist language ideology needed to make sense to all Japanese nationals, and to achieve this it would need powerful supporters. Such support was also necessary because this novel idea of a national language, equally shared and mastered by all, was notably incongruent with the sociolinguistic situation of the time.

Ueda Kazutoshi: Japan's First Modern Linguist

Born in Edo, renamed Tokyo one year later, Ueda Kazutoshi (1867–1937) grew up speaking the local language variety from which Standard Japanese was to evolve. He enrolled in Tokyo Imperial University in 1885, where he studied Japanese literature (*wabungaku*), under the guidance of tutors including Tsubouchi Shōyō (1859–1935), author of *The Essence of the Novel*. On entering Tokyo University, Ueda initially wished to become a novelist, but changed his mind after attending the linguistics classes of Basil Hall Chamberlain (1850–1935). The young Ueda was particularly impressed with Chamberlain's *A Handbook of Colloquial Japanese*, as the spoken language of Japan at that time was still widely considered to be lacking in rules, and thus unworthy of scholarly attention (Yamamoto, 1981: 428–430). Ueda completed his undergraduate studies in 1888 and subsequently worked as an English teacher. At the same time, Ueda began studying at graduate school, where he specialized in language didactics (Nakamura, 1987: 212). Despite his decision to become a linguist, Ueda Kazutoshi continued to move in literary circles and, in 1889, published a German-into-Japanese translation of the Brothers Grimm fairytale Ōkami (in English, *The Wolf and the Seven Little Kids*) using the *genbun itchi* style. Already the young Ueda was an impressive intellectual figure. Nevertheless, it was not until he returned from a study tour to Europe that he emerged as the most important authority on Japanese language and society of the day. The reasons for this were twofold: firstly, Ueda was responsible for the dissemination of novel and thus-far incompletely understood western ideas, and secondly, the fact that these ideas had already been effectively put into practice in the west and thus seemed all the more sensible to many of his contemporaries (Ramsey, 2004). Let us begin by examining the language ideologies Ueda encountered during his studies abroad.

Studies Abroad

In 1890, Tokyo University President Katō Hiroyuki (1836–1916) ordered Ueda Kazutoshi to travel to Europe to study linguistics. The objectives Ueda was to pursue included conducting an examination of ways in which the Japanese language might be adapted to the modern age, and the creation of a standard grammar for Japanese (Shi, 1993: 131). In Germany, Ueda studied comparative linguistics at Berlin and Leipzig Universities, under the guidance of such eminent scholars as (in Berlin) Heymann Steinthal (1823–1899) and Georg von der Gabelentz (1840–1893), and (in Leipzig) August Leskien (1840–1916), Karl Brugmann (1849–1919), Eduard Sievers (1850–1932), Hermann Osthoff (1847–1909) and Wilhelm Wundt (1832–1920). He moved to Paris in 1983 and returned to Japan the following year.

Upon his return, and despite being only 27 years old, Ueda was appointed professor of linguistics at Tokyo University. While studying the methodology and theory of comparative linguistics abroad, Ueda also encountered ideological notions about language popular in Europe. He was conversant with the ideas of speech community (*Sprachgemeinschaft*) and national community (*nationale Gemeinschaft*), and thus with the notion that a national language might be employed as a powerful symbol of national unity. More practically, Ueda had acquired the skills necessary to orchestrate linguistic research at the national level (Koyama, 2003: 854) – such knowledge and skills had not been available in Japan before – and he wasted no time in spreading them on his return to Japan.

One crucial lesson Ueda had learned in Europe was that a national language could not depend too heavily on other languages if it was to be considered as authentic. Of critical importance in shaping his opinions about national language were the attempts to 'purify' German of French and Latin influence he had witnessed first hand in Germany. Ueda closely followed the debate surrounding language purification in the name of Germanization (*Verdeutschung*), as promoted by the General German Language Association (*Allgemeiner Deutscher Sprachverein*). Having diagnosed German as being in a state of decay, and this being based on a lack of national self-esteem, the German Language Association set about cleansing German of foreign influences. In order to 'cure' the language (and the attitudes of its speakers), a policy was developed under which foreign words were not to be used where the same meaning might be expressed in authentic German (*auf gut deutsch*) (see Barbour, 2000; Coulmas, 1997; Townson, 1992 for more details).

Upon returning from Europe, Ueda stressed the importance of national languages to the emergence of nation-states in Europe, and called for a mobilization of the intellectual elite towards the establishment of a Japanese national language. He asserted that the German national language and, by extension, the German nation-state, could not have developed without the works and activities of writers such as Johann Wolfgang von Goethe (1782–1832) and Friedrich von Schiller (1759–1805), and of scholars such as Wilhelm von Humboldt (1767–1835). He also highlighted the importance of such things as Otto von Bismarck's (1815–1898) decision to have compulsory school education conducted entirely in German. Furthermore, scholars were involved in the study of German at more than 20 universities, and all of these scholars took pride in their national language. Of greater significance still was that the German government itself took responsibility for the national language, being well aware that confusion over language would ultimately weaken the state (Ueda, 1895a).

Ueda's influence cannot be overemphasized. Already an 'enthusiastic state-language-ideology advocate' (Shi, 1993: 133) before his studies in

Europe, Ueda now began to actively shape Japanese language policy according to his ideas, serving in numerous bureaucratic institutions concerned with language and education. He was the driving force behind the establishment of the National Language Research Council, and hugely influential in determining its research agenda. Ueda also had a lasting influence on the establishment of modern linguistics in Japan, himself training two generations of Japanese linguists. And, most importantly perhaps, he was responsible both for the creation of the new school subject, *kokugo* (national language), and played a key role in developing its curriculum (for more general information on Ueda and his legacy in Japanese linguistics, see Doi, 1977; Eschbach-Szabo, 1997; Heinrich, 2002; Inamura, 1987).

Ueda as a Language Ideology Broker

Ueda was of seminal importance in the creation of a plethora of language studies characterized by language nationalism (Osa, 1998: 90). Language nationalism drew on the heightened sense of national pride that had emerged after Japan's victory in the Sino-Japanese War and by Japan's becoming a colonial power in 1895. As an effect of the Treaty of Shimonoseki, ratified between Japan and China on 17 April 1895, Taiwan had been ceded to Japan. The revision of the so-called Unequal Treaties between Japan and the western powers (see Chapter 2), the Japanese victory in the Russo-Japanese War in 1905, and the annexation of Korea in 1910 further bolstered Japanese nationalist pride, and weakened the general sense of scepticism about the idea of a Japanese language that had been prevalent during the time of Mori Arinori's proposal (Chapter 3). The fact that Japan had joined forces with the western powers seemed to prove the language sceptics wrong, and the Japanese language no longer seemed to present the insurmountable obstacle to modernization it once had. Now, it was on a par with western languages.

The significance of the Japanese victory over the Chinese was so great that 1895 also marks a turning point in Japanese language history (Lee, 1996: 86), and Ueda Kazutoshi lost no time in jumping on the bandwagon of Japanese nationalism. Immediately after his return from Europe, he gave a series of seminal lectures, five of which will be studied in detail below (Ueda, 1895a–d, 1903). The most famous of them is undoubtedly 'National Language and the State' (*Kokugo to kokka to*) (Ueda, 1895a), which is characterized by Shimizu Yasuyuki (2002: 145) as a 'declaration to raise the curtain' on language planning in Japan.

One of the key concepts Ueda (1895a) popularized in his lectures was that of the mother tongue (*Muttersprache*). Going beyond *Muttersprache*, Ueda also provided the metaphor of national language as mother, specifically, as the mother of a national polity. The mother tongue, Ueda asserted, accompanied its speakers from their first day to their last, thereby nurturing love and respect for the Japanese nation. All Japanese, therefore, should respect their mother tongue, their national language. Such respect for the national language was considered a foregone conclusion in Europe, where Welsh and Gaelic had been banned by the British Government, Basque and Breton by the French, and Polish, Danish and French by the German. These languages were outlawed precisely because the national language alone could exist as the language of the state. In all the countries of the Occident, Ueda concluded, efforts to encourage pride in national, standard languages were being made, and if Japan, too, wished to establish a standardized national language, it should follow the European model.

According to Ueda (1895a), Japan's successful resistance against the threat of western imperialism and its victory in war against China proved that the Japanese, unlike the Chinese or the Koreans, possessed a strong sense of nationhood and a common national character. Furthermore, he asserted that this could be attributed to their sharing a mother tongue, and that the spirit (*seishin*), thought (*shisō*) and emotions (*kanjō*) of the Japanese nation found their expression in the national language. Ueda thus subscribed to the Herderian ideology that languages are nothing but a product of the people who speak them (see Chapter 1) and that the existence of a shared mother tongue makes brothers in spirit. The basic premise of Ueda's language ideology is summarized in the first line from the cover page of his 1895 book *For the National Language* (*Kokugo no tame*), which reads, 'the national language is the fortification of the Imperial Household – the national language is the affectionate mother of the nation' (*kokugo wa teishitsu no hanbyō nari – kokugo wa kokumin no jibo nari*).

Of course, the idea of seeking to restore the national language to its 'rightful place' demanded that some pre-existing elements be removed, or at the very least downgraded in importance. Resisting such change, Ueda warned, was evidence of an improper attitude towards language, nation and state. Thus, Ueda's promotion of Japanese as the national language for Japan was accompanied by a conscious and deliberate effort to weaken the status of Chinese and western languages in Japan. Ueda believed that scholars of Chinese and western languages in particular lacked the right attitude towards Japanese, and he saw this as particularly damaging, given the fact that such scholars were usually employed as teachers, and thus well placed to further disseminate their unpatriotic ideas. Despite the awakening of Japanese popular nationalism and the new sense of superiority over China, Chinese Studies continued to be massively popular, however. Doi Toshio (1977: 163) reports that about 300 different textbooks on the Chinese language were in circulation during the Meiji period (1868–1912) alone, meaning Japan had in all probability the largest number of students of Chinese-as-a-foreign language in the world then. However, Ueda strongly objected to the idea that Chinese should continue to exert such a dominant influence over Japanese, and that it was embarrassing to see the national language not receiving the respect it deserved.

Ueda (1895a) argued that Japan, having risen to the status of an imperial world power, ought to have a national language worthy of its glory. Accordingly, he called for emancipation from the perception that Sino-Japanese words (*kango*) were superior to the indigenous Japanese lexicon (*yamatokotoba*) (Ueda, 1895b) and, inspired by German efforts to purify their national language, Ueda strongly supported the idea that Japanese be liberated from what he perceived as the yoke of Chinese loanwords (just as German had been liberated from French and Latin influence). In so doing, however, Ueda insisted that one ought not to follow the advice of those pre-modern nativist scholars (*kokugakusha*) who had turned exclusively to the language of the Japanese classics as a means of curtailing Chinese influence over the national language (see Burns, 2003 for details). According to Ueda, too much enthusiasm for antiquated language might prove troublesome. Instead, a new common language should be refined, and integrated into both spoken and written language.

Ueda (1895c) stressed the importance of writers for achieving language modernization – of people like Martin Luther (1483–1546) and Wolfgang von Goethe (1782–1832) to the modernization of German, and Geoffrey Chaucer (1343–1400) and William Shakespeare (1564–1616) to that of English. He also believed that the best way to develop a standard language would be to allocate superiority to an existing language variety over all other varieties and to subsequently refine it. In 1903, Ueda illustrated this point with an examination of language modernization in Germany. Although in pre-modern Germany there were many instances in which French could just as easily be used, Germans began to deliberately use their own language of German instead. Faced with a choice between using the elegant (*jōhin*) language of French or the more rough (*soya*) German, the German people opted for the latter, believing their own 'rough language' to better capture the soul of their nation. What further strengthened their conviction in doing so was the belief that, once refined, this rough language would evolve into something beautiful (*migoto na mono*).

Ueda's outlook (1895b) drove him to challenge existing educational practices. He was suspicious not only of teachers of Chinese and western studies, but also of instructors of national language and literature, doubting that they were sufficiently knowledgeable about matters relating to contemporary

Japanese. In order to tackle their shortcomings, Ueda argued in favour of the expansion and contemporization of national language study. In no uncertain terms, he stressed the need for compulsory school education to be focused on the national language rather than on Sino-Japanese writing (Ueda, 1895a), and was a key figure in the movement to establish *kokugo* (national language) as a fully fledged school subject, with the aim of cultivating contemporary use of national language at the Japanese school (Ueda, 1895d).

Only too aware that many of his ideas about language and society were controversial, Ueda anticipated resistance. His knowledge of the work of Dwight Whitney (1827–1894), who characterized language change and reform as a manifestation of the struggle between conservatives and progressives, had prepared Ueda for the counter-attack, however. Ueda agreed with Whitney's comments about conservative obstruction of language change and its reliance on education, in particular on a knowledge of and respect for classical literature (Suzuki, 1994: 132). On returning to Japan, and with this in mind, Ueda set about encouraging writers, actors, educators, lawyers and politicians to get involved in language reform (Ueda, 1895a, 1895c, 1895d), that is to say, to what might be referred to today as prestige planning (see Haarmann, 1990). With regard to the development of a modern written language variety, Ueda (1895c) indicated that those responsible for the creation of that variety would be remembered as the patriots who had laid the foundations of Japanese cultural progress.

Above all, Ueda (1895a) sought to introduce linguistic uniformity across Japan, stressing the importance of developing Standard Japanese not as a language variety to be used only by the educated elite, but as a national language spoken universally by the entire Japanese population, then some 40 million in number. In this we find evidence of Ueda's nationalist leanings, as we may also in his tendency to downplay linguistic diversity within a nation he envisioned to be unified in language. In fact, Ueda chose to ignore all of Japan's linguistic and cultural minorities (Shimizu, 1990: 123), despite the country's long history of linguistic and cultural diversity (Maher & Yashiro, 1995; Oguma, 2002). In 'National Language and the State', Ueda (1895a) explicitly denied the existence of other languages and ethnic groups, depicting Japan's linguistic reality as a one-to-one relationship between Japanese language, Japanese nation and Japanese state. He even cited this as evidence that Japan was even more suitable for modernization than the more heterogeneous states of Europe, and as a reason for Japan's success as an emergent empire.

Seeing Japan as monolingual, Ueda (1903) asserted that, unless invaded by foreigners, a nation always used the language handed down by its forefathers. As we shall see in chapters that follow, it was this ideology – based on the perception of Japan as a monolingual state – that caused language shifts among all of the autochthonous minority speech communities in Japan, a reminder of how dominant ideologies often become self-fulfilling prophecies (see Chapter 7).

Ueda as a Language Planner

Ueda was nothing if not pro-active in putting his ideology to work. One way in which he did so was through the establishment of state-funded institutions for the research of national language, such as the Seminar for National Language Studies (*Kokugo Kenkyū-shitsu*) at Tokyo University, as well as the National Language Research Council (*Kokugo Chōsa I'inkai*). He also proved influential in shaping the research agenda for such study. In 'National Language and the State', Ueda (1895a) dictated that the study of the national language should address 10 issues: language history, contrastive grammatical studies, pronunciation, the history of language studies, script reform, the status to be given to *futsūbun* (general-purpose written style), foreign words in Japanese, Japanese and foreign language didactics, ways of limiting the influx of foreign words, synonyms and lexicography. He stressed that the relative lack of understanding of these subjects at the time of his speech hindered language reform. What is more, and what was entirely new, he declared that the state should be responsible for funding such research (Ueda, 1895d).

As we have seen, standardization of the Japanese language was Ueda's primary objective. Highlighting the importance of carrying out research into the establishment of a standard language, Ueda (1895d) pointed out that it was so far unknown even how many vowels and consonants existed across the various Japanese language varieties, and which of these sounds (*oto*) were used only in certain regions. It was necessary, therefore, to draw up maps showing the distribution of all sounds across Japan, a task which, Ueda decreed, should also be undertaken with school-based language instruction in mind, for he believed problems related to pronunciation to be particularly prevalent in schools. To Ueda's mind, to allow local school teachers to decide matters of pronunciation would be to imply that something as important as central education (*chūō kyōiku*) was not being taken seriously by the Japanese government. Rather, Ueda believed that such issues should be dealt with at the highest level, and that rules of pronunciation should then be introduced first to normal schools (where the teachers of tomorrow were being trained), and gradually to all schools throughout Japan. With regard to writing, Ueda strove to establish a standard orthography for compulsory school education as quickly as possible, pointing out that a uniform education was impossible in the absence of a standard orthography. Existing orthographic difficulties at the time included kana variants (*hentaigana*) and the hitherto unsolved question of whether kana orthography should follow historic or phonetic principles.

For Ueda, standardization implied the unification of language use. In promoting the development of a standard language suitable for all regions and social strata (Mizutami, 1996: 26), language modernization as advocated by Ueda demanded the development of some elements of Japanese and, simultaneously, a simplification of others. Ueda decreed that compulsory education required the establishment and spread of a spoken and written language variety which could be mastered by all. For this reason, he supported the idea of *genbun itchi*, promoted the increased use of Japanese words (*yamatokotoba*) at the expense of Sino-Japanese words (*kango*) and supported the idea of restricting the use of Chinese characters in writing (Clark, 2002: 138). Through such measures, Ueda was convinced that Japanese could be 'brought back' to the common people (Osa, 1998: 94), restored to its rightful position as a national language worthy of such a title. Towards the end of linguistic unification, Ueda even considered the eradication of local dialects an acceptable means of achieving this end (Hōryoku, 2002: 26).

Because Ueda served as a director to the Ministry of Education's Bureau of Higher Education (*Senmon Gakumu-kyoku*), he was able to implement several language reforms in school education. Most significant was his influence on the Elementary School Ordinance (*Shōgakko-rei*) of 1900, which redefined the structure and curriculum of compulsory school education. Amongst other things, the Elementary School Ordinance regulated matters of pronunciation, kana form (*kana jitai*), kana orthography and written style, and limited the number of Chinese characters to be studied (Takebe, 1977: 262). Without doubt, the most significant achievement, however, was the establishment of a school subject called *kokugo* (Kurashima, 2002: 10). It is important to note that the *kokugo* curriculum at the time also included lessons on spoken language. By integrating *kokugo* into the school curriculum, for the first time in its history the Ministry of Education assumed responsibility for providing a definition of national language which stated that it was (quoted from Clark, 2002: 196): 'to be the common, spoken language and, [...] to (employ) characters and phrases known in everyday life'. In April 1901, Ueda's educational reforms began, and their effects were seen in school textbooks from 1902 onwards. In 1903, the first state textbook for Japanese language education, the *Common Elementary Reader* (*Jinjō shōgaku dokuhon*), was published (Galan, 2001: 137), thus firmly institutionalizing the national language and facilitating the continuous reproduction of language use and ideology Ueda had envisioned. The gap between language ideology and the sociolinguistic situation on the ground had begun to close.

Ueda's Ideological Legacy

Under Ueda's guiding hand, the idea of what a language ought to be changed considerably. His speeches and publications played a pivotal role in creating a link between national language (*kokugo*), state (*kokka*) and nation (*kokumin*), and this connection was reinforced in the minds of the Japanese through national education (*kokumin kyōiku*). Successfully adapting the Tokyo language variety of educated speakers to the communicative needs of the modern age was only one aspect of language modernization. Just as important was the creation of the perception that all pre-existing social and regional language varieties spoken in the Japanese Archipelago were in fact part of that one, unified national language. Additionally, the creation of an authentic national language demanded a reduction in Chinese influences, for two important reasons. Firstly, a greater sense of distance from the Chinese emphasized Japanese linguistic independence, and thus enhanced the sense of authenticity. Secondly, it facilitated greater access to the language for formally less well-educated Japanese nationals. This was of great importance to Ueda's vision, because he believed that the national language should serve two new important roles, both of which transcended issues of communication before the Meiji restoration: it should be a symbol of Japanese unity and it should serve as a means of defining the Japanese.

It is because the Standard Japanese language was intended to unite Japan's people that Tanaka Katsuhiko comments thus:

> National language requires the recognition of its standards by all people. That is to say, such recognition has to pay tribute to the nation-state with regard to obedience, respect and loyalty [of all nationals P.H.] towards the ideological structure of the nation-state. (Tanaka, 1978: 246)

Tanaka here refers to the fact that the development of a national language included the creation of a wide range of ideological attitudes about language form and function, and that these reflect the modernist imagining of the Japanese nation. Similarly, Masiko Hidenori (1997: 68–70) mentions several such effects on language. For example, the speech of the educated in Tokyo came to be seen as good language, and all other local varieties as deviations thereof. The grammar of the standard variety was treated as a continuance of the grammar of written Japanese, and also provided a link to the past and to Japan's cultural achievements. By defining the standard variety as the model for the written language, the sense of unity through national language was further enhanced. In turn, the norm and prestige of the written language were instrumental in sustaining this superiority of the standard language over other varieties. Sibata Takesi (1977: 29), too, has noted that the negative image of regional Japanese dialects was created in the early years of the 20th century precisely at the time when Ueda and the National Language Research Council set about establishing Standard Japanese. Dialects, Sibata writes, came to be viewed as incorrect (*tadashikunai*), bad (*warui*) and old-fashioned (*furukusai*), indeed, as the exact opposite of Standard Japanese, which was seen as good (*ii*) and correct (*tadashii*).

The creation and dissemination of the idea of Standard Japanese as the national language brought to an end the concept of disunity and unattended linguistic diversity in the Japanese Archipelago, a diversity that had once been accepted to give clues to the regional, social, occupational and educational status of the speaker. Inoue Miyako has described this shift in language ideology in the following way:

> Prior to Ueda, standardization was understood, more or less, as the immediate application of, and the dissemination of, the speech of the Tokyo educated. From Ueda's point of view, standard language [...] could no longer be reduced to actual or tangible speakers of the educated middle-class. Transcending the materiality of the individual by the normalizing notion of national language (*kokugo*), standard language signifies the abstract community, or the nation, and it is the voice of the imagined speaking subject of the imagined national community. (Inoue, 1996: 60–61)

Indeed, Ueda (1895c) insisted that the standard language ought to be purged from its dialect odor (*hōgen no kusami o dassuru*), the effect of which was to partially detach the language from its concrete speakers. The representation of the national language by Standard Japanese ultimately came to serve as a yardstick of correctness against which all language use would be measured. In other words, a standardized national language, detached from its speakers and loaded with nation-imagining ideology, would be forced upon all Japanese nationals, and their every utterance evaluated according to this linguistic yardstick. This is the very means by which language ideology affects language use, and its results were language change and language shift (see Chapter 7 for details).

By making this newly created standard/national language both a subject of compulsory education and its medium of instruction, no excuse remained for not being able to speak Standard Japanese (and, by extension, the national language) properly. This was important, as a lack of proficiency in the national language was more than a mere linguistic issue. Language ideologies are morally and politically loaded too, as Judith Irvine

(1989) stresses. Therefore, speakers lacking proper control over their national language are likely to be perceived as lacking the proper attitude (see Chapter 5). While Ueda successfully established ideologies concerning what the Japanese language in the modern age ought to look like, his ideologies and the kind of language use he promoted were still in need of legitimization. This was achieved through the work of the National Language Research Council, and it is to the activities of the council that we shall now turn our attention.

The National Language Research Council

The establishment of the National Language Research Council marks the beginning of organized, structured, state-supported language planning in Japan. Such measures are far from inexpensive, and the establishment of the council only came about as a result of concerted lobbying. This process itself produced much in the way of commentary related to language ideology. Let us consider this briefly, before moving on to the activities the council undertook once in place.

Establishing the National Language Research Council

In 1899, Ueda set forth his proposal for the creation of a state-funded institution responsible for research on the national language. The Ministry of Education quickly approved it and appointed seven researchers, among them Maejima Hisoka (1835–1919) and Ōtsuki Fumihiko (1847–1928), as well as Ueda himself, to serve in what was known as the National Language Council (*Kokugo I'inkai*). At Ueda's behest, in 1900 the Imperial Society for Education (*Teikoku Kyōiku-kai*) drafted a Petition Concerning the Reform of National Script, National Language and National Writing (*Kokuji kokugo kokubun no kairyō ni kansuru seigansho*), claiming that the Japanese language was badly in need of reform but that this could not be achieved without prior research (Takebe, 1977: 273). During question time in the Upper House of the Diet, Tokyo University president Katō Hiroyuki presented the petition, and outlined some of the language problems his country faced. Katō saw the national language as being in a state of disarray, and believed that national education was suffering as a result. He believed, too, that comparison of the written language in Japan to the written languages of the west suggested a Japanese language reform, and commented on the need for clarification of such terms as national language (*kokugo*), the language of the country (*kuni no kotoba*) and dialect (*hōgen*) (Mizutami, 1996: 27). Katō's presentation, then, covered both what he saw as deficiencies in the language corpus and conceptual uncertainties regarding language in Japan, and thus dealt with matters not only of language proper, but also of language ideology.

Owing to a lack of sufficient funding, however, the National Language Council was dissolved before any research had been carried out. Setting this setback aside, Ueda continued to lobby, eventually succeeding in convincing the influential Imperial Society for Education to continue to support his scheme of state-sponsored national language research. The Imperial Society for Education subsequently established several research groups devoted to linguistic issues, the most important of which was the Genbun Itchi Club (*Genbun Itchi-kai*), which included many eminent linguists, of whom Ueda was one. In drawing a parallel between the *genbun itchi* movement and the emancipation of European national languages from Latin, the Genbun Itchi Club saw the wholesale implementation of *genbun itchi* as an essential part of the creation of an authentic and independent Japanese national language. In 1901, the Genbun Itchi Club drafted a new petition titled 'Petition Regarding the Implementation of *genbun itchi*' (*Genbun itchi no jikkō ni tsuite no seigansho*), which stated that a state-funded language research institution would contribute greatly to the cause of national unity and civilisation through the simplification of Japanese. In support of this argument, the Genbun Itchi Club referred to various instances in which European countries had simplified and standardized their national languages. It also argued that in following the western example, Japan would distinguish itself from other Asian nations (Twine, 1991: 168–169).

The Genbun Itchi Club's petition was passed by both houses of the Diet in March 1902, and the National Language Research Council (*Kokugo Chōsa I'inkai*) was established as an advisory body to the Ministry of Education in the same year. Again, 12 members were appointed to sit at the council, with Katō Hiroyuki as its head, Ueda Kazutoshi as its managing director and Ōtsuki Fumihiko as its head researcher. Through the council's creation, the Japanese state took responsibility for developing, cultivating and maintaining the national language (Mizutami, 1996: 28–29), setting quite a precedent, for no previous administration had ever acted in such a way. Although the council's members did not always agree, its research activities advanced steadily. By the time the council was eventually disbanded in 1913, the place of both the national language and Standard Japanese in everyday life was secure, and the history of their creation and dissemination hidden behind ideologically mediated common sense. Ueda's language ideology as a *une verité à faire* had come to be accepted as truth, *une verité tout court*, if you will.

In order to decide its objectives, the research council met nine times between April and June 1902. These meetings resulted in a two-fold research agenda, the first half of which covered four areas (Ōno, 1976: 260):

(1) The use of an alphabetic writing system, including consideration of the advantages and disadvantages of using kana or the Latin alphabet for writing Japanese.
(2) The feasibility of unifying spoken and written language (*genbun itchi*).
(3) The phonology of Japanese.
(4) Japanese dialects, with the aim of creating a standard language.

In addition to these four research topics, the National Language Research Council set out to undertake an investigation into six further issues related to language education:

(1) The possibility of abandoning Chinese characters.
(2) The possibility of adjusting *futsūbun* (general-purpose written style).
(3) Collecting material on *shokanbun* (epistolary style) and the characteristics of other written styles in common use.
(4) Kana orthography of the national language.
(5) Phonetic orthography of the national language.
(6) The transcription of foreign languages.

Yasuda Toshiaki (1999a: 105–106) points out that the first four research aims of the research council were interpreted in different ways, particularly with regard to the development of Standard Japanese, which was taken by some to mean that a hybrid of several dialects was to be developed into one standard language, but by others as an indication that the aim was to choose one dialect to fulfil that role, which may or may not later also incorporate elements from other regional varieties. In fact, the somewhat obscure nature of the research agenda gave little clue as to the real objectives of the research council, and to this day, scholars remain divided as to its real purpose (see Kurashima, 2002: 11–12; Osa, 1992: 8 for discussions).

Oddly, the language variety of the Tokyo educated is never explicitly mentioned. This is all the more surprising given that it was already the medium of compulsory school education, following the Elementary School Ordinance (*shōgakko-rei*) of 1900. Actual research conducted by the research council, and a paper by a substitute member, Hoshina Kōichi (1902), suggest that the Tokyo variety was already considered Standard Japanese by the council's members. Hoshina (1872–1955), a student of Ueda, argued strongly in favour of the Tokyo variety as the basis for Standard Japanese all the same.

Further insight into the development of a standard language and the general aims of the National Language Research Council may be gained by considering its research in more detail.

The Research of the National Language Research Council

The sheer volume of research undertaken by the National Language Research Council is astounding, and a considerably body of texts was created from the extensive field work and philological studies its members carried out. Between February 1902 and July 1903, the research council drafted no less than 36 directives (*hōan*), which served as the basis for its research activities thereafter (see MKK, 1949: 65–68 for a complete listing). It is worth noting, however, that these directives did not cover all of the council's research objectives. There were, for example, no directives concerning the abolition of Chinese characters, the adjustment of *futsūbun* (general-purpose written style) or the collation of *shokanbun* (epistolary style). Moreover, no record of any discussion on the use of an alphabetic writing system exists. In view of the fact that these were primary objectives of the council's actual research agenda, this is unexpected to say the least, and is indicative of the fact that the actual work of the National Language Research Council was less radical than its stated intentions might have suggested. What is revealed by the directives is the council's dedication to the task of developing Standard Japanese through the adoption of *genbun itchi*, to conducting a comprehensive survey of local language varieties throughout Japan, to limiting the number of Chinese characters in use, and to selecting and codifying rules of grammar and orthography.

The activities of the National Language Research Council led to the publication of no less than 18 works, listed below (MKK, 1949: 70–71):

(1) (1904) *Chronicle of Articles on National Language and National Script Reform* (*Kokugo kokuji kairyō ronsetsu nenpyō*).
(2) (1904) *Test Reports on the Difficulties of Reading and Writing Katakana and Hiragana* (*Katakana hiragana yomikaki no nan'i ni kansuru jiken hōkoku*).
(3) (1904) *Dialect Survey Handbook* (*Hōgen saishū-bo*).
(4) (1904) *Overview of the Merits of Kana and Latin Alphabets* (*Kana-ji rōmaji yūretsu hikaku ichiran*).
(5) (1905) *Report on Phonological Field Work*, 2 volumes (*On'in chōsa hōkokusho*).
(6) (1905) *Report on Uncertainties in Kana Orthography* (*Kanazukai gimon ni tai suru tōshin*).
(7) (1906) *Research Report on Common Grammar Reform Measures* (*Genkō futsū bunpō kai-teian chōsa hōkoku no ichi*).
(8) (1906) *Field Work Report on Spoken Language*, 2 volumes (*Kōgohō chōsa hōkokusho*).

(9) (1907) *Declensional Kana Orthography (Okurigana-hō).*
(10) (1908) *Outline of Chinese Characters (Kanji yōran).*
(11) (1909) *Historical Material on the Development of Kana Orthography and Kana Form (Kanazukai oyobi kana jitai enkaku shiryō).*
(12) (1911) *Research Report on the Epistolary Spoken Style (Kōgotai shokanbun ni kansuru chōsa hōkoku).*
(13) (1911) *Reflections on Kana Origins,* 2 volumes *(Kana genryū-kō).*
(14) (1911 & 1914) *Research on the Heike Monogatari,* 2 volumes *(Heike monogatari ni tsuite no kenkyū).*
(15) (1911) *Reflections on Ancient Sounds and Rhyme Evidences from the Shūdai Period (Shūdai ko'on-kō oyobi inchō).*
(16) (1912 & 1915) *Uncertainties of Kana Orthography,* 2 volumes *(Gimon kanazukai).*
(17) (1916) *A Grammar of the Spoken Language (Kōgohō).*
(18) (1917) *Supplement to the Grammar of Spoken Language (Kōgohō bekki).*

The works listed above reflect the council's real research objectives more faithfully than do the original directives, a quick look at the contents of which will show that only works on the feasibility of abandoning Chinese characters and transcribing foreign words are missing from the list above. Clearly, in practice the partial or total abandoning of the use of Chinese characters proved to be too radical a measure for the council's research, while the transcription of loanwords was perhaps seen as too specific a topic to deserve its own dedicated publication. What is undeniable, however, is that these 18 publications formed the foundation of linguistic research and language ideology in modern Japan.

Three of the council's publications were of particular importance to achieving the end of selecting and codifying Standard Japanese: the *Dialect Survey Handbook (Hōgen saishū-bo)* of 1904, *A Grammar of Spoken Language (Kōgohō)* of 1916 and the *Supplement to the Grammar of Spoken Language (Kōgohō bekki)* of 1917. The publication of the *Dialect Survey Handbook* made available a wealth of linguistic data from the research council's surveys. *A Grammar of Spoken Language* is notable for its commentary on the spoken language, and the *Supplement to the Grammar of Spoken Language* provides a grammar on what became non-standard forms. It will be useful to examine the importance of these three books in more detail, though given their relative size and complexity, I shall take the liberty of restricting this to a consideration of the four areas most significantly affected by the process of modernization: personal pronouns, conjunctions, honourifics and gendered particles (see Inoue, 2006; Sanada, 1987; Tanaka, 1983, 1999, 2001; Wetzel, 2004).

Dialect Survey Handbook (1904)

The *Dialect Survey Handbook* is a 310-page glossary based on Ueda's former instructor, Georg von der Gabelentz's *Aufnahme der fremden Sprachen* (*Survey of Foreign Languages*) and of *Outline Dictionary* by Oxford University's Max Müller. The handbook was distributed to schools across Japan and local teachers asked to collect data and forward their results to Tokyo. In order to gather such data, however, the research committee first had to establish certain writing conventions and a linguistic point of reference. It settled on the writing conventions as defined by the Elementary School Ordinance, and on the Tokyo language variety, both already being in use in schools. The fieldwork for the handbook thus produced a series of glossaries by which Tokyo Japanese could be compared with other local language varieties. This methodology inevitably resulted in the perception of differences between these local language forms and the Tokyo variety, the standard against which they were measured. Consequently, these local varieties were perceived as deviations from written Japanese as modelled on the Tokyo variety, or Japanese *tout court*. The question, then, of whether a single regional dialect should be chosen as a model for Standard Japanese, and if so, which that should be, already appears to have been decided by the time the *Dialect Survey Handbook* was conceived, and certainly the conviction that this role should be filled by the Tokyo language variety was strengthened by its publication. Once it had been agreed that surveys would be carried out in this way, the ideology by which all other language varieties were rendered as variants of a unified national language was firmly in place.

Let us now consider the handbook in relation to the four linguistic features mentioned above. We find no reference to honourific language in the book, and though there is an extensive list of sentence final particles, none of these are linked to gendered speech. With regard to personal pronouns, the handbook gives the following entries on personal pronouns (KCIIK, 1904: 133–135):

First person singular	*watashi,*
Second person singular	*naji*
Third person singular	*kare*
First person plural	*watashira*
Second person plural	*nanjira*

Note that no form is given for the third person plural and that *naji* and *najira* would later become outmoded forms. In addition, *kare* today signifies only 'he', 'she' being *kanojo* in Standard Japanese.

With regard to conjunctions, we find the following entries (KCIIK, 1904: 223):

arui wa (or)
moshiku wa (or)
mata (moreover)
mata wa (or, besides)
narabi ni (and)
shikaru ni (but, however)
shikashi (but, however)
shikashinagara (but, however)
keredemo (but, however)
sarinagara (yet)
sore yue (accordingly)
sore de aru kara (accordingly)

Of these entries *moshiku wa, narabi ni, shikaru ni* and *sarinagara* became elements of literary language. Thus, while the handbook took the Tokyo language as its point of reference for the collation of information on regional dialects, the standard forms in the handbook did not necessarily become Standard Japanese, some of these forms falling into disuse and others being used only in formal or literary contexts. Of even greater significance to the codification and modernization of Standard Japanese was *A Grammar of Spoken Language*, published 13 years after the *Dialect Survey Handbook* during a time of rapid language change (see Sugito, 2009).

A Grammar of Spoken Language (1917)

A Grammar of Spoken Language was written by Ōtsuki Fumihiko, head researcher of the National Language Research Committee and a recognized authority on Japanese grammar. By the time of its publication, most of the questions about what Standard Japanese should eventually look like had already been answered. The book's introduction states clearly that it is to take the language of Tokyo's educated elite as its model, and that historical, social and regional variation would be dealt with in a partner work, the *Supplement to the Grammar of Spoken Language*. Nanette Twine stresses the significance of these two publications to the standardization process, observing that:

> It is true that there had been earlier grammars of colloquial Japanese, but these were the first to carry the weight of state authority. Their prescriptive definition of *Tōkyōgo* [Toyko language P.H.] as the standard ended this phase in the modernization of the language. (Twine, 1988: 453)

Indeed, debate about which language variety the new standard language should be based on would virtually disappear from popular discourse after the publication of *A Grammar of Spoken Language*. This was not as a result of any consensus having been reached, however, but rather, as E.P. Thompson (1990) reminds us, because ideologies are most successfully disseminated when backed by power. The state's support for *A Grammar of Spoken Language* was decisive in bringing to an end the first phase of language modernization. Thus, rather than seeking to actively craft a new standard to represent the national language, the National Language Research Council's primary objective was to legitimize the language ideology of Ueda and his associates, and the body of academic work represented by the council's research only added to its credibility.

A Grammar of Spoken Language also played a significant part in the codification of Standard Japanese. Consider its treatment of personal pronouns, for example. In Japanese, the appropriate personal pronoun is chosen based on the addressee's social status relative to the speaker (KCIIK, 2000: 7) (Table 4.1).

This listing deviates considerably from the entries of the *Dialect Survey Handbook*, with the forms given in *A Grammar of Spoken Language* being much closer to those of Standard Japanese. It is worth noting that the use of *omae* (you) gave way to *anata* after World War II, as a result of reforms aimed at the 'democratization' of Japanese (see Lewin, 1979). Variation was further reduced by the first person plural *watashi-tachi* becoming unmarked. These

Table 4.1 Personal pronouns in *A Grammar of Spoken Language*

	Same or lower status than speaker	Same or higher status than speaker
First person singular	*watakushi*	*watashi*
Second person singular	*anata*	*omae*
Third person singular	*kono/sono/ano kata*	*kono/sono/ano hito*
First person plural	*watakushi-domo* *watakushi-tachi* *watakushi-ra*	*watashi-domo* *watashi-tachi* *watashi-ra*
Second person plural	*anata-gata*	*omae-gata* *omae-tachi* *omae-ra*
Third person plural	*kono/sono/ano kata-gata*	*kono/sono/ano hito-tachi* *kono/sono/ano hito-ra*

later changes aside, it is clear that *A Grammar of Spoken Language* was highly influential in establishing the rules of personal pronoun use.

With regard to conjunctions, *A Grammar of Spoken Language* lists the following forms (KCIIK, 2000: 114–115):

keredomo (but, however)
shikashi (but, however)
soshite (and, then)
sore ni (besides, moreover)
mata wa (or, besides)
de (and so)
suru to (whereupon)
dakara (therefore)
dakeredomo (but, however)
demo (but, yet)

Once again, these forms correspond closely to today's Standard Japanese. Furthermore, the expressions *moshiku wa, narabi ni, shikaru ni* and *sarinagara* – included in the *Dialect Survey Handbook*, but absent from the list above – are today regarded as literary language, rather than as everyday expressions. In addition, two conjunctions included in *A Grammar of Spoken Language* became seen as being part of informal language, namely *suru to* and *dakeredomo*.

Considering the complexity of the subject, the book's coverage of honourific language is cursory, to say the least. As we have seen, however, no such examination was included in the *Dialect Survey Handbook* at all. In *A Grammar of Spoken Language*, we find a short list of plain and polite verb forms (KCIIK, 2000: 37) (Table 4.2). Yet again, these forms reflect the norms of contemporary Standard Japanese, the only exceptions being *kuu* and *yaru*, both of which became features of informal speech.

Much of *A Grammar of Spoken Language*, almost 100 pages in fact, is dedicated to an analysis of particles. Let us consider the book's examination of the particles *ze, zo* and *ne/nee* in some detail. According to *A Grammar of Spoken Language, ze* and *zo* are to be 'used for emphasizing what is being said' (KCIIK, 2000: 162), whereas the particles *ne/nee* are to be used when 'asking for confirmation' (KCIIK, 2000: 200). While this is generally speaking true of modern Japanese today, *ze* and *zo* are associated with male speech while *ne* and especially *nee* are features of female speech (Tanaka, 2004). Information about the gendered use of these particles is absent from the book, however, despite the fact that research by Inoue (2006) shows that women's language forms, including the gendered use of *ze/zo* and *ne/nee*, first appeared around the same time as Standard Japanese.

Table 4.2 Polite and plain verb forms in *A Grammar of Spoken Language*

Polite form	Plain form	English
mōsu	iu	say
itasu	suru	do
itadaku	morau, kuu, nomu	receive, eat, drink
agaru	hōmon suru, iku	visit
mairu	iku, kuru	go, come
ukagau	kiku, tazuneru	ask
ageru	yaru	give
moshiageru	iu	say
taberu	kuu	eat

Thus, while *A Grammar of Spoken Language* did not codify all aspects of Standard Japanese, in particular those issues associated with style (e.g. gendered speech, levels of politeness), it did set down many of the standard forms still in use today. More importantly, however, *A Grammar of Spoken Language* virtually ended the debate surrounding the development of a standard language. Further still, by treating even language deviating from Standard Japanese as part of the national language – albeit non-standard uses thereof – the book further supported the ideology of a linguistically unified Japan. Non-standard forms of the national language were the topic of the third and final publication of the National Language Research Council that we shall consider in more detail next.

Supplement to the Grammar of Spoken Language (1917)

The organization of the *Supplement to the Grammar of Spoken Language* is identical to that of *A Grammar of Spoken Language*, and the two volumes are essentially two halves of the same book, the supplement describing those forms of the national language henceforth to be regarded as historical, regional or formal. It is essentially a grammar of marked language. In addition, the supplement records historic forms of what had 'evolved into' unified Standard Japanese. As such, the standard forms set out in the grammar appear at the apex of a linear historical development of language change and unification, whereby the process of selecting one language variety to stand above all others, and the countless debates about what written and spoken language ought to look like associated with that process, suddenly disappeared behind the newly created history of language. The arbitrary nature of the decisions about what was standard, and what constituted a deviation thereof, was thus concealed, and the National Language Research Council played a crucial role in this process.

Let us consider how this relates to the four linguistic features we have chosen to address in detail here. With regard to personal pronouns, the *Supplement to the Grammar of Spoken Language* lists entries from the Muromachi period (1338–1573) to the Edo period (1602–1868), and thus includes many glosses not found in the Grammar (KCIIK, 1980):

First person singular	*ore, ora, konata, nishi*
Second person singular	*sonota*
Third person singular	*aitsu*
First person plural	*orera, washira, watsura*

Although not all these forms have fallen in disuse, they have all become features of non-Standard Japanese. In modern Japanese, *ore* and *orera* infer informality, *ora, washira* and *watsura* are features of regional dialects, *konata* is an elegant form, *nishi* and *sonata* are historic, and *aitsu* is today considered slang. That these forms were not part of Standard Japanese did not imply that they were also not part of a unified national language. We can see from this example, then, how the idea of an unrestricted linguistic continuum, which had so troubled language ideology brokers in the early Meiji period (1868–1912), had by now given way to the view that variation in language was not necessarily in contrast to the idea of a unified national language. As a result of such a fundamental shift in language ideology, all language forms other than those which were to become part of Standard Japanese were rendered as regional, historical or social variations of the national language.

Regarding conjunctions, the *Supplement to the Grammar of Spoken Language* gives the following forms not listed in *A Grammar of Spoken Language* (KCIIK, 1980: 305–307): *tadashi* (but, however), *sono ue* (besides, moreover), *shikaru ni* (however), *tsuite wa* (therefore), *shikashinagara* (but, however), *to wa iu mono no* (but, however), *nominarazu* (furthermore, besides) and *ga* (but, however). Of these, only *shikaru ni* and *nominarazu* are considered non-standard today, both now being regarded as literary language. In this case, then, the stipulated norms of Standard Japanese turned out to be too narrowly defined, and variation was not restricted to the degree that these two partner texts seem to have anticipated.

Concerning honourific verb forms, the *Supplement to the Grammar of Spoken Language* gives its usual historical and regional *tour d'horizon*. This includes advice on the use of polite forms, stating that *mōshiageru* is politer than *mōsu* (to say), *tsukamatsuru* politer than *itasu* (to do) and *sashiageru* politer than *ageru* (to give) (KCIIK, 1980: 152). This time, it was *tsukamatsuru* that became literary language alone. As in two publications studied earlier, the *Dialect Survey Handbook* and *A Grammar of Spoken Language*, very little information at all is given on the subject of honourific language.

The *Supplement to the Grammar of Spoken Language* also provides several examples concerning the correct use of the particles *ze* and *zo* (KCIIK, 1980: 365–366). Although there is no mention of gender, the speakers in the examples given (such as, *komatta mono da-ze* (that's a problem, for sure) or *iu koto o kikanai-zo* (just ignore what's being said)) could today be identified as male speech. Other examples for *ne/nee* evoke associations with female speech, for example, *hana ga saku-ne* (the flowers are blossoming, aren't they?) (KCIIK, 1980: 506). This notwithstanding, gendered speech as such is not a topic of the *Supplement to the Grammar of Spoken Language* either. Matters of style, too, do not receive much attention, but rather the focus is on issues related to linguistic unification.

Imagining a Unified Speech Community

In this chapter, we have seen that neither Standard Japanese nor the national language (*kokugo*) came into existence spontaneously. Rather, the deliberate implementation of one specific language ideology, though among many others (see Chapters 2, 6 and 8 for alternatives), was of critical importance to their development. This ideology, introduced to Japan by Ueda Kazutoshi after his study tour in Europe, claimed that Japan was linguistically unified to such a degree that the very essence of Japanese identity could be attributed to the sharing the same mother tongue by all Japanese nationals, and thus Japanese became the national language of Japan. While this imagined national language contained variation, this became seen as being variations of Standard Japanese, that is, of educated Tokyo speech. In this way, variation no longer contradicted the idea of a Japanese nation unified by national language. Variation could be explained (away) by reference to region and time. In fact, of course, national language was only unified in ideology.

To truly create linguistic uniformity throughout Japan, notions of language ideology that could rationally support it as a worthwhile goal for Japanese nationals to achieve were needed. It was for this reason that a link between linguistic uniformity and social and individual well-being was subsequently invented. This ideological linkage resulted in those whose speech represented deviation from uniform national language being put under pressure to correct their 'deviance' in the name of progress. Rather than language ideology being an effigy of the sociolinguistic field it claimed to account for, the sociolinguistic field had to adapt to dominant language ideology. The data on variation within the language gathered by the National Language

Research Council, as well as the results extrapolated thereof, were useful to the language planners in supporting their ideology and thereby coercing speakers of non-standard forms to conform.

Ueda had envisioned a uniform and egalitarian speech community and championed the cause of the contemporary spoken language. However, in making claims of linguistic equality when in reality the opposite – linguistic variation and multilingualism – was in place, discrimination against all those deviating from the norms of Standard Japanese was inevitable. In order to illustrate this point, and the effects of such an ideology, we will turn our attention from the brokers of language ideology to the linguistic margin of the imagined homogenous speech community in the following chapters. In the next chapter, we will look closely at two such marginal groups and their experiences of the spread of Standard Japanese, the linguistic minorities of Ainu Mosir (Hokkaido) and the Ryukyu Archipelago.

5 The Linguistic Assimilation of Ryukyuans and Ainu

In the opening pages of this book we examined the various contradictory views held about Japan's linguistic situation, and we have seen how these contradictions relate to the schism between language ideology and the sociolinguistic field, for ideology is incongruous with that which it claims to represent. This is not to say that the two are not interconnected, however, for language ideology manifests itself in language use. One specific characteristic of language ideology is that the existence of contradictions thereof rarely results in correction of, or even reflection on, ideological beliefs. Rather, the reverse is the case, the contradictions to dominant ideology becoming the subject of correction and re-adjustment, resulting in language change and language shift.

In this chapter, we will consider the effects of Japanese nation-imagining ideology on linguistic minorities in Japan. Such an investigation serves a dual purpose, on the one hand deconstructing ideas about nation and national language, and on the other revealing the lack of awareness of minority languages in Japan. The effects have been different for the people of Ainu Mosir (Hokkaido) than for those in the Ryukyu Islands, and this difference belies two further characteristics of dominant language ideology. In the case of the Ainu, we see the ability of the dominant ideology to erase alternatives, while for the Ryukuans, it was ideology's ability to 'make sense' in order to align individuals to participate in social and linguistic change, in particular after World War II, which came into play. Ultimately, however, the effect is the same: sociolinguistic realities adapt to accommodate ideology. Linguistic uniformity, viewed by many as evidence of unity amongst Japanese, is such an example.

In Chapter 1, we also learned that the key to the success of a language ideology is how successfully it conceals the power relations that sustain it, for without doing so it cannot function ideologically. Once being aware of the power inequalities behind a dominant ideology, and by shifting the focus to what we call the linguistic margin, both the arbitrary nature of ideology and the concealment of such arbitrariness become visible. In a word, the ideological spell is broken. Exposing language ideology thus requires the existence of doubt over what the dominant ideology claims, that is, ontological doubt. The relationship between language, nation and state is thereby revealed as being different from what national language ideology claims it to be. Rather than language defining nation, and the boundaries of the national speech community defining state borders, it is in fact the state that defines those living within its borders as nation and then enforces national language upon them.

This chapter takes a closer look into how the Japanese language was spread by way of defining the borders of the Meiji state and, by extension, the boundaries of the Japanese nation. The first part of this chapter will consider Japanese language spread in the Ryukyu Islands from the Meiji restoration to the end of World War II, while in the second part we shall look at how the same process occurred, over the same period of time, in the lands of the Ainu. Though the Ryukyu Islands were under US occupation from 1945 until 1972, the spread of Japanese continued unabated, and so in the final part of this chapter we will discuss the post-war Ryukyus as well.

Japanese Language Spread in the Ryukyu Islands between 1868 and 1945

The Ryukyu Islands once constituted an independent and unified kingdom. Contact with China, to which tributary missions were sent, and trade with South-East Asia brought to the Ryukyu Kingdom a golden age of material and cultural prosperity. All this would change with the advent of early modernity (*kinsei*) on the Japanese mainland (*yamato*). During Japan's attempts to conquer Korea in the early-16th century, the powerful warlord Toyotomi Hideyoshi (1536–1598) urged the Ryukyu Kingdom to provide troops for his army, but the Ryukuans refused to comply with his demands. This refusal, and the subsequent failure of Hideyoshi's Korea campaign, paved the way for an invasion of the Ryukyu Kingdom in 1609, by the Japanese Satsuma Clan. The Ryukyu Kingdom thus became a vassal state (*zokkoku*) of Satsuma, though a façade of independence was maintained, largely to conceal Satsuma's influence over the Ryukyus to China.

The ambiguous status of the Ryukyu Kingdom changed quickly after the Meiji restoration of 1868. In seeking to secure its borders, the young Meiji government openly claimed the Ryukyu Kingdom for Japan, and forcibly annexed it to the Meiji state, as Okinawa Prefecture, in 1879. King Shō

Tai (1843–1901) was forced into exile in Tokyo in the same year, and Matsuda Michiyuki (1838–1882), chief secretary of the Japanese Home Ministry, was put in charge of the development and implementation of completing the total integration of the Ryukyu Islands into the Meiji state. Throughout all of this, the opinion of the Ryukyuan leadership was never once consulted (see Kerr, 1958; Smits, 1999 for details on Ryukyuan history).

Language was to play a key role in the subsequent transformation of Ryukyuans into Japanese nationals. The Ryukyuan languages and Japanese are two distinct branches of the Japonic language family. The Ryukyuan branch of the Japonic language family can be further divided into the northern and southern Ryukyuan languages (Miyara, 2010b), the northern branch comprising the languages of Amami, Kunigami and Uchinaa (Okinawa), and the southern branch those of Miyako, Yaeyama and Yonaguni (UNESCO, 2009). None of the Ryukyuan languages is mutually intelligible with Japanese, and lexicostatistical evidence (Hattori, 1954) confirms a linguistic distance between Japanese and the Ryukyuan *abstand* languages exceeding that between both the Romance languages and between the Slavic languages. In a seminal paper, to recall, Heinz Kloss (1967) distinguishes between two sociolinguistic types of languages. *Abstand* languages (languages by distance) can be identified via their intrinsic linguistic distance to one another, while *ausbau* languages (languages by development) are languages made distinct through the selection and codification of differences in what would otherwise be seen as constituting one language. Danish, Swedish and Norwegian are textbook examples of *ausbau* languages, while the Ryukyuan languages are typical examples of *abstand* languages. Needless to say, the existence of such linguistic distance between Japanese and the Ryukyuan languages had to be downplayed in order to support the nation imagining ideology as established in the Meiji period, and the politics of language and its reinforcement through national linguistics (*kokugogaku*) – a discipline established by Ueda Kazutoshi – was crucial to this.

The Politics of Language

Max Weinreich's (1945: 13) assertion that 'a language is a dialect with an army and navy' is as over-used as it is accurate. In his negotiations with the Ryukyuan, Japanese and Chinese authorities, Ryukyu Disposition Superintendent (*Ryūkyū shobun-kan*) Matsuda Michiyuki highlighted historical, cultural and linguistic similarities between Japan and the Ryukyu Islands, which, he concluded, were evidence of the fact that the language used in the Ryukyuan Islands were simply varieties of Japanese (see Oguma, 1998: 28–29).

The first linguist ever to conduct research on the Ryukyuan languages, Basil Hall Chamberlain (1850–1935), drew quite different conclusions, however. While Chamberlain (1999) found evidence of a shared Ryukyuan – Japanese genealogy, he saw the relationship between the Japanese and the Ryukyuan languages as similar to that between Spanish and Italian, or Spanish and French. In other words, Chamberlain defined the Ryukyuan language varieties as languages in their own right. Faced with the same information, Japanese scholars of national linguistics (*kokugogaku*) would however fall in line with nation imagining ideology. This is hardly surprising, given that the very discipline of national linguistics (*kokugogaku*) was founded by Ueda Kazutoshi with the explicit aim of institutionalizing national language as a shared bond between all Japanese nationals (Yasuda, 2000b: 152–153).

The new ideology of the national language demanded new ways of studying language, too, ones that took notions of state and nation as their point of reference, and defined national language accordingly. National linguistics was part of what today is called the politics of language, and from the outset, never contained any expression of doubt over the conviction that the only language spoken in Japan was the national language, that is, Japanese. Departing from their belief that nation and state were autonomous, real and entirely natural concepts, scholars of national linguistics set out to prove that the borders of the state and the borders of the national speech community were the same, and therefore that the territory held by the state was equal to that inhabited by the Japanese nation. In this way, the discipline of national linguistics found a way to be of service to the ideology of language nationalism. Thus, ideology was taken as the ontological basis from which research was to depart, and linguistic data was made to fit the ideological framework. Throughout the 20th century, mainstream Ryukyuan linguistics would be conducted in this way.

The linguistic distance between the Ryukyuan languages and Japanese meant that it was no easy job to use their similarities as the basis of an argument in support of national language ideology. Indeed, it took several decades of research, analysis and interpretation to make the argument a convincing one. Tōjō Misao (1884–1966), a student of Ueda and widely regarded as the 'founding father of Japanese dialectology', was the first to offer an academic solution to the problem of bringing Japan's sociolinguistic field in line with the dominant ideology of language, nation and state. Tōjō's efforts to do so involved creating new meta-language relating to national language. In his groundbreaking *Dialect Map of Greater Japan* (*Dainihon hōgen chizu*), Tōjō confirmed Chamberlain's view that the Ryukyuan language varieties were genealogically related to Japanese. Contrary to Chamberlain, however, he classed them together as a greater dialect (*dai-hōgen*) of the national language, the other greater dialect consisting of mainland Japanese language varieties.

Tōjō's work may be considered circular, in that his research is forced to support what dominant language ideology claims, as we can see in the following quote:

> Since [Ryukyuan P.H.] is a language which has split from the same ancestor language [as Japanese P.H.] and, in addition, the use of the language is limited within the boundaries of the same state, I would like to regard it as one dialect of the national language. (Tōjō, 1927: 18)

In a later publication, Tōjō further substantiated this line of reasoning, by defining dialect (*hōgen*) in the following way:

> If a national language is broken up into a number of language groups (*gengo-dan*) which differ with regard to pronunciation, lexicon and grammar according to the different regions in which they are used, these various groups are called a dialect. (Tōjō, 1938: 6)

Something that is clear from this quote is that Tōjō never questions the appropriateness of the concept of national language for Japanese nationals, for by this time, both the idea of national language and the inclusion of the Ryukyuan languages within it had passed smoothly from ideology to ontology. In other words, ontological knowledge was established on the basis of national language ideology. Scholarly work in the tradition of national linguistics was not expected to produce anything other than new methods and means by which the Ryukyuan language varieties could be incorporated into the national language, resulting in new and rather clumsy definitions like 'greater dialect' or 'language group'.

Such definitions were hastily abandoned by Tōjō's successors, such as Hattori (1932), who simply used the term dialect (*hōgen*) when referring to the Ryukyuan language varieties, but while this has been the norm in Ryukyuan language research for a very long time, it has not gone entirely unchallenged. An early example is the case of Kinjō Chōei (1902–1955). Kinjō, whose first language was Uchinaaguchi (Okinawan), observed that the view of Ryukyuan languages as greater dialects of Japanese had much support within national linguistics. His objection was to the fact that (Kinjō, 1944: 6) 'this has never been treated as a tentative view, but has, from the outset, been accepted as fact'. One effect of this acceptance was that the Ryukyu Islands were primed for the dissemination of Japanese in the name of language standardization. Let us consider now how the Japanese language was spread in the Ryukyus.

Language Planning Measures

After the Meiji restoration, initial contact between the Japanese and the Ryukyuans was characterized by communication problems between the two sides, and subsequently by efforts to overcome these problems. The historian George Kerr (1958: 412–413) gives the following description of the situation in the year 1870: 'The Japanese could converse with the educated leaders at Shuri and Naha, but could not make themselves understood in the countryside'. Following this early phase, the Japanese language gradually spread throughout the islands during the 1880s, by which time the aim of the Meiji government was to force the Ryukyuans to adapt to mainland Japanese customs, thereby rendering them effectively Japanese (Shinzato, 2001: 241). The implementation of measures towards achieving this end began with the inauguration of compulsory school education in Okinawa Prefecture in 1880.

Even a cursory glance at some of the institutions responsible for spreading Japanese throughout the Ryukyus reveals the political backgrounds on which that policy rested. Initially, the Bureau of the Ryukyu Domain (*Ryūkyū-han Jimu*) was responsible for language issues. In September 1872, jurisdiction over the bureau was transferred from Kagoshima Prefecture (the former Satsuma Domain) to the central government's Ministry of Foreign Affairs (*Gaimushō*). In the same year, a Foreign Ministry Branch Office (*Gaimushō Shutchōjo*) was established at Shuri, but Tokyo's insistence that the Ryukyu Islands were in fact Japanese, and it's eagerness to assert this fact in the face of criticism by the Chinese, led to the office being brought under the control of the Home Ministry (*Naimushō*) and its subsequently renaming as a Branch Office of the Home Ministry (*Naimushō Shutchōjo*), just two years later, in 1874. Finally, in 1879, the Branch Office became the home of the Okinawa Prefectural Government (*Okinawa Kenchō*), the bureaucrats employed at which were largely recruited on the mainland, usually in Kagoshima Prefecture (Oguma, 1998: 20). Thus, the years between 1872 and 1879 came to be known as the period of the Ryukyu disposition (*Ryūkyū shobun*), during which administration of the Ryukyu Domain was transferred from local to central authorities, and then from foreign to home affairs.

Following the reorganization of the Ryukyu Domain into Okinawa Prefecture, the vice minister of the Ministry of Education, Tanaka Fujimaro (1845–1909), was dispatched to the new prefecture tasked with the development and implementation of educational policy (Kerr, 1958: 412). Upon his arrival in Uchinaa, Tanaka decided that the Ryukyuans would most readily acknowledge the authority of the central government in Tokyo if they received their orders in Japanese. Since this presupposed their understanding Japanese, in February 1880, Tanaka gave orders for the establishment of a

Conversation Training Centre (*Taiwa Denshūjo*) (Okinawa Kyōiku I'inkai, 1965–1977: 20). Unlike teacher-training facilities on the mainland, the Conversation Training Centre in Uchinaa was also given the responsibility of compiling a Japanese language textbook. Japanese officials employed at the prefectural Department of Education produced the book, titled *Okinawa Conversation* (*Okinawa taiwa*), which was subsequently used for instruction in all prefectural schools from 1880 onwards (Fujisawa, 2000: 193).

Okinawa Conversation was a bilingual textbook, making it the first ever Japanese-as-a-foreign-language textbook in history. Neither the concept of national language (*kokugo*) nor that of Standard Japanese (*hyōjungo*) was well-known in late-19th century Japan, and so the Japanese language was spread under the label of Tokyo language (*Tōkyō no kotoba*) (Hokama, 1971: 52–54). Consider in this context, too, the following excerpt from *Okinawa Conversation* (GOH, 1981: not paginated), which features a conversation between a mainland Japanese person (line 1) and an Uchinaanchu (Okinawan) (line 2). In the following, (a) denotes Japanese, while (b) is Uchinaaguchi (Okinawan).

(1a) *Kihō wa Tōkyō no kotoba de o-hanashi dekimasuka?*
(1b) *Unjoo toochoo nu kutuba shaai uhanashi unami sheebiimi?*
(2a) *Nakanaka yoku wa hanasemasen.*
(2b) *Aa shikatto hanashee nayabiran.*

The English translation would be as follows:

(1c) Do you speak the language of Tokyo?
(2c) I do not speak it well at all.

Evidence that Japanese was initially taught as a foreign language in Uchinaa is to be found in the personal recollections of those such as Iha Fuyū (1876–1947), the 'founding father of Ryukyuan linguistics', who testified that he first learned Japanese at the age of 11. Iha (1975: 456–457) further recalled that the number of Japanese speakers in Uchinaa at that time was roughly equal to the number of those speaking English there. *Okinawa Conversation* was replaced by the second, and last, bilingual Japanese – Uchinaaguchi textbook for Ryukyuan pupils, the *Common Primary School Reader for Okinawa Prefecture* (*Okinawa-ken yō jinjō shōgakkō dokuhon*), which was used until the end of the 19th century.

Efforts to spread the Japanese language were accompanied by attempts to repress Ryukyuan language use, such as the prohibition against using indigenous languages in public, and the 1907 Dialect Regulation Ordinance

(*Hōgen torishimari-rei*) (ODJKJ, 1983: 443–444). As its title suggests, the ordinance defined Ryukyuan languages as dialects, and dialects in need of regulation at that. It is worth noting that no other dialect of Japanese was deemed to be in need of such an ordinance. Its remit is indicative of the difficulties Ryukyuans faced in acquiring Japanese, and it was by way of an attempt to tackle these difficulties that local languages, viewed by the authorities as no more than very strong dialects, became the subject of deliberate and concerted repression. One notorious method of punishing Ryukyuans for speaking their own languages, and therefore not Japanese, was the so-called dialect tag (*hōgen fuda*). School pupils who had used their local language in class were expected to wear the dialect tag around their necks. Usually there was only one dialect tag in each class, and the student already wearing it was responsible for passing it on to the next pupil who broke the rules of the ordinance, thereby encouraging peer-group monitoring of Japanese language use in schools. Those pupils who were found to be using local languages too frequently were admonished, or their parents urged to encourage them to cooperate more closely with language education efforts (Kondō, 1997: 38–39).

Methods of spreading Japanese in Okinawa Prefecture reached new levels of sophistication with the creation of the Movement for the Enforcement of Normal Language (*Futsūgo reikō undō*) in 1931. Following the period of Tokyo language (*Tōkyō no kotoba*), Japanese was briefly spread under the label of normal language (*futsūgo*), before it came to be represented by standard language (*hyōjungo*) in the second half of the 1930s. This movement had much support from teachers throughout Okinawa Prefecture, and developed, for the first time, schemes for spreading the Japanese language in the private domain. In 1937, it was renamed the Movement for the Enforcement of Standard Language (*Hyōjungo reikō undō*), and in 1939, it compiled, in collaboration with the prefectural Department of Education, a policy known as the Programme for Education in Okinawa Prefecture (*Okinawa-ken kyōiku kōryō*). This policy initiative emphasized the importance of Japanese language spread, and committees responsible for directing the spread of Standard Japanese were subsequently set up in every local community (Nakamatsu, 1996: 42). Thereafter, the Movement for the Enforcement of standard language pushed to make standard language part of everyday life (*hyōjungo no seikatsugo-ka*) and to improve the atmosphere in which Standard Japanese was used (Hokama, 1971: 84–89). In line with this aim, the use of Standard Japanese was promoted through the organizing of debates and presentation circles at schools, which the families of the pupils were invited to attend. Schoolchildren involved in such debates risked punishment if they failed to use Japanese, and speaking local languages at such events was generally understood to be unpatriotic (Iha, 1975: 458).

The true nature of this policy of encouraging the spread and use of the Japanese language in order to force Japanese language and identity upon the Ryukyuans is most easily understood by examining the close links between the Movement for the Enforcement of Standard Language and the National Spiritual Mobilization Movement (*Kokumin seishin sōdōin undō*) in the period between 1938 and 1945. Research conducted by Kondō Kenichirō (1999, 2000), reveals a marked increase in the use of dialect tags after the outbreak of the Sino-Japanese War in 1937 (Table 5.1).

In February 1939, the Movement for the Enforcement of Standard Language, in collaboration with the prefectural government, organized a Week of Enhancing Japanese Spirit (*Nihon seishin hatsuyō shūkan*), during which the purpose of spreading the Japanese language spread was outlined as follows (quoted from Kondō, 1997: 31): 'Enforcement of the Standard language is in accordance with the enhancement of the Japanese spirit and is of great importance to the lives of prefectural citizens'. The Movement for the Enforcement of Standard Language also created slogans to encourage the use of the standard language for the sake of national unity, progress and development. Consider these examples (Kondō, 2006: 225):

Standard language – anytime, anywhere (*itsu demo doko demo hyōjungo*).
Towards attaining the steadfast support of the unified prefectural citizens for the standard language (*hyōjungo e kenmin itchi no chikarakobu*).
One country, one mind, one language (*ikkoku, isshin, kotoba mo hitotsu*).
Everywhere, everyone, standard language (*kogoto, hitogoto, hyōjungo*).
Standard language – the whole family as one (*ikka kozotte hyōjungo*).
Standard language – familiarization from infancy onwards (*nyūji kara narase hyōjungo*).
Standard language – uniting a hundred million hearts and minds (*ichioku no kokoro o musubu hyōjungo*).
Standard language – especially in close relationships (*shitashiki naka koso hyojungo*).
An advanced Okinawa begins with language (*shinkō okinawa kotoba kara*).

Table 5.1 Use of the dialect tags in Okinawa Prefecture in 25 schools on Yaeyama and Miyako

	Use of dialect tag	No Use of dialect tag
1910–1919	4	21
1920–1929	13	12
1930–1939	17	8
1940–1945	13	12

In Chapter 1, we looked at how language-related discourse becomes ideologically loaded via the linking of language with non-linguistic matters, an arbitrary process designed to achieve goals other than linguistic ones. This characteristic of language ideology is evident in Japanese language spread in the Ryukyu Islands, in the slogans above, for example.

Efforts to unify Japan linguistically included measures intended to eradicate the Ryukyuan languages completely. This clearly went beyond what was required for effective communication between mainland Japanese and Ryukyuans. The main objective, of course, was not to encourage communication, but rather to foster national unity in line with the ideology of a monolingual Japan united by national language. The gradual escalation in severity of these attempts to forcibly discourage local language use led to the characterization of pre-war language education in Okinawa Prefecture as hysteric (ODJKJ, 1983: 320), and by the end of World War II it had literally become a matter of life or death. During the Battle of Okinawa, a military decree was passed whereby anyone caught using Ryukyuan languages, unintelligible to speakers of Japanese, would be treated as a spy, resulting in the shooting and stabbing to death of local language users by the Japanese military (Nakamatsu, 1996: 58; Oyafuso, 1986: 38).

There was thus no unity in language such as national language ideology would claim. The contradiction between language ideology and linguistic realities in the Ryukyus meant that using Japanese only as a *lingua franca* did not go far enough. As Japanese gradually spread under the guise of standardizing the national language, the Japanese nationals came to view all other languages as inconsistent with dominant language ideology and therefore in need of suppression. Despite the downgrading of the Ryukyuan languages from languages in their own right to dialects of the national language, the use of such dialects was repressed even in the private domain. Language ideology smoothed the way, rationalizing that repression and linking Japanese monolingualism with unity and progress. Japanese language spread, and the attack on Ryukyuan languages, was justified because it was a necessary part of the process of giving all Ryukyuans a place within the Japanese nation. That the validity of their place was openly challenged after World War II only led to further efforts to eradicate Ryukyuan languages (see below), though that time the movement originated from within the Ryukyus, rather than from the mainland.

Before examining how the Ryukyuans themselves spread the Japanese language within their families and neighbourhoods in the post-war era, let us first consider the fate of the Ainu in the period between 1868 and 1945. Many similarities to the language policies implemented in the Ryukyu Islands exist, but they were legitimized in an altogether different way. This difference is of great importance, for it illustrates that ideology is not a fixed body of ideas, but a generative principle which forever produces new meaning for its own defence, justification and protection. Undoing ideology may never be achieved simply by describing its manifestations, but requires a comprehensive understanding of how language ideology works. In an effort to arrive at such an understanding, let us now consider the case of the Ainu.

Japanese Language Spread in Ainu Mosir between 1868 and 1945

Colonization always starts with the taking of new territory linguistically, for geography is invariably in the service of power, that is in the service of the state (see Jones et al., 2006). It is hardly surprising, then, that the very name Hokkaido (literally 'North Sea Circuit') was created at the time of its colonization by Japan. Hokkaido is the only administrative unit in Japan named in this way, having previously been known by pre-modern Japanese as Ezochi, literally 'alien land'. During the early modern period (1602–1867), the Japanese viewed Ezochi as being somewhere between a foreign land and the outer circle of their still vaguely defined cultural sphere, a view informed by notions of increasing foreignness and barbarianism over space as handed down from China (Walker, 2006: 39–40).

Ezochi was officially renamed Hokkaido at the inauguration of the Hokkaido Development Agency (*Kaitakushi*), which was subsequently responsible for the planning and organization of Japanese migration to settlements in the North Sea Circuit. Many Ainu avoid using the term Hokkaido today, preferring instead the indigenous word, Ainu Mosir, meaning literally 'the peaceful land of the Ainu'. Originally, Ainu was not used as an ethonym but simply signified 'human being(s)'. While the term Ainu Mosir reflects the fact that the land it designates was once the undisputed territory of the Ainu, it also implies a sense of linguistic, political and cultural unity among the Ainu, which in reality did not exist prior to its colonization. In the absence of any politically neutral alternative, however, the term Ainu Mosir will be given preference over Hokkaido where it is possible.

With regard to language, a broad distinction can be made between the Ainu language varieties of Hokkaido, the Kurile Islands and Sakhalin. While the difference between Kurile Ainu on the one hand, and Hokkaido and Sakhalin Ainu on the other, is said to be most distinctive (Tamura, 2000: 2), insufficient data exist to verify the linguistic distance between them. With regard to the difference between Ainu on Hokkaido and on Sakhalin,

Hattori's groundbreaking Ainu dictionary provides glottochronological data of 13 Ainu dialects on Hokkaido and of five Sakhalin dialects. Hattori's data show that the rate of shared cognates between the Hokkaido and the Sakhalin dialects is never more than 80%, and averages 73% (see Hattori, 1964: 19). Rather than one unified Ainu language, therefore, there existed three, unroofed, *abstand* languages (languages by distance): Kurile Ainu, Sakhalin Ainu and Hokkaido Ainu. To date, no genealogical relations between Ainu and other languages have been established, and it is best, therefore, to view these three as language isolates (Lewis, 2009). As the languages of the Ainu are typologically polysynthetic (Shibatani, 1990) and therefore typologically very different from the agglutinating Japonic languages, it would be rather problematic to claim that they are dialects of Japanese, and in fact no such claims have been made. Rather, we will discuss in more detail below, how, from very early on, the Ainu languages were earmarked for language loss.

Early Assimilation Efforts

Even though contact between mainland Japanese and the Ainu predates the Meiji restoration of 1868, the Ainu were not subject to linguistic assimilation by the Tokugawa Shogunate (1602–1868). Some of the Ainu acquired a certain level of proficiency in Japanese, and also in Russian, as a result of trade with their neighbours during this period (Walker, 2006: 10, 142, 173), and there were thus individual Ainu over several generations who were multilingual before the modernization of Japan, a fact which serves as a reminder that the idea of monolingual uniformity is neither natural, normal nor historically accurate. Rather, modern Japan's emphasis on linguistic homogeneity intended to bring all those defined as Japanese nationals within its ideological framework, and as such linguistic minorities like the Ainu were seen to constitute a problem. Problems, of course, demand solutions, and in Ainu Mosir that solution too was linguistic assimilation. In line with national language ideology, the Ainu were forcibly encouraged to abandon their native languages.

Japanese language spread amongst the Ainu population evolved in two stages. Between 1868 and 1898, developments were rather low-key and poorly organized, but from 1899 onwards, more concerted efforts to assimilate the Ainu into the Japanese society, albeit as an underclass, were made (DeChicchis, 1995). The incorporation of Ainu territories into the Japanese nation-state made its first linguistic mark in 1869, when the Japanese orthography for Ainu place names was standardized (Maher, 2001: 328), thereby doing away with Ainu etymologies for place names and replacing them with ad-hoc allocations of Chinese characters denoting Japanese versions of Ainu toponyms. The piecemeal erasure of Ainu languages was further intensified through the forced relocation of Ainu communities to reservations in order to make way for Japanese settlements in Ainu Mosir, as a result of which many established speech communities were broken up. When the practice of traditional Ainu rituals like hunting, tattooing and funeral ceremonies was outlawed in 1871, the argument that all Ainu should learn spoken and written Japanese was also raised (Oguma, 1998: 54). In the same year, the Ainu were designated as Japanese citizens (*heimin*), a move that implied total assimilation in line with nation-imagining ideology, that is, assimilation into Japanese monolingualism.

One early attempt at assimilating the Ainu into the Japanese majority was made in 1882, when 35 Ainu were sent to Tokyo to study Japanese language and customs. The aim was to have them become leaders and role models for their respective Ainu communities, and thereby to spread Japanese language and culture in this way. The plan failed miserably, however, with the majority of those sent to Tokyo leaving before they could acquire any significant level of proficiency (Kuroda, 2002: 14). The advent of school education in 1875 proved far more effective (Maher, 2001: 329). In 1879, Aboriginal Education Centres (*Dojin Kyōikujo*) were established and language textbooks for use by Ainu compiled (Kuroda, 2002: 14). Compared to similar activities being conducted in the Ryukyu Islands during the same period, however, these efforts were relatively innocuous. Clearly the assimilation of the Ainu, with a population of around 17,000, was seen as a less pressing issue than that of 600,000 Ryukyuans, and not until the 1890s would the Japanese language education of the Ainu come to be seen as a matter of national interest. Once this was the case, special schools for Ainu were established and a standardized curriculum specific to them developed (Peng & Geiser, 1977: 184). To combat the low school attendance figures, compulsory school education for Ainu – conducted in Japanese – was introduced in 1898, heralding the next phase of the language assimilation policy, which now set its sights firmly on dissolving Ainu language and culture. This policy was characterized by the authorities as an act of benevolence.

Assimilation as an Act of Benevolence

The years between 1899 and 1901 mark a watershed in the linguistic assimilation of the Ainu. In 1899, the Hokkaido Former Aboriginal Protection Act (*Hokkaidō kyūdojin hogo-hō*) was promulgated and two years later the Ainu Education System (*Ainu kyōiku seido*) came into being. The Hokkaido Protection Act, 'the keystone of an imperialistic assimilation policy' (Siddle,

1995b: 149), mainly concerned itself with farming and education, its aim being to integrate the Ainu into the Japanese nation as farmers. Under the act, Ainu languages, traditional hunting techniques and Ainu festivals were largely banned. Richard Siddle (1995a: 87) describes the act as 'instrumental in institutionalising the paternalistic view of the authorities of the Ainu as [...] "former aborigines"', and as a consequence 'gave credence to, and further reinforced, an image of a doomed, inferior race'. This general perception of the Ainu as racially inferior, and fit only for assimilation, changed little even after many of the restrictions of the 1899 act were lifted in the period from 1919 onwards. Since the Ainu could not easily be assimilated into the Japanese nation due to the considerable linguistic and cultural differences between the two, they were instead characterized as a dying people (*horobiyuku minzoku*), and the problems they faced with regard to successful assimilation were consequently seen as manifestations of the struggle for survival of an inferior race (*rettō no jinshu*). Assimilation, therefore, was seen as the only way out of their misery, by offering them acceptance into a race superior to their own (*yūtō no jinshu*). To Japanese policy-makers, therefore, this constituted an act of benevolence (*buiku*).

Following the implementation of the Hokkaido Former Aboriginal Protection Act, 21 National Schools for Former Aborigines (*Kokuritsu Kyūdojin Gakkō*) were established by way of advancing assimilation of the Ainu (Peng & Geiser, 1977: 184). Compulsory school education was conducted only in Japanese, with Ainu children learning Japanese as a foreign language, albeit under the label of national language (*kokugo*), as was the case in the Ryukyu Islands. This strategy was bolstered by the 'success' already achieved in the Ryukyus, and clearly strengthened efforts to dissolve the Ainu language and culture. Most importantly of all, it was a way of promoting the ideological vision on what the Japanese nation should be – united and uniform in language and culture. While assimilation of the Ainu into the Japanese nation was carried out in the ideological belief that it represented an act of benevolence, existing inequalities pertaining to economic well-being, access to education, or in Japanese language skills between the Ainu and the Japanese resulted in continual economic, social, cultural, political and linguistic discrimination.

Inequality was of various kinds. It included economic well-being, social participation, health, access to education and other social goods. Closer to the topic of this book, linguistic and cultural capital manifesting in proficiencies in the dominating language Japanese must be mentioned. One thing such inequalities had in common was that it affected the assessment of those who lack power. When lacking power, difference is interpreted as obsolesce, and progress is associated with assimilation to the dominating community.

Segregated school education for Ainu and Japanese was firmly established with the enactment of the 1901 Ainu education system. The practice was abolished in 1908, but later reintroduced between 1916 and 1937. The education of Ainu children prioritized Japanese language over other school subjects, with history, geography and science not taught at all in Ainu schools. Pupils were also encouraged to give up what were seen as inferior Ainu habit, and a concerted effort was made to foster obedience to the Japanese nation and to the emperor (Koshida, 1993: 3). Needless to say, the very existence of segregated school education points to the gap between nation-imagining ideology and the sociolinguistic realities within the Meiji state. While the ideology promoted the view that all Japanese citizens were linguistically homogenous, national language proved not to be the unifying bond it was supposed to be, with *kokugo* language education demanding the compilation of bilingual textbooks and specific curricula in both the Ryukyu Islands and in Ainu Mosir, and national language ideology requiring the establishment of schools specifically for Ainu for several decades after the beginning of Japanese migration to Ainu Mosir.

Owing to being told at school that theirs was an inferior race, the Ainu soon developed negative attitudes towards their own ethnicity, language and culture. The late Ainu culture and language activist Kayano Shigeru (1923–2006) shows how the decline of Ainu language and culture was the result of ideological coercion, rather than a free and rational choice on the side of the Ainu:

> The Ainu have not intentionally forgotten their culture and their language. It is the modern Japanese state that, from the Meiji era on, usurped our land, destroyed our culture, and deprived us of our language under the euphemism of assimilation. (Kayano, 1994: 153)

Underlying the oppression of minority languages and cultures in modern Japan was the very idea that uniformity equals equality and progress, which made the decline of minority languages and cultures seem an unavoidable and entirely natural consequence of successful modernization. A place for linguistic and cultural distinction was never envisioned as part of the Japanese nation. Unsurprisingly therefore, attempts at maintaining and revitalizing minority languages and cultures in present-day Japan are largely attempts at overcoming such self-imposed ideological restrictions (see Chapter 9).

Natural intergenerational transmission of linguistic and cultural knowledge was interrupted rather easily and quickly in Ainu Mosir. Documents collated by the Hokkaido prefectural government suggest that such transmission began to fall apart in the period between 1910 and 1930. In contrast to reports written before this period, Ainu language problems go largely unmentioned, suggesting that language shift was well under way and that Ainu children had started speaking Japanese as their first language by that time (Kuroda, 2002: 15, 19). Although the Ainu shifted to using Japanese in both the public and private domains relatively quickly (see Chapter 7), some opposition to the Japanese language policy had existed. Of such opposition, Siddle (1999: 146) writes that '[these] men and women [...] sensitive, educated and articulate but ultimately unable to escape categorization as "natives" – reacted to their marginalization by attempting to create a new sense of pride and worth in being Ainu'. In spite of such attempts at emancipation, however, those speaking out in support for Ainu were already subjugated under the dominant ideology by then. Due to the imbalance of power between the brokers of the dominant language ideology and those speaking in support of Ainu emancipation, the call to take pride in being Ainu largely fell on deaf ears.

Conscious of the fact that the Ainu neither shared the same language, culture nor customs as the Japanese demanded that their case be managed differently from that of the Ryukyuans, where it was deemed possible to rebrand the indigenous language and culture as Japanese. While assimilation of the Ryukyuans was presented as a necessary component of their adaptation to the modern world, no such subtleties disguised the overt substitution of Ainu language and culture with their Japanese equivalents. That is not to say that it was not deemed necessary to legitimize this process in some way, for as we have seen above, rationalization was sought in the struggle for survival narrative (*seizon kyōsō*), a concept that had been readily accepted by Japanese intelligentsia during the Meiji period (Swale, 2000: 188–219). Following the Spencerian logic of the survival of the fittest (*yūshō reppai*), a theory that held great sway in the Meiji period Japan, Japanese domination over the Ainu was seen as inevitable, for the former was perceived to constitute a superior race, and the latter an inferior one. Furthermore, by ignoring the disastrous effects of previous restrictions placed on the Ainu by the Japanese prior to the Meiji restoration, which had left the Ainu disease stricken, malnourished and dependent upon the Japanese for aid, the Meiji state believed wholeheartedly that they were indeed acting benevolently towards the people of Ainu Mosir (Walker, 2006).

Firmly rooted in this survival narrative, the steady decline of Ainu language vitality was seen to be inevitable, and the number of native Ainu speakers dropped in line with the progress of their assimilation. Japanese language spread among the Ainu was, therefore, a conscious attempt to readjust the sociolinguistic reality of Ainu Mosir to incorporate the dominant national language ideology. The linguistic assimilation of the Ainu into the imagined national speech community thus proved to be *une vérité à faire*. With regard to language ideology, the lesson to be learned thereof is this. Firstly, we understand that that which does not agree with the dominant ideology, rather than being seen to undermine the legitimacy of that ideology, is characterized as a deviation in need of remedy. In the case of the Ainu, the remedy entailed linguistic and cultural loss. In other words, faced with a challenge from the west, mid-19th century Japan's efforts of emancipation by becoming a modern nation cost those at its newly defined margins dearly.

Having looked at the situation in pre-war Ainu Mosir, we shall now return to the Ryukyu Islands, this time to consider events there post-World War II. We shall thereby examine a further aspect of language ideology: its interrelation to the well-being that accompanies specific language choices. As we are about to see, the same national language ideology that was employed to repress Ryukyuan autonomy before 1945, in fact proved to be a powerful tool for defending social and personal rights and freedoms after the war. This was because Ryukyuans found themselves under US occupation between 1945 and 1972, and within this new context the same ideology that had justified their oppression in the pre-war period was now directed against the Americans, in the name of Ryukyuan emancipation. Such a paradigm shift in the function of an ideology is not entirely surprising, however, for ideologies must make sense, and sense emerges only in response to its specific contexts.

Japanese Language Spread in the Ryukyu Islands under US Occupation

The Ryukyu Archipelago was a decisive location at the beginning of Japanese expansionism, and at its end, with the decisive battle of the Pacific War being fought on Uchinaa, between April and June 1945. The Battle of Okinawa and the archipelago's subsequent occupation by the United States mark a massive turning point in Ryukyuan history. Before Japan's surrender to the Allied Powers in September 1945, a military government for the Ryukyu Islands was established, rendering the Ryukyu Islands a political orphan. Detached from the Japanese mainland from June 1945 to May 1972, the US military controlled the archipelago, though 'residual sovereignty' stayed with Japan.

By the time the Korean War broke out in 1950, it had become clear that the United States intended to keep the Ryukyu Islands occupied for an extended period of time, in order to serve its geopolitical interests. As a result, a popular movement advocating a return to Japanese rule emerged in the Ryukyus. In 1950, Taira Tatsuo (1892–1969) won the gubernatorial election in Okinawa Perfecture through his taking just such a stance, and by extension, therefore, rejecting both the idea of Ryukyuan independence and that of continued US occupation. From the 1950s onwards, the movement called for the Japanese language to be spread to families and local neighbourhoods (Heinrich, 2010a), and the use of Japanese, that is, national language, in the Ryukyus was used to prove to both the United States and to Japan that Ryukyuans were truly Japanese and that the Ryukyu Islands should therefore be returned to the fatherland (*sokoku*), Japan.

The decision to promote Standard Japanese in all domains, as a means of fostering a Japanese identity amongst the Ryukyuan population, was pitched against two alternatives: political independence or continued occupation by the United States. In support of the latter of these alternatives, some sought to highlight the differences between Ryukyuans and Japanese. On the other hand, a popular sense of Ryukyuan nationalism never developed, partly due to the fact that residual sovereignty over the islands still rested with Japan, thereby effectively restricting the choice to one of rule either by the Japanese or the Americans. Taira Koji summarizes the arguments and the circumstances which led to chose reversion as follows:

> Why, from all the possible alternatives, Okinawa chose reversion to Japan requires an understanding of how the international environment during the 1950s and 1960s, especially US-Japanese relations, restricted Okinawan choice. The Cold War made any political stance in Okinawa other than co-operation with the *status quo* a subversive one, and thereby subject to repression. Any criticism that defined US rule in terms of colonialism was regarded by USCAR [United States Civil Administration of the Ryukyu Islands P.H.] as part of a (imaginary) communist conspiracy. This threat effectively killed freedom of speech for Okinawans, while at the same time the possibility of extending political autonomy to Okinawa was denounced as a fantasy by the longest-serving High Commissioner, General Caraway (in office 1961-4). (Taira, 1997: 160)

Given the situation described above, return to Japanese rule appeared to be the most viable way out of occupation and US control. With the trauma of the Battle of Okinawa (Ota, 2000) and the memory of Japanese discrimination against Ryukyuans in general (ODJKJ, 1983: 518) still fresh in the minds of many Ryukyuans, however, the popular reversion movement took several years to gather large-scale support. Immediately after the Battle of Okinawa, genuine consideration was given to the idea of banning the

Japanese language from the Ryukyu Islands indefinitely (Nakamatsu, 1996: 62–63). At the same time, the US authorities supported the use of Ryukyuan languages, both in the public domain and as a medium of education, at least in the early years of the occupation. Let us briefly examine these early years of ambiguity, and the insights they give into the possible alternatives to Japanese monolingualism that were later pursued in the Ryukyu Islands.

Years of Ambiguity

Language planning was mainly driven by two parties in the post-war era. On one side, the US military authorities encouraged both the use of Ryukyuan languages and of English at the expense of Japanese, while on the other, predominantly Ryukyuan civil servants attempted to restore Japanese to its pre-war place. Let us consider the Americans first. General Douglas McArthur (1880–1964), the Supreme Commander of Allied Forces, personally supported the idea that the Ryukyuans were not Japanese, and that an education policy promoting the Ryukyuan languages ought to be developed (Motonaga, 1994: 184). As a result, the US authorities re-evaluated the status of Ryukyuan languages when devising a language policy for the occupied islands, and rejected outright the idea that the Ryukyuan languages were part of the Japanese national language. Their decision was largely based on a report compiled by anthropologists from Yale University which was titled *The Okinawans of the Loochoo Islands, a Japanese Minority Group*. The report pointed to exploitation and discrimination of Ryukyuans at the hands of the Japanese, and defined the Ryukyuans as an ethnic, cultural and linguistic minority (OCNO, 1944). But the American administration soon began to lose interest in issues of language, and so in the end no substantial language policy was ever developed. With the communist victory in China of 1949 and the outbreak of the Korean War in 1950, the window of opportunity for the status of Ryukyuan languages to change closed. From the 1950s on, it was the Japanese language that would again dominate the public domain.

Initially US authorities considered the promotion of English as the official second language of the Ryukyus. This, too, was never realized. The idea was that the Ryukyus might serve as a bridge between the United States and Japan (Morita, 1967: 207), and indeed some efforts to spread English through school education were made, but these proved ineffective and short-lived. In December 1950, a directive was passed by which (quoted from Fisch, 1988: 100) 'instruction in the English language for all natives is a prime necessity, but this is not to be construed as discouraging instruction on native languages and culture'. Such aims notwithstanding, compulsory English language education was quickly abandoned, partly due to a serious shortage of qualified teachers (Kamegawa, 1972: 208–209). Interestingly, the directive also gives priority to local languages, and thus ignores the ideology of Japanese national language and its allusion to linguistic homogeneity. Regardless, all attempts to initiating language status change, whether of the Ryukyuan languages or of English, proved to be ineffectual.

While the first manoeuvres of post-war language planning were taken by the US administration, Ryukyuan bureaucrats and educators soon took over. This was part of the drive to hand over administrative power quickly from US officers to Ryukyuan public servants. Pivotal in this respect was a proposal by the occupation forces to establish an Okinawan Advisory Council (*Okinawa Shijun-kai*) in 1945. The council comprised 12 departments, one of which was dedicated to educational affairs. According to directive 86 of the US Naval Military Government, the Okinawa Department of Culture and Education (*Okinawa Bunkyō-bu*) was responsible for the following matters:

> Educational affairs insofar as they concern actual operations of schools, including planning of curriculum, preparation of texts, appointment and removal of principals and teachers and other personnel, inspection of schools, allocation of personnel, maintenance of records, and general administrative detail are placed under an Okinawan Department of Culture and Education, staffed by Okinawans but supervised at the Headquarters level by Military Government personnel who retain the final discretion. (Quoted from Fisch, 1988: 277)

It is worth noting that this directive did not specify which language should be used for school instruction. Rather, this important matter was left for the Okinawan Department of Culture and Education to decide.

That Japanese would be the medium of school education was certainly not a foregone conclusion. By way of making this decision, the Textbook Compilation Division (*Kyōkasho Henshūbu*) was established at the Department of Culture and Education. This group discussed the feasibility of developing Ryukyuan textbooks, but arrived at the conclusion that such an endeavour was unrealistic and impractical (Nakamatsu, 1996: 62–63). That any attempt to develop Ryukyuan language-based teaching materials faced a multitude of potential hurdles is indisputable. For example the multilingual makeup of the Ryukyu Archipelago presented a major problem. No Ryukyuan unifying standard language existed, nor did any standard dictionary or grammar of any of the Ryukyuan language at that time. Since all communicative functions related to written language had been assigned to Japanese pre-1945, no fixed orthography or written materials, on which such textbooks could be based, were available either. In addition, there were enormous lexical gaps due to the restriction of the Ryukyuan languages to the private domain after 1880. The Textbook Compilation Division encountered the very same problem that mainland Japanese language planners had met in the 19th century, namely that of adapting the existing languages to the communicative necessities of the modern age.

While Japanese language ideology brokers successfully lobbied for the development of the Tokyo variety to meet these demands, Ryukyuans opted to preserve the pre-war linguistic order and use Japanese in the public domain. At a conference of school directors in 1950, it was decided that school education in the occupied Ryukyu Islands should exactly follow that of mainland Japan (Motonaga, 1994: 185–188), and from 1951, textbooks were imported from Japan to be used in the occupied Ryukyus. Thus, after a short period of uncertainty surrounding language education in schools, the pre-war *status quo* was resurrected, with the only difference this time around being that Japanese language education was no longer called *kokugo*, but was referred to as reading class (*yomikata*) instead.

Japanese Language Spread from Within

The period of occupation marked a turning point in Ryukyuan identity, with most islanders identifying themselves as Japanese by 1950. Under American rule, the Ryukyuans became more aware of how much they had in common with mainland Japanese, but their desire to return to Japanese rule was also fuelled by the unfavourable conditions in the Ryukyus as compared to those in mainland Japan (Taira, 1997). Since all Ryukyuans were bilingual after 1945, it is interesting to note that later changes in patterns of language choice did not have problems of communication at their root, but rather sprang out of the unresolved question of nationality and by extension, therefore, out of the question of whether or not the occupation of the Ryukyu Islands could legitimately be continued.

In many ways, the rise in status of Japanese after 1945 followed much the same pattern as that which occurred in the pre-war era, accompanied as it was by measures, albeit less drastic ones, designed to oppress local Ryukyuan languages (see Tanaka, 2001). This time, too, this was only possible because language spread was presented as part of the process of standardization, rather than as a precursor to local language loss. Yet another similarity is that Japanese language spread after 1945 relied on a popular movement, this time with its roots in the call for a return to the fatherland (*sokoku fukki*) that featured prominently in 1950s Ryukyuan politics. There emerged a group calling itself the Movement for a Return to the Fatherland (*Sokoku fukki undō*), which claimed many local school-teachers among its supporters (Oguma, 1998: 563). Echoing the agenda of the pre-war Movement for the Enforcement of the Standard Language, the Movement for a Return to the Fatherland also lobbied for the exclusive use of Japanese in public and private domains.

The Movement for Return to the Fatherland also found many sympathizers both in prominent Ryukyuan political parties and in the mainland-based Movement for the Return of Okinawa (*Okinawa henkan undō*). The Okinawa Teachers' Association (*Okinawa Kyōshokuin-kai*) would also prove influential in promoting Japanese after 1945. In addition to the Japanese language, the Okinawan Teachers' Association also fostered symbols of Japanese nationhood like the *hinomaru*, the Japanese flag, and the national anthem (Oguma, 1998: 564), and promoted an irredentist policy that stressed the importance of the spread and proper use of Japanese as a means of ensuring re-unification with the mainland (Anhalt, 1991: 45).

In the face of US attempts to define the Ryukyus as a nation in its own right, many Ryukyuans espoused the ideology of Japanese national language, believing that by identifying themselves as Japanese they could effectively render the US occupation illegitimate. In 2001, the popular magazine *Edge* published the minutes of a number of teaching committees, in which the promotion of the Japanese language under US occupation was discussed (see Oguma, 2001: 38–95). These materials reveal how little attitudes towards Japanese and the Ryukyuan languages had changed. A meeting of the Okinawan Teachers' Association in 1957, for example included the presentation of a comprehensive report on language life in a local school, and called for the enactment of the following measures to ensure correct use of Standard Japanese:

> Explain the necessity of the standard language, encourage the use of the standard language by means of student circles, display slogans, reflect on recent language use during morning circles in classes, and create an atmosphere in which the standard language is used spontaneously. (Quoted from Oguma, 2001: 57)

It is not difficult to see how closely this approach mirrors efforts to afford Japanese greater prestige than the local Ryukyuan languages during the pre-war era.

Given these similarities with Japanese language spread before 1945, it is not surprising that any interference from local languages on the use of Japanese by Ryukyuan speakers was condemned as bad language (*fusei-go*).

Writing in 1964, Narita (2001: 245) reports that the use of Ryukyuan languages in private domains was widely acknowledged as the main cause of a lack of achievement in school. The natural response, yet again, was to view the repression of local languages as inevitable. Indeed, the dialect tag was experiencing a renaissance, with research conducted by Itani (2006: 140–166) providing evidence of dialect tag use in the Ryukyu Islands well after 1945. Then, in 1963, the school subject National Citizen Education (*kokumin kyōiku*) was established in the Ryukyu Islands, following the lead of mainland Japanese schooling. The adoption of this subject was motivated partly by anti-American and anti-militaristic sentiments, but it was also evidence of the increasingly Japanese nationalist leanings of the Ryukyuans (Karimata, 2001: 39–40).

Ultimately, the events described above resulted in the monolingual Japanese model sweeping across the multilingual Ryukyu Islands, even at a time when the archipelago was politically separate from mainland Japan. Three factors proved crucial to all this: (1) the absence of efforts to modernize Ryukyuan languages before 1945; (2) resistance to the US occupation; and (3) the internalization of oppressive pre-war language ideology. US endeavours to strengthen Ryukyuan identity by encouraging the use of Ryukyuan languages only led to a heightened sense of loyalty towards Japanese, and so language shift continued unabated (see Chapter 7). This shift was triggered by unfavourable attitudes towards local Ryukyuan languages as a result of the ideological attacks launched against them in the pre-war period (see Clarke, 1997).

It was thus by way of ending the US occupation, and thereby improving their well-being, that the Ryukyuans chose to embrace a Japanese identity. By imagining themselves to be part of the Japanese nation as defined by a historically shared language bond, they completed the national language ideology and put it into practice. To return to Japan, the Ryukyuans choose to prove that they were Japanese, and as the ability to speak Japanese was the main prerequisite thereof, Ryukyuans needed only to dispose of their own linguistic heritage to fulfil the prophecy of a monolingual Japanese nation as imagined in the Meiji period (1886–1912). In doing exactly this, ideology turned into reality, confirming the validity of ideology as an effect.

In the last part of this chapter, then, we saw how the Ryukyuans used an ideology oppressive of local languages to rid themselves, formally at least, of the US occupation. The case of the Ryukyu Islands demonstrates how language ideology may be employed to inspire and motivate specific groups to pursue their interests against those of other groups. Language ideology may be employed to achieve non-linguistic goals, in this case, a return to Japanese rule. Note also that the arbitrary nature of language ideology has two interlinked components: a specific language, and its specific ideological loading (e.g. notions of identity, morality or progress). We also saw, in Chapter 2, how early language modernizers doubted the suitability of Japanese for the communicative requirements of modernity. These doubts, against which an emancipative Japanese national language ideology was developed (see Chapters 3 and 4), were to return after Japanese defeat in World War II. This manifested itself, among other things, in a call to abandon Japanese in order to build a 'true civilization' in Japan. To this end, in 1946 it was proposed that French should be adopted as the national language of Japan, and it is to an investigation of this proposal that we shall turn next. In doing so, we will see that there are two sides to every ideology: on the one hand, a striving for emancipation, and on the other, the oppression which inspired it.

6 The Most Beautiful Language in the World

However absurd it might seem, it would be a mistake to simply dismiss a proposal to completely replace one language with another. Such radical linguistic proposals deserve our attention, for they tell us much about the language ideology that inspires them, particularly when they have been put forward by powerful language ideology brokers like Mori Arinori. Another such broker was Shiga Naoya (1883–1971), who in 1946 proposed that French be adopted as the national language of Japan. Following Japan's defeat in World War II, just as in the early part of the Meiji restoration, notions of culture, tradition and language were the subject of much debate. In particular, national language problems (*kokugo mondai*) re-emerged as a topic of discussion, leading to the re-examination of many issues thought to have been settled by the successful modernization of Japan and the adoption of Japanese as the national language early in the 20th century.

The dominant language ideology came under pressure in the post-war years because modernist ideology identifies itself with, and is legitimized by, notions of progress. In light of the disastrous outcome of Japan's involvement in World War II, the ideologies and practices of the past were re-evaluated to determine just how progressive they had actually been. Language was no exception, especially given the pivotal role that it had played in Japan's modernization. The post-war period was thus one of reflection, and Shiga's essay, which is to be discussed in this chapter was one such example of re-evaluation. It is important for students of ideology to study such periods of reflection as the Meiji period (1868–1912), the period of US occupation (1945–1952) and the so-called lost decade (the 1990s) – the rather catastrophic collapse of the Japanese economy in 1990/1991 and its by now two-decade long impact on all aspects of life in Japan, for reflection is invariably a quest for alternative ideologies and practices that would otherwise have been drowned out by the dominant ideology. It is perhaps unremarkable, then, that all proposals relating to language planning developed during the Meiji period also saw a revival after 1945 (see Carroll, 2001: 51–71).

Perhaps the most famous and influential contribution to language-related discourse in the post-war period was that of Shiga Naoya, who submitted a four-page essay to the influential journal *Kaizō* in March 1946. While Mori Arinori's proposal to introduce English is both well known and frequently made reference to (e.g. Coulmas, 1985; Lee, 1990, 1996; Neustupný, 1995), Shiga's proposal attracted relatively little attention among linguists. Nevertheless, Shiga's proposal deserves our attention because his essay illustrates the fundamental principles at work in language ideology, and because it played a defining role in the re-affirmation of Meiji language ideology in post-war Japan.

Shiga's suggestion to replace Japanese with French was in many ways even more adventurous than Mori's 1872 proposal to replace it with English. In the late-19th century, Japanese faced a multitude of problems related to its development and adaptation to the demands of modernity. No such problems remained unsettled by 1946; in the words of Florian Coulmas (1991: 8), the Japanese 'language crisis' was over. The last residues of the pre-modern diglossia, manifested in government documents (*kōyōbun*) were easily dealt with in that all new documents were written henceforth in the 'spoken standard', that is in *genbun itchi* style (Inoue, 1991), and modest script reform (Gottlieb, 1995) had settled the debate over whether Japanese written language was undemocratic by nature or not (Lewin, 1979). But these post-war language reforms should not distract us from the fact that far more radical measures, like the possible replacement of Chinese characters with kana or Latin script (Unger, 1996), the feasibility of a second *genbun itchi* movement (Neustupný, 1974: 42), and the elimination of honourific language (Carroll, 2001: 70) were all considered at the time. And so, too, did the most radical solution of all to Japan's perceived language problems, the replacement of Japanese with another language, return as a topic of popular debate, with Ozaki Yukio (1859–1954), a well-known journalist and politician, adding his own voice to Shiga's in arguing for the abandonment of Japanese in favour of a western language.

Kokugo Mondai: The National Language Problem

Of the many post-war debates related to the Japanese language, it was Shiga's proposal that sparked new ideological debate about the relative pros and cons of using Japanese. Part of the reason for this was the status Shiga enjoyed as a writer and intellectual in Shōwa period Japan (1926–1989).

Shiga is, to this day, considered the most important exponent of the I-novel (*shi-shōsetsu*), a genre he also helped establish (Suzuki, 1996). By the 1930s, Shiga had already turned many of his personal experiences into works of literature and was heralded by his peers as God of Fiction. The linguist Kindaichi Haruhiko (1913–2004) comments on his reputation in the opening pages of his bestselling book *The Japanese Language*:

> Shiga was a man of some stature, referred to as the God of Fiction. Once, during the good old days before Japan was thrust into a doomed war, Shiga appeared in a newsreel, and one literature-mad youth cried out, 'Hats off to Shiga Naoya'! (Kindaichi, 1978: 19)

The idea of replacing Japanese with French thus seems all the more radical as it was proposed by a man popularly known as the 'God of Japanese fiction', a skilled craftsman of modern Japanese. It was in fact partly the shock Shiga's proposal caused that motivated Kindaichi (1957) to write *Nihongo*, an appraisal of the strengths and qualities of Japanese, which thereby constituted a rebuttal of Shiga's argument. *Nihongo* sold 800,000 copies, and was one of the first books in Japanese about Japanese to be translated into English (Kindaichi, 1978). Clearly, *Nihongo* dealt with a subject of enormous public interest, which transcended the concerns of professional linguists. It addressed the issue of what Japanese ought to be, and re-affirmed modernist language ideology in the face of the renewed doubts that surfaced in the immediate aftermath of the Japanese defeat. Shiga's and Kindaichi's respective commentaries on the nature, and the future, of the Japanese language inspired a significant amount of public interest in linguistic discourse in the decade following the end of the War, described by contemporary observers Yoshizawa Norio (1955) and Matsumura Akira (1956) as a 'language boom'. It is within this context that Tessa Carroll (2001: 66) also considers the establishment of the National Institute for Japanese Language (*Kokuritsu Kokugo Kenkyūjo*) in 1948 is related to Shiga's essay, writing that the institute was 'probably at least partly' a reaction to Shiga Naoya's pessimism about the adequacy of Japanese as a modern national language.

The magnitude of none other than Shiga Naoya putting his weight behind such a radical proposal cannot be underestimated: an equivalent in European terms would be if Thomas Mann had suggested the abolition of German or Émile Zola the replacement of French with another language. Kindaichi (1978: 19) moved to counter Shiga's argument in no uncertain terms, and begins his book: 'Soon after World War II, Shiga Naoya wrote an article entitled "Japanese Language Problems" for the magazine *Kaizō*, which shocked the Japanese people'. That Shiga was usually conservative in linguistic terms, cautioning his countrymen against the negative effects of written language reform, for example, only heightened the sense of shock amongst his contemporaries that his proposal inspired. What is more, Shiga's point-blank admission that he did not know how such a scheme might be realized caused much confusion. In contrast to Mori Arinori, who was a fluent speaker and prolific author of English, Shiga had little proficiency in French. In light of this, Roy Andrew Miller accuses the Japanese critics of the day for failing to realise that Shiga's proposal may well have been an ironic one:

> Apparently no one in Japan has even considered the mere possibility that Shiga may have been having a wry joke at the expense of the badly frayed national nervous system as it existed in the dark days of 1946. No one who commented upon the incident [...] ever suggests that perhaps Shiga may have been indulging in some literary figure such as irony or satire. (After all, he was a man of letters, and men of letters *have* been known to indulge in literary figures). (Miller, 1982: 113, emphasis in the original)

However, an understanding of Shiga's literary oeuvre suggests that his proposal was completely serious. Like all the writers of the I-novel genre, Shiga wanted his readers to sympathize with the protagonists of his works. For this reason, he addressed his readership as honestly as he could, making every effort to disclose as much in the way of detail to his audience as possible (Ueda, 1976: 104). Shiga also rejected the idea that an author could deceive his audience as to his true intentions when writing, and took great pains to assure his own readers of the authenticity of his work (Hijiya-Kirschnereit, 1981: 244). Because that work deals exclusively with personal experience and autobiographical events, it is difficult to distinguish Shiga the man from Shiga the character. This is important when weighing up the seriousness of his proposal, as is the fact that his literary work largely deals with man's drive to overcome personal hardship by relying on his instincts of sense and reason. Shiga thereby appealed to his contemporaries to seek, in a calm and rational way, the best solution to the problems of the Japanese language, just as his protagonists sought the solutions to their own problems. Rather than an attempt at irony, then, the essay in which he set out his proposal to replace Japanese with French is an example of the stance taken by those of the *shi-shōsetsu* school of literature.

Shiga's proposal was certainly taken as genuine. Ōno Susumu (1919–2008), a Japanese linguist known well beyond the confines of his academic discipline, was appalled by it, and when introduced to Shiga in the mid-1950s, he wasted no time in questioning the latter's motives. Shiga is reported to have replied that he had been motivated by the fact that Japanese was not an international language, and that Japan thus suffered as a result of being unable to communicate with other nations. Shiga believed that having a language that was not international would be harmful to Japan, and that this had played a role in the outbreak and escalation of the Pacific War (1937–1945). As the Japanese language continued to present a barrier to international exchange after the War, Shiga was afraid that history might repeat itself if this problem was not effectively dealt with (Agawa, 1994: 175), and it was this which drove him to propose the abandonment of Japanese in favour of French in 1946. Let us turn now to Shiga's 1946 essay, here translated into English for the very first time.

National Language Problem

Never has Japan experienced such hardship. All kinds of calamities rain down on us ceaselessly. To lapse into a state of abject lethargy would be understandable under such conditions. The lack of food is the greatest cause for concern. Suddenly, our dinner tables are bare again. One begins to feel melancholic when one remembers how – just one year ago – the lack of food affected our physical and psychological condition. Then there are the problems of inflation, education and unemployment, each of these serious enough by itself, never mind in combination with the others. I wonder how our compatriots in the former Japanese territories are getting on, particularly those in the north of Korea and in Manchuria. We have not even the slightest news of their well-being. Epidemics have erupted in the streets. All forms of crimes occur, and with such frequency as to seem almost commonplace, while not a single measure is taken to combat these. We are grateful merely to be free to speak our minds, and to go to bed knowing that we can sleep sound until the next morning.

In addition to all these problems, each of them serious enough to demand that action be taken immediately, there is yet another problem, and a far more serious one at that: the problem of the national language. Finding a solution to this problem is perhaps less of a pressing concern than finding solutions to those others, nevertheless, it represents the greatest threat to the future of Japan. But because we are immersed in our existing national language from infancy, we are unable to see that there is no other language in the world as incomplete and harmful to a nation's prospects as the national language of Japan. When one considers, however, just how much our national language has hampered the development of our culture, one soon realizes the gravity of the situation, and how important it is that we find a solution as quickly as possible. If we fail to do so, it is no exaggeration to say that there is no hope for Japan's future and its prospects of becoming a truly civilized nation.

While I am unable to describe in concrete terms the extent to which the national language of Japan is incomplete and inconvenient, I have become painfully aware of this fact over the 40 years I have spent writing. What, then, can be done to solve this problem? Although there are well-established movements that call for writing to be done by means of kana, or even in the Latin alphabet, we cannot consider such schemes to be viable alternatives. And while there are numerous well-known public figures who promote, in particular, the use of the Latin alphabet, its widespread use fails to materialize in any meaningful way. This, I think, is due to its shortcomings as an idea.

During the War, I repeatedly remembered Mori Arinori's attempt to introduce English as the national language 60 years ago. I have asked myself what would have happened if Mori's proposal had been realized. I imagine that the development of Japanese culture would have been more substantial than it has ever been, and even that the War might have been avoided. We might well have improved the quality of our education, and we would have more favourable memories of our schooldays as a result. All these ideas have crossed my mind. As children today no longer learn the old Japanese system of quantifying measures and weights, we would not have learned the old national language, but would have spoken and written English without considering it a foreign language. In all likelihood, many words specific to Japan would have developed, words which do not appear in English dictionaries. It is even possible that many more people would have read the *Man'yōshū* and the *Genji monogatari* in English than have read it in Japanese. The benefits of having adopted English as the national language at that time would have been countless. Doubtless, it would be an almost unbearable strain to separate myself from the existing national language at the age I am now, but if this had happened 60 years ago, with hindsight, I cannot help but see how much better things might have been.

Everyone agrees that the national language needs reform. In recent times, a number of societies have urged me in calling for language reform. Nevertheless, I am pessimistic about efforts to maintain and complete the existing national language by making various amendments. Perhaps I take such a stance because I myself do not have a good idea of how we might reform the national language. Regardless, I remain pessimistic about the effectiveness of such a strategy. I am of the opinion that nothing satisfactory can ever be made of the national language we have at present, and I am doubtful of whether there really exists a viable proposal for its reform. I risk appearing irresponsible by giving my opinion without a sound knowledge of such issues, but I do not hold out much hope for the success of such proposals.

That is why I have given so much thought to what might be if Japan would only have the courage to choose the best and most beautiful language in the world, and adopt it, without alteration, as its national language. Further to this, I ask whether French might not be the best language for such a scheme. Why not finally put into practice the proposal put forward by Mori Arinori some 60 years ago? This would certainly be more effective than half-baked reforms of the current national language. Although the realization of such a proposal would have been difficult in Mori's time, it is far from unachievable now. Of course, many feel differently about such an undertaking, and if it is in fact possible to improve upon our existing national language, then this would be favourable. But if this proves not to be the case, then now is the time to take a leap of faith, and for the sake of those children born a century or two hence, we must discard our sentimentality and stop clinging to our past.

I am not well versed in foreign languages, and do not speak French well enough to promote it confidently. Nevertheless, French springs to mind as an example of a successful national language because France is a country with a developed culture and because, when reading French novels, one gets the impression that there is something that the French and Japanese share in common. It is said that there are similarities between French poetry and elements of *waka* and *haiku* poetry, and that French is a language that was given its structure by men of letters. For these reasons, I believe that French would be most suitable. When examining the present situation, and with Mori Arinori's proposal in our minds, the adoption of a foreign language seems a sounder, more promising, and therefore more appropriate solution than the continued use of a crippled language that will only cause confusion for many years to come as a result of ineffectual language reforms.

While I also have no knowledge of the practical aspects of replacing a national language, I cannot believe that this would be all that complicated. Once teachers had been trained in French, it could then be used as the national language in schools, beginning with the first-year classes. How was that actually done in Korea when Japanese replaced Korean?

While my six children use the metric system, I stubbornly continue to use the Japanese system for weights and measures. Regardless of how the national language might change, I can no longer separate myself from our present national language. However, when reflecting upon how easy the instruction of elementary schoolchildren has become since the introduction of the metric system, it is my greatest wish that the problems of the national language likewise be solved, for the sake of our children, or in my case, of my grandchildren.

We are well aware of how hard the present times are for Japan. Although we are painfully conscious of problems such as shortage of food and inflation, however, we cannot say with confidence that we truly understand the extent of our difficulties. We are like a person wounded gravely, who – contrary to what one might expect – does not feel pain, as if the nerves have been desensitized. We should be grateful for our ability as human beings to adapt in this way, but though our wounds are severe we must not rely on our capacity to judge effectively under such duress, for by doing so we will only fail to grasp the truth about our suffering. One must not be misled into believing that the problems of our national language affect us less than the shortage of food, for example, much less that no such problems exist. But if we do not take bold action now, the negative consequences of such neglect will be felt for a hundred, perhaps even a thousand, years. Today, Japan is at a more critical juncture even than when Chinese script was first introduced, or when Mori Arinori urged the adoption of English as our national language. We must be conscious of this when we consider the problems of the existing national language.

There can be no doubt that separating ourselves from our existing national language will be painful, but this would only be temporary, and in 50 or 100 years, our countrymen will no longer feel that pain. Putting our trust in our Japanese blood, and resisting the temptation to be governed by our sensibilities, we must consider, without prejudice, the problems of our national language and how they relate to the future of Japan.

Language Ideology in Shiga's Proposal

We have seen that language ideologies are the result of connecting language structures and language use with specific, non-linguistic phenomena such as the concepts of nation, enlightenment, civilization or progress. Due to the making of such connections, the study of language ideology is largely concerned with the history of thought, and linguistic issues often take a back seat in language ideological discourse as a result. Frequently, language is but the arena in which issues related to nation, culture or progress are debated. That language often becomes the major field to settle largely non-linguistic issues is due to various reasons. One prominent motive is the political and moral loading of language through ideology, and another the deeply rooted view that controlling language implies control over what is being discussed (see Cameron, 1995: 219). Shiga's essay is a case in point.

Shiga never informs his readers of exactly how the problem of Japanese being incomplete or obstructive is manifested in concrete terms. Nor does he provide evidence to support his claim that French is well ordered. Indeed, his commentary on the structure and use of both languages is generic and lacking in specific detail. At the same time as failing to supply such evidence, however, he argues the case for the superiority of French over Japanese, stating the latter is both incomplete and obstructive. It is important, especially given the scope of this book, to note that Shiga's view was neither unique to him, nor novel in Japan. Already the national philologists (*kokugakusha*) of the Edo period (1602–1867) had entertained such beliefs, and saw the origin of the problems of Japanese as rooted in the influence of the Chinese language (Burns, 2003). Such a perception of Japanese had also developed in the west following modernization there and the birth of Orientalism (see Chapter 1), and had become accepted in Japan after being transmitted via contact with western scholars and ideology. In fact, Japanese modernist language ideology developed as reaction to such negative appraisal of the Japanese language (Chapter 4), a process which required, among other things, the creation of a unified style of writing, which subsequently passed as being Japanese, or national language, *tout court* (Chapter 3).

That Shiga's proposal came at a time when the Japanese language had both been modernized successfully and had become the accepted means of everyday communication renders it even more radical than Mori's scheme. Not only had all the obstacles to adapting Japanese to the needs of modernity been overcome, Japanese language modernization had begun to serve as a model for that of other Asian national languages, such as Chinese and Vietnamese. In other words, the ideology of one's deficiency in the Japanese language was no longer perceived to constitute a problem by 1946. What did remain, however, was a sense of the inferiority of Japanese to the national languages of the west. Shiga, like many, believed the Japanese language to be defective, while perceiving western languages to be perfect means of communication, and it is the popularity of this perception at the time that made him feel that he did not need to back up his radical assessment with evidence.

In the preceding chapters, we also saw how the ideological upgrading of Japanese as a modern language was an essential part of wider Japanese modernization. The very concept of contemporary Japanese as a language deserving of pride and respect was virtually non-existent in the early Meiji period (1868–1912), such notions being the product of as much careful crafting as the corpus of the national language itself (see Chapter 4). It was perhaps inevitable, therefore, given the deep connection between the Japanese language and Japanese modernization that the crisis of Japanese modernization that followed defeat in World War II created a crisis of the national language. The idea of the Japanese language somehow being an obstacle to the Japanese nation was a product thereof, but this is where Shiga's ideology differs from Mori's, in that the former's incorporates a sense of both the hurdles that must be surmounted by way of modernizing Japanese, and of the ideological set pieces of the ensuing emancipative discourse in the defence of Japanese.

It is this mixture that renders Shiga's essay so important to our attempts to understand the effects of language ideology in modern Japan.

From his appraisal of Japanese as an obstacle best done away with completely, it is clear that Shiga, like Mori before him, considers language to be a utilitarian tool for information exchange. If language is a tool and that tool is found to be defective, logic dictates that it should be replaced with another, better tool. In contrast to Mori, however, Shiga displays a strong emotional attachment to Japanese, and he makes no attempt to hide the fact that the replacement of Japanese would cause him, and his fellow speakers of Japanese, much pain. But this is a manifestation of language loyalty, the by-product of a specific language ideology propagated in Japan from the 1890s on. Recall the strength of Ueda's conviction that the Japanese language was as deserving of emotional attachment and respect as one's parents, and one may gain some understanding of the quandary Shiga faced, thus torn between two radically conflicting views about his language. On the one hand, he restricts his definition of language to that of a tool for communication, while on the other he expresses his sentimentality and attachment to Japanese. These views are contradictory, and denote his inner conflict, which is evident from his assertion that to solve the problems of the national language through reform would be preferable, even while he lacks confidence in the potential of such reform.

At the heart of Shiga's quandary of language the tool versus language the object of emotional attachment, is the legacy of an ideology according to which some languages were seen as unfit for modernization. These were typically non-western languages, hence Shiga's call to replace the non-western language Japanese with a western alternative, French. Such an outlook hints at Shiga's belief in this ideology, at his doubt over whether Japanese could ever be sufficiently developed and adapted to cater for new functions. That is to say, to Shiga a language was inevitably and unalterably either of good or of poor quality. Shiga's attempts to balance the importance of the Japanese language to the country's modernization against the disastrous consequences of Japan's involvement in World War II lead him to conclude that the hard times that befell his country were partly the consequence of using a fundamentally defective language. Shiga thus subscribed to the same prejudiced view of non-western languages so popular in the 19th century. By extension, therefore, Shiga also believed in the utilitarianism of language, and that the fate of a language's speakers was bound to the quality of its language. In Shiga's view, therefore, the success of any strategy aimed at improving a nation – at becoming 'truly cultivated' – rested on making the right choice vis-à-vis the language that nation employed. Departing from such a language ideological standpoint, no other choice than 'the best language of the world' makes sense. Thus, in spite of the emotional strain that the loss of the 'present national language' would cause, language reform alone would not suffice. Active and deliberate development and adaptation of language is not possible under the utilitarian language ideologies held by Mori and Shiga. Rather, to replace Japanese with a western language – in Mori's words, a 'good' language, in Shiga's and 'ordered' and 'complete' one – seemed to be the only rational solution.

A still deeper conflict at work within Shiga's 1946 proposal relates to how one defines a national language and its relationship to the idea of a nation. One of the most important components of the language ideology developed by German Romanticists like Herder (1744–1803), Grimm (1785–1863) and von Humboldt (1767–1835), is that nation came to be defined on the basis of language. According to such an ideology, language – in conjunction with other factors such as climate, religion, politics, and so on – was seen as defining, shaping and giving character to a nation (Formigaria, 1999). Although these ideas were spread throughout Japan during the 19th and 20th centuries, however, Shiga's definition of national language was in fact quite different. For him, the term national language merely referred to that language used unequivocally by a particular nation. Any sense that a national language is part of what defines a nation is absent from Shiga's views on language. This is only possible, of course, because the Japanese nation had already been invented on language ideological grounds at the time of Shiga's essay, thereby allowing him to portray a collective shift by the Japanese nation from using Japanese to using French as nothing more than that, a shift to French as the national language of Japan.

While the modernist ideology of language defining nation is absent from Shiga's proposal, however, the idea of replacing Japanese by French nevertheless depends upon set pieces of modernist ideology. Shiga still believed in one uniform language for all Japanese, only that the uniform language in question be French. In this way, Shiga was in fact arguing the case for the dissolution of the Japanese language nation, for his proposal dictated that the Japanese people could no longer be defined by the language ideological belief that they all, and only all of them, spoke the same uniform language and, equally important under language nationalism, that they had always done so. This sets him apart from Mori, who, while making similar claims, lacked both the ideas of national language and of a language nation (Lee, 1990). At the same time, Shiga's choice of French belies his understanding of the connection between language and nation, because he is of the opinion, when reading French novels, for example, that there are similarities between the French and the Japanese. It is this that Shiga identifies as his reason for selecting French over other western languages as an ideal replacement for

Japanese. Shiga saw French as reflective of the Japanese national character, and it is through this that Shiga's exposure to the ideology of a nation being defined by its national language becomes visible. In contrast to Mori, Shiga Naoya was a thoroughly modern man.

Language ideologies are many and varied, and where they appear uniform and complete this is due to the power support that underpins the spread and acceptance of dominant ideologies (Chapter 1). The plurality of language ideology manifests itself in Shiga's essay, and it is this, and the subsequent ideological hybridity of his proposal, which is responsible for the reaction it provokes among its readers. As we have seen, this hybridity results in prominent contradictions in the language ideological notions underlying the proposal. Unfortunately for Shiga, contradiction is bad, ideologically speaking, because it fails to fulfil the most important characteristic of any successful ideology, namely, that it makes sense. In Shiga's essay, ideology is visible. As a result, the essay ultimately achieved little more than sparking off a call for reaffirmation of Meiji period language ideologies during the post-war years. This was most famously articulated by Kindaichi Haruhiko, in his bestselling 1957 monograph *Nihongo*.

In countering Shiga's appraisal of Japanese as defective and incomplete, Kindaichi carefully examined the Japanese language with regard to its origins, variations, pronunciation, vocabulary and morphosyntax. His investigation led him to this conclusion:

> How should we evaluate the Japanese language when thus viewed in all its aspects? Japanese does have various defects, but it is also true that we can say and write whatever we think in Japanese. Fortunately, we can use it to write scientific theses and business papers, and it would be neither possible nor advisable to abandon this language. (Kindaichi, 1978: 279–280)

Furthermore, he urged speakers of Japanese to remain loyal to Japanese, and to further its development and refinement. The closing chapter of his book contains the following admonition:

> On the one hand, a language is a natural development, but, on the other, it is something created. Even German, which is said to be a model among systematic languages, is a creation of the German people over a period of several generations. We who are living at the present time cannot help feeling a heavy responsibility for the future of the Japanese language. (Kindaichi, 1978: 280)

While Kindaichi's book was favourably received by the Japanese public readership, US Japanologist Roy Andrew Miller (1982) was so irritated by it that he wrote an entire book on what he defined as 'language myths' of Japanese. Therein, he accused Kindaichi, and other contemporary Japanese linguists, of treating the Japanese language ideologically. Miller took an especial dislike to linguists who took a stance that

> sometimes stresses that the language around which it [the myth P.H.] has been erected is perfect, unique, and superior to all other languages; but simultaneously, and from her ends, it may equally stridently announce that the Japanese language is imperfect, vulnerable, and visibly coming apart at the seams, hardly likely to last the night. (Miller, 1982: 8)

In another book, titled *Nihongo – in Defense of Japanese*, an obvious reference to Kindaichi's bestseller, Miller repeated his criticism, reproaching Kindaichi for deliberately setting up deficiencies of Japanese as a rhetorical device, in order to then argue to the contrary, writing that Kindaichi's

> concept of "defending Japanese" is to debunk, as gently as possible, his own suggestions that the language is inferior, while at the same time urging the Japanese to re-arm themselves by renewing their self-confidence and self-esteem, particularly as these qualities relate to their language. In a word, Kindaichi's defense seems to us no defense at all, because the "problems of language" as he describes them are mere strawmen, set only up to be shot down. (Miller, 1986: 245)

What Shiga, Kindaichi and Miller all fail to realize is that they are themselves involved in the creation and discussion of language ideology. Their lack of awareness is furthermore exaggerated by the fact that all three view ideology very differently. Shiga's sense of an innate reason best guiding the interest of individuals, the central topic of his literary oeuvre as reflected in his 1946 essay, belies an enlightenment perspective on ideology. In other words, Shiga saw ideas about language as matters of right and wrong, and sought to free language from the shackles of wrong ideas, setting his sights on a view of language free of ideology, as espoused by the pioneers of ideology study such as Bacon, Locke and Hume (see Chapter 1). Students of ideology will be well aware that such an opinion on ideology is unlikely to find much success in practice, for ideology is primarily a discursive behaviour, there to safeguard and promote specific interests. This, in turn, requires power. In light of this, one cannot help but wonder whose interest the introduction of French might have served, and exactly where the power to back it up was to have come from. Shiga thus faces a dual challenge, both drawing inaccurate conclusions about language problems in post-war Japan by accepting prejudiced western views of Japanese, and at the same time adhering to a view of ideology as lacking in effectiveness as his proposal to replace Japanese with French.

Miller, on the hand, is a textbook example of traditional ideology, that is, that which is conceptualized on the basis of truth. Here, this leads him to take what we call a pejorative view of ideology, in that he perceives all but himself to be ideological. To Miller, Kindaichi's ideas are simply wrong, and he attempts to correct them. Lastly, Kindaichi may be seen to be engaging in empowering ideology, in that he is 'making sense' of why the Japanese language ought to be maintained, developed and respected in the face of standing doubts over its quality. Given such differing ideological views and practices, it is perhaps of little surprise that these three discourses do not easily align, thereby illustrating the need for a comprehensive understanding of ideology, which distinguishes between such differing perspectives on, and behaviour towards, language ideology.

Despite the fact that Shiga's essay proved to be of little consequence in transforming language ideology in modern Japan, it nevertheless deserves attention with regard to the matters discussed in this book. It testifies to a re-emergence of doubts about Japanese language and culture post-1945, doubts that could only be quietened through a reaffirmation and strengthening of that language ideology developed in the Meiji period (1868–1912). Furthermore, it asserts that language ideological views are not always invisible and may be susceptible to such doubt. Established language ideologies may very well be challenged, transformed or reinstated, and doing so renders language ideology visible, exposing the gaps between language ideology and the sociolinguistic field. At the same time, language ideologies are truly remarkable for their capacity to evade questioning of their appropriateness and legitimacy. We come to understand that language ideologies are flexible and generative dispositions, rather than being a fixed body of ideas, and are able to adapt to changing contexts and allow for new meaning within such contexts. In so doing, language ideologies can survive in constantly changing environments, and thereby continue to pass themselves off as fact. It is just such a flexible generation of permanently new meanings in changing contexts that makes language ideologies invisible, which makes ideologies appear to be common sense. Accordingly, language ideologies can never be rigidly defined, nor can they be replaced by 'singling out' contradictions. Ideology is always in the business of hiding or bridging the gap between what it claims, and what it neglects or simplifies in doing so.

In order to understand a particular language ideology and its effect on language, we must therefore shift our attention to the way that language ideology functions. Thus, the most important issue for us to consider with regard to Shiga's proposal is that language ideologies consists of two sides in fundamental opposition to each other, if not contradictory. Language ideology demands an understanding of a perceived language problem, and also a solution to that problem. In the case of the Japanese language, the problem was seen as an inability of Japanese to serve the functions of modernity, coupled with the view that no non-western language could ever fill such a role. Emancipation from such a negative appraisal, and the development of Japanese as a modernized national language, form the reaction to the problem. Ideology never emerges without a purpose, only creating meaning as a reaction to a specific problem. All the while, though the problem could in fact be made to disappear through the careful crafting of an empowering language ideology, as well as through the ability of language ideology to create new language structures and uses, awareness of the problem always remains. The problem, therefore, may no longer remain in the language, but it will in ideology. It was this lack of real 'deficiencies' in Japanese, against which Kindaichi sought to defend the language, that frustrated Miller so much, deficiencies that for the most part only appeared in ideology during the post-war era.

It is still too soon to consider how modernist language ideology continues to stress what it has already achieved, for we have yet to see how language ideology turns into reality, and to thereby gain a comprehensive understanding of how language ideology works. So let us turn our attention to this issue next, by examining how one of the central pillars of Japanese modernist language ideology is turning into reality. We shall look, therefore, at the issue of language shift and language loss in modern Japan, and the crucial role that language ideology has played in increasingly shifting Japan from a multilingual to a monolingual state.

7 Language Ideology as Self-Fulfilling Prophecy

Language ideology is not about ideology alone, but rather functions as a self-fulfilling prophecy, influencing language structure and use. Over the last 20 years, sociolinguistic research has gradually begun to expose some of the fundamental mechanisms at work in the language shift of ethnolinguistic minorities in modernized nation-states (see e.g. Bradley & Bradley, 2002; Brenzinger, 2007; Fishman, 1991; King, 2001). This research has shown that language shift is usually part of a larger socio-cultural enterprise. In modernity this goal was progress, and progress was linked with homogeneity (Bauman, 1992), including linguistic homogeneity (Blommaert & Verschueren, 1991; Rampton, 2006). This is equally relevant in the case of language in Japan (Heinrich & Galan, 2011a). Given such a modernist outlook on progress, ethnolinguistic minorities are seen as constituting disorder and therefore become the subject of remedial action, for modernity, writes Zygmunt Bauman, knows only two ways of dealing with contradictions to its imagined ideal of homogeneity, monotony and clarity: assimilation and exclusion (Bauman, 1997: 18). As we saw in Chapter 5, both of these orientations can also be found in Japanese modernity.

We understand today that linguistic diversity is the product of the expansion, movements and organization of societies across history, and that modernity – as a means of giving structure to society – has been a significant cause of reduction of linguistic diversity. Jean Aitchison correctly asserts that language shift is primarily a social phenomenon whereby the extinct language usually 'faded away because it did not fulfill the social needs of the community who spoke it' (Aitchison, 2001: 246). Others, for example Coulmas (2005), Edwards (1985), Ladefoged (1992) and Mufwene (2003), draw similar conclusions. At the same time, however, we are aware that these social needs were deliberately created in modernized societies, following ideological lines that viewed multilingualism among ethnolinguistic minorities not as an asset, but as a sign of 'backwardness', a barrier to assimilation and the total membership to the ideological construct of the nation that assimilation would grant them. This assimilation became the default solution to addressing the 'disorder' represented by ethnolinguistic communities and where it failed or was resisted, then the second option of exclusion was resorted to. Of course, this problem of language loss in modernized nation-states is something of a 'chicken and the egg' conundrum. It is not the language shifts among ethnolinguistic minorities which create a monolingual environment, but loss of linguistic diversity is rooted in a modernist ideology that shapes linguistic behaviour and thereby influences the linguistic ecology.

For the sake of its own legitimacy, modernist ideology in search of homogeneity was deliberately linked with notions of progress, specifically, that kind of progress which lies always in the future and required efforts of ordering in order to achieve it (Albrow, 1996). It was precisely this idea of uniformity and the promise of progress that made language shift and language loss seem an inevitable side effect of modernization, and made efforts to maintain language seem regressive by comparison. Sue Wright (2007) has convincingly argued that language use is an indicator of power, language shifts in modernized nation-states being manifestations of the imbalance of power between communities coming into contact with each other. Minority language speakers, invariably positioned at the weaker end of the power divide, therefore shift to the language of the dominant group. Language vitality may have more to do with issues of power and control over resources than with the utility of any given language, which is itself determined by the socio-cultural, economic and political environment resulting from that power structure. Since ideology is not about false ideas, but a means of making sense to which even those subscribe whose interests are disregarded thereby, such ideological notions influence language uses and structures. As a result, the utility of the languages of marginalized communities is undermined, and language shift is the result.

The study of language ideology reveals that the rise and fall of languages have little to do with the merit of these languages per se. The endangerment and subsequent extinction of minority languages are consequences of the successful enforcement of the idea that state, nation and language form a unified whole. In this chapter, we will see how this is no less true in the case of autochthonous minority languages in Japan. We will begin by examining how the national language, represented by written Standard Japanese, has purposefully been assigned positive attributes and the ways in which minority languages are portrayed as everything that standard language is not. We will examine language ideology at work in a debate over policies designed to encourage Japanese language spread in the Ryukyus, and later turn our attention to a more detailed analysis of the role of language ideology in the gradual erosion of marginalized languages. More specifically, we consider some of the ways in which language shift creates its own dynamics by constantly degrading language utility and, based on these insights, we will look closely at the language shifts that occurred under Japanese modernity amongst the Ainu, the Ryukyuans and the Ogasawara Islanders. Let us begin, then, with a further language ideological debate.

The Great Dialect Debate

With regard to the spread of Standard Japanese in the Ryukyu Islands, a wide-reaching and intense debate began in January 1940, eventually running for more than a year. It would later become known as *hōgen ronsō* (dialect debate). As is to be expected from language ideological debate, more was at stake than language alone, with the issue of language education providing the arena for a discussion on national unity, the value and position of the Ryukyuan languages in the Japanese state, and the place of the Ryukyus within the modern Japanese state. For the purpose of our examination, however, we shall restrict our examination of the dialect debate to language ideological views alone. For those who would like to look beyond this limited scope, see Clarke (1997), Steele (1995) and Tanigawa (1970).

In the following, a total of 18 publications will be considered with regard to the language ideological notions expressed therein (Higashionna, 1940; Iha, 1940; OKGB, 1940a–c; Sugiyama, 1940a–c; Sugiyama & Tanaka, 1941; Tōjō, 1940; Yanagi, 1940a–e; Yanagita, 1940; Yoshida, 1940a, 1940b). These selected publications were central to the debate, and there are a great many cross-references between them. The 18 texts were penned by a total of eight different authors. Yoshida Shien (1910–1989), head of the Educational Department at Okinawa Prefecture, and Sugiyama Heisuke (1895–1946), a well-known critic from the mainland, advocated the spread of Standard Japanese in a way that required oppression of the local languages. Higashionna Kanjun (1882–1963) and Iha Fuyū (1876–1947), two very influential scholars of Okinawan Studies, argued for a more relaxed stance towards the local languages. They were assisted by the mainland scholars of folklore, Yanagita Kunio (1875–1962) and Tanaka Toshio (1914–1953), as well as by the linguist, Tōjō Misao (1884–1966). Yanagi Muneyoshi (1889–1961), who had established the Folk Craft Society (*Nihon mingei kyōkai*) in 1934, was the most outspoken defender of the Ryukyuan languages, and urged speakers of these language varieties to take pride in their linguistic skills.

The debate has its origins in a discussion forum about mainland tourism to Okinawa Prefecture, held on 7 January 1940 at Naha City Hall. When government officials urged renewed efforts to further the spread of Standard Japanese in the prefecture (see Chapter 5), Yanagi and other members of the Folk Craft Society objected, and complained about the oppression of local languages. The discussion quickly escalated, with the Department of Education revealing its intention to spread Standard Japanese throughout all domains in Okinawa Prefecture, leaving no room for local language use, in the face of calls from the mainland visitors for the Ryukyuan languages to be valued and supported accordingly. Events at Naha City Hall were reported in the local newspaper editions of the following day, and the Department of Education took this as an opportunity to reassert its support for Standard Japanese, and opposition to local languages, publishing a newspaper article on its meeting with the Folk Craft Society two days later (OKGB, 1940a). The dialect debate was underway.

In defending its language education policy, the Department of Education exhibited the same utilitarian view of language as the Meiji period modernizers of the Japanese language (see Chapters 3 and 4), which held that language was both a means of expression and a tool for achieving non-linguistic goals such as economic development or political and social mobilization (OKGB, 1940a; Yoshida, 1940a, 1940b). This view was supported by Sugiyama (1940a), who himself asserted that not all language varieties were equal to this task, and it was therefore of benefit to speakers of ineffective language varieties to be relieved of the burden of their use. To Sugiyama (1940b), regional languages were peculiar (*tokushu na gengo*), painful to read and to listen to. Consistent with this was his belief that the influence of local language varieties on the standard language constituted a threat to the latter's purity, and by extension, therefore, such language varieties should be oppressed accordingly.

Even those who criticized the methods by which Standard Japanese was spread did not necessarily disagree with Sugiyama's rationale. Higashionna (1940) took a view similar to that of both Yoshida and the Department of Education, in that he, too, thought that the degree of utility between languages or language varieties differed. However, he also believed that to imagine that the people of Okinawa would rejoice when praised for their proficiency in Standard Japanese was false, pointing to the fact that such an idea was rooted squarely in a mainland Japanese psyche. Higashionna added that pride in a language could be fostered, even where that language was of little utility. His sentiments are echoed by Iha's contribution to the debate. Iha (1940) stated that one should not meddle in matters of language, as this might have grave psychological consequences for its speakers. This notwithstanding, Iha agreed that some language varieties were more useful than others, which is perhaps the reason for his belief that regional language varieties could not be spread in the same way as Standard Japanese. The dialectologist Tōjō (1940) was more reserved in his opinions, believing that all language varieties had a cultural value, and he acknowledged that they all constituted cultural treasuries and were therefore a means to unlocking cultural issues.

Yanagi's argument is quite different from those above. He not only called for greater tolerance towards local languages and cultures – he actively praised them. Furthermore, he frequently and directly addressed the local population in his contributions, urging his readers to strive towards achieving the same goals as he himself did. In return, Yanagi (1940b) promised to inform his mainland audience about the merits of Ryukyuan culture and language. Yanagi offers us a wealth of language ideological commentary. The existence of Standard Japanese as a language for interregional communication, Yanagi (1940d) wrote, was both essential and advantageous to Japan. As such, he saw it as the duty of all Japanese nationals to study Standard Japanese. But Yanagi (1940a) juxtaposed the functional aspects of the standard language against the cultural values of local languages. Since local languages were passed on through generations of speakers, he saw them as the embodiment of local beliefs and culture. Therefore, Yanagi asserted, local languages ought to be valued highly by their speakers, and speaking a regional language should be seen as a joyful activity. In contrast, the oppression of local languages was no less than a curse (Yanagi 1940b). Yanagi (1940a) believed that people were not limited to speaking only one language, and he thought it necessary to encourage Ryukyuans to maintain and take pride in their local languages as a result (Yanagi, 1940b). Improving the utility of local languages should be the goal, and might be achieved, for instance, by using local languages to create literary works.

Such opinions about Standard Japanese and the Ryukyuan languages as emerge from these kinds of language ideological statements should be treated together, as one invariably relates closely to the others. According to those who supported the methods of spreading the Japanese language employed at the time, Okinawa Prefecture had a language problem – a problem that had to be solved for the good of the prefecture's citizens. Yoshida (1940b) argued that local language varieties incomprehensible to speakers outside the prefecture were unsustainable. According to the Department of Education (OKGB, 1940a), local languages were regressive and hindered the expression of thought. In contrast to this negative appraisal of the Ryukyuan languages, Standard Japanese was seen as conducive to the cultivation of progressive attitudes among its speakers, and was therefore promoted as a means of improving oneself, and of expressing one's ideas cordially. Standard Japanese was seen to further the development of the prefecture, and it was believed that school education had become more efficient due to its increased use, while greater proficiency in Standard Japanese had made Okinawa's citizens happier and more confident.

Sugiyama (1940a–c) had similar views on the place and value of local languages in Okinawa. He believed that the prefecture's inhabitants should be liberated from their 'old language', for its continued use would only handicap them in the future. Furthermore, an incomplete command of Standard Japanese and the mixing of local language varieties with Standard Japanese would inevitably be perceived as inferior by mainland Japanese. Sugiyama commented that the conversations of commoners in Okinawa were inferior even to the gibberish (*chinpun kanpun*) spoken in Akita and Aomori Prefectures, two prefectures well-known for their 'thick accents', and he perceived attempts to maintain Ryukyuan languages as ill advised and potentially damaging.

The critics of the policy of language spread within the Ryukyus, particularly Yanagi, were more imaginative still in the associations they made between Standard Japanese and local languages. Higashionna (1940) admitted, albeit without giving details, that local languages had some inherent inconveniences, but pointed out that at the same time they were a valuable subject matter for academic study. Yanagita (1940) commented that responsibility for learning the national language was a heavy burden for the pupils of Okinawa Prefecture to bear, and although he too believed that there were problems with local languages, he repeatedly drew attention to the trouble caused by attempts to find a solution. Tōjō (1940) expressed similar views, indicating that he could not imagine how the loss of local languages could be seen as a cause for joy, as had been claimed, and expressing concern that the languages be lost before there had been an opportunity to study them in detail.

Yanagi, as the most outspoken of those questioning the dominant language ideology, argued that local languages should be recognized and respected as part of the national language. This assertion was supported by his conceptualization of a country as the sum of its constituent parts, that is, of its regions. If a given region is weakened, Yanagi (1940a) explained, so too is the country. He went further, saying that of all Japanese regions, Okinawa Prefecture could boast the culture of greatest worth, for no other part of Japan was so rich in culture. A Japan without regional languages, he continued, would be dull and culturally poor. Yanagi (1940b) was driven by the conviction that a lack of understanding of the culture and languages of Okinawa Prefecture was the reason for negative appraisal thereof, and argued forcefully for a shift in focus, away from Okinawa Prefecture's economic poverty to its cultural richness. He hoped to foster the idea of a strong Okinawa Prefecture, and appealed to the people of the prefecture to support his efforts. He saw great value in the local languages and felt that using them to write literary works might contribute greatly to the prestige of Okinawa Prefecture, and of Japan as a whole (Yanagi, 1940b). Yanagi (1940a) also expressed the belief that speaking only the language of Tokyo, as he himself did, ought to be considered a handicap, and he praised Ryukyuans for speaking both a regional language and what he referred to as the 'central language'.

His opinion of Standard Japanese was both less enthusiastic and less liberal. According to Yanagi (1940a), the so-called standard language (*iwayuru hyōjungo*) was in need of further standardization and refinement, and towards achieving this end he urged the creation of a correct standard language (*tadashii hyōjungo*). He believed that the incorporation of western loanwords was undermining the purity of Standard Japanese, and saw potential in the local languages of Okinawa Prefecture for the crafting of a more authentic and pure standard language, for they contained many elements of Old Japanese that might well find a place in the 'correct standard language' he promoted.

Based on such widely divergent assessments of Standard Japanese and the Ryukyuan languages, it is not surprising that a number of different possibilities for a future language order were suggested. The supporters of the policies already in place encouraged monolingualism, and saw no place for Ryukyuan language use in Japan's linguistic future. The Prefectural Department of Education categorically ruled out the possibility that use of the standard language could be promoted in a way that was respectful of local languages (OKGB, 1940a). Yoshida (1940b) stated that language varieties nobody understood outside the prefecture were unsustainable, and Sugiyama (1940a) supported the prefectural government's policy of simultaneously spreading Standard Japanese whilst oppressing local languages. Although opponents to existing educational practices repeatedly asked for these views to be justified, they never were. Yanagi (1940a) even went as far as ridiculing his opponents, asking if there was indeed something inherently barbarian about the language of Okinawa Prefecture (or superior about Standard Japanese), or whether, in fact, the supporters of the official line were simply afraid that local language speakers would forget the standard language if they did not speak it at home.

Those contributors to the debate, who were critical of the policy of local language oppression, advocated greater tolerance. Iha (1940) pointed out that promoting Standard Japanese did not demand such intolerance and oppression. Similarly, Yanagita (1940) proposed a reconsideration of existing practices, and

Tōjō (1940b) added his disapproval of prohibiting local language use. Yanagi's alternative to the regimentation of languages in Okinawa Prefecture (1940d), whereby local languages would be respected as part of the national language, contained a proposal to use Standard Japanese in official domains, while allowing local language use in private domains. In this way, mutual coexistence of both local languages and standard language might be achieved.

As we have seen, debates concerned with language ideology are never about linguistic matters alone, and we can identify two main reasons for this. Firstly, language ideology always involves non-linguistic elements, because language discourse can only become ideologically loaded through the forging of such extra-linguistic connections, and secondly, any ideological debate is inextricably linked to struggles for authority and power. In line with this, the victorious side in any such debate will always be that backed by the most powerful social agents. What is more, the victors will invariably conceal their links to power and thus claim their view to be normal, for by doing so they can most effectively 'make sense' of their position. Ultimately, what made the most sense in 1940 was essentially the position taken by dialectologist Tōjō, that the Ryukyuan languages were effectively greater dialects (*dai-hōgen*) of the national language (see Chapter 5). This view led administrators to argue that any dialect unintelligible to speakers in the rest of Japan could not be maintained and should therefore be suppressed. Having thus emerged from the great dialect debate victorious, this ideological standpoint went on to survive the US occupation both of mainland Japan (1945–1952) and of the Ryukyus (1945–1972), and has only recently found itself under pressure (see Chapter 8). In this way, it was the ideologies promoted by Yoshida and Sugiyama that came to describe most accurately the linguistic order which would emerge in the Ryukyus under the order of modernity.

Ultimately, the great dialect debate did little to change the general perception of the Ryukyuan languages. To do so, and to thereby alter the destiny of the Ryukyuan languages would have required a shift in the balance of power between the centre and the margin. This was even commented upon in the debate, exposing the struggle for power and its corollary authority that was going on behind the scenes. Yanagi (1940c) raised the pivotal question of whether those measures implemented to encourage the spread of the standard language were effective, thereby openly questioning the credentials of those responsible for language education in Okinawa Prefecture. Higashionna (1940), too, reproached the prefectural authorities for having failed to provide a justification of their educational policies. Yanagi (1940a) asked why local languages were not to be used at home, and saw the lack of such consideration as evidence of the fact that the prefectural policies had failed to acknowledge the place of Ryukyuan culture within the culture of Japan (Yanagi, 1940c,

1940d). Towards the creation of a more appropriate policy, and by way of concluding the debate, Yanagi (1940a) proposed that a discussion forum be held, which was to be attended by his main opponent, Yoshida, as well as local intellectuals and members of the public. Unsurprisingly, no such debate ever took place. As we have seen, it is not arguments that settle ideological debate, but power employed in the service of making sense.

In such a debate as this, the credibility and integrity of the less powerful are questioned incessantly. We saw this earlier, in our discussion on the debate about *genbun itchi* (Chapter 3), and we can see it here again in 1940. From the very outset, the Department of Education (OKGB, 1940a) declared the details of the Folk Craft Society's argument unimportant, and questioned their legitimacy and qualifications with regard to their criticism of official prefectural policy. The Department (OKGB, 1940b, 1940c) branded criticism of its policies as noise (*satsuon*), and sought to portray the goal of the Folk Craft Society – to spread Standard Japanese while remaining respectful of local languages – as unfeasible. In later contributions, and apparently in reaction to Yanagi's call for local support, the Department of Education (OKGB, 1940b, 1940c) stressed its cooperation with the popular Movement to Enforce the Standard Language in Okinawa Prefecture. Yoshida (1940b) commented that linguists and the Folk Craft Society should not interfere in policy-making, and focus instead on what he saw as their real duties, that is, the study of language and culture. Scholars, he asserted, tended to view things only from their own narrow professional position, and this was insufficient for the demands of policy-making. Yanagi's proposals were portrayed as lacking practicality, and local educators all agreed that his views were unhelpful, according to Yoshida.

Emancipation demands a successful shift of authority and a readjustment of power relations, and it was by failing to achieve this that Yanagi and his supporters were ultimately unsuccessful. Their challenge to the oppression of local languages came during the general mobilization campaign – a period of time which turned out to be ill-suited for debating a redistribution of power and cultural capital. Rather, the debate is a clear case of a struggle where power shifts away from ideology towards coercion. With the publication of an article written collaboratively by Sugiyama – the folk art scholars' most ardent critic – and Tanaka – chief editor of the society's journal *Gekkan mingei* (*Monthly Folk Craft*) – in April 1941, the debate came to an end (Sugiyama & Tanaka, 1941). The academic methods of the Folk Craft Society had been effectively denounced, and a more pragmatic approach adopted. This final contribution to the great dialect debate serves as a reminder that the days in which open debate on policies were possible had come to an end.

The place of Ryukyuan languages in the modern Japanese state as debated here cannot be considered in isolation from the comments and ideas expressed with regard to Standard Japanese. This is particularly important when looking at the connections between language and non-linguistic issues that are revealed during the course of the debate. For example Standard Japanese is portrayed as an emblem of national unity, modernity and progress, the use of Standard Japanese thereby rendering its speakers Japanese, modern and progressive. Ryukyuan languages, on the other hand, are presented as all that the standard language is not, as representative of regionalism and retrogression. By using Ryukyuan languages, therefore, the speaker rendered himself provincial, old-fashioned and backward.

In his analysis of the debate, Clarke concludes,

the overwhelming force of argument seems to have come down in favour of the prefecture's policy of vigorous promotion of the standard language. The reason for this can be divided into the two broad categories of external political pressure of the state on the one hand and the internal desire of the Okinawans themselves for economic and social advancement. (Clarke, 1997: 207)

Clarke's conclusions are certainly accurate. Nevertheless, we must also acknowledge that language ideology relies on the deliberate linking of linguistic and extra-linguistic issues. Thus, students of language ideology are aware that there is no natural and obvious connection between, say, language choices made in one's home or neighbourhood and economic and social advancement. In the absence of language ideology, we can see that these issues are in fact completely unrelated. In seeking to understand how such a connection comes into being, there are three important factors to consider. Firstly, the loading of a language with empowering ideology must take into account the presence of other languages and language varieties, for empowerment of one language variety demands the disenfranchisement of others. The denigration and stigmatization of other languages become the mechanisms by which the empowered language is made distinct. Secondly, this kind of stigmatization is not concerned with language alone, but extends to the speakers of those other languages and language varieties. Thirdly, ideology does not only exist in the realm of ideas and conceptions, but also affects patterns of language structure and language use. Ideology thereby triggers language change, which in turn supports the claims ideology has made, among them, that some languages present an obstacle to communication, for example, or to the well-being of their speakers. We shall now take a closer look at these three issues at work in the context of Ryukyuan languages, and see how they have manifested themselves in concrete terms.

The Progressive Erasure of Ryukyuan Languages

The influence of ideology is gradual and may be best understood within the framework of progressive erasure. The progressive erasure of languages through language shift occurs in four stages: fragmentation, marginalization, sublimation and subordination. All these stages are driven by dominant language ideology, which in turn is reinforced and validated by the effects of progressive erasure. In order to conceptualize the role of language ideology in language shift processes, Tsitsipis (1998, 2003) proposed the progressive erasure model as a means of studying the consequences of ideologically driven language change. This approach highlights the way in which declining languages are gradually and exponentially put under pressure by the dominant language. In this case, that language is Japanese. Let us consider the first stage of language shift, that of fragmentation.

Fragmentation

Fragmentation is characterized by the gradual restriction of a language to limited functions. In other words, it defines a loss of domains of use. Through fragmentation, the cultural and linguistic coherence of a language are reduced, or as Tsitsipis writes, the 'indexical totality, as one might call it, between linguistic and extralinguistic order is fragmented' (Tsitsipis, 2003: 550).

The fragmentation of the Ryukyuan languages was largely brought about by three developments linked to Japanese modernization. These were (1) administrative reforms; (2) the emergence of news reporting and modern literature; and (3) the introduction of compulsory school education. Two of these three have pre-modern origins. After the Satsuma Domain's invasion of Uchinaa (Okinawa) in 1609, Japanese became one of two languages used for writing administrative documents, the other being Chinese, and from the time of the Ryukyu disposition (*Ryūkyū shobun*) on, it was the only language used for this purpose. The establishment of Okinawa Prefecture in 1879 resulted in the complete reorganization of administrative, educational and executive institutions, but at no stage were any of the Ryukyuan languages considered for use in official domains.

From there, Japanese soon became accepted as the medium for all forms of written texts, from official publications to newspapers, books, periodicals and public signs (Matsumori, 1995: 40). Furthermore, since those functions of language related to modernity were handled in Japanese, use of the Ryukyuan languages was restricted to matters considered, at the time, as generally unimportant and of little prestige, and turned thus into what is known in diglossia theory as low varieties (Ferguson, 1959). Note, however that no fixed complementary allocation of language functions resulted from the fragmentation of the Ryukyuan languages. Neither diglossia nor any other kind of stable multilingualism emerged as a consequence of Japanese language spread into these domains.

The establishment of local newspapers further accelerated the spread of Japanese through writing, and further fragmentation of the Ryukyuan languages followed. All the prefecture's local newspapers were published exclusively in Japanese, from their very first issues on. The daily newspaper *Ryūkyū shinpō*, for example, was founded in 1893 by members of the ancient ruling class, and with a circulation of 400–500 copies per day, sought to contribute to the development of Okinawa Prefecture by openly promoting assimilation into the Meiji state (ODJKJ, 1983: 886). In 1905, the *Okinawa shinbun*, and in 1908, *Okinawa mainichi shinbun*, were founded with similar objectives. As was the case with prefectural bureaucracy, a lack of relevant professional qualifications and Japanese language ability led to recruiting employees from the mainland, while through the publication of these local newspapers, Japanese became the accepted medium for news coverage, and, by extension, of political and economic debate. Fragmentation duly increased.

Another means by which the Japanese language spread was the novel. In comparison with mainland Japan, the novel got off to a late start in Okinawa Prefecture. This was not only due to the difficulties encountered by local people in reading and writing, but also to a lack of opportunity to publish. The local newspapers, in particular the *Ryūkyū shinpō*, invested greatly in the promotion of modern Ryukyuan literature. The modern Ryukyuan novel was written exclusively in Japanese (Okinawa Kyōiku I'inkai, 1965–1977: 737–739). In 1932, the first of Ryukyuan novel to be read widely outside the prefecture was Kushi Fusako's *Horobiyuku ryūkyū onna no shuki* (*Memoirs of a Declining Ryukyuan Woman*). It centred on the lives of Ryukyuans living in Tokyo who had chosen to denounce their Ryukyuan identity in order to avoid discrimination, and appeared in the popular mainland magazine *Fujin kōron* (*Women's Forum*). While work depicting the reality of the Ryukyuan daily experiences thus began to reach the mainland audience, it did so, and was only able to do so, through the medium of Japanese.

Newspapers, novels and bureaucracy aside, by far the most important factor in the fragmentation of the Ryukyuan languages was the establishment of compulsory school education (see Chapter 5). Teaching staff from mainland prefectures were employed in great numbers because there were not enough teachers of Japanese native to Okinawa Prefecture (Ahagon, 1980). The decision to use Japanese as the medium of school education hugely affected the status of the Ryukyuan languages, detaching them from the domains of learning and academic study. From that point on, discussing intellectual matters, not to mention writing about them, would be done only in Japanese.

The developments described above demonstrate how the utility of a language is gradually eroded through fragmentation. While Ryukyuan languages would continue to be used as a means of verbal communication in the private domain for many decades to come, the impact of fragmentation on the use and structure of those local languages was permanent, and led to the second stage of progressive erasure – marginalization.

Marginalization

Marginalization is the process by which the subordination of a language and its speakers through fragmentation is further reproduced and reinforced. Consider Tsitsipis' explanation of marginalization using the language of Arvanitika (Greek-Albanian) as his example: 'It is silently assumed that Arvanitika people will "naturally" switch [from Arvanitika to Greek P.H.], given the subordinate status of their language and, through indexication, of its speakers' (Tsitsipis, 2003: 552). This quote contains a number of points relevant to the discussion at hand. It reveals how language ideology uses the status of a language to index its speakers. Subsequently, this indexication forces speakers to make certain predetermined language choices, specifically, ones that favour the dominant language and thereby sustain the inequality between two languages and their respective speakers. Finally, Tsitsipis' comments reveal how this phenomenon is triggered by an imbalance of power, the very same imbalance that creates the difference in status in the first place, and which is reproduced and made common sense through the pattern of specific language choices it generates. Let us consider some concrete examples of how this ideological process works on the field.

In the Ryukyu Islands too, Ryukyuan speakers were responsible for language accommodation of Japanese monolinguals. The decision over whether to use Ryukyuan languages or Japanese in contact situations was never formally discussed, but from the very beginning it was generally accepted that Japanese should be used where mainlanders were present (see Iha, 1916 for a critique). In a visit to the Ryukyu Islands in 1893, the pioneer of Japanese and Ryukyuan linguistics, Basil Hall Chamberlain, shrewdly observed that the Japanese language textbook *Okinawa taiwa* had been published 'by the prefectural authorities, with a view to aiding Luchuans [Ryukyuans P.H.] in the acquisition of the speech of their Japanese masters' (Chamberlain, 1999: 1).

Behind both fragmentation and marginalization lies an unequal division of power, and marginalization not only reaffirms that inequality but magnifies it too. Furthermore, marginalization is not merely restricted to matters of language choice, but may be observed at all levels of language. Let us consider two concrete examples.

With regard to phonology, a study conducted by Nagata (2001) on Yonaguni Island reveals the influence of Standard Japanese on the phonological system of the local language. Nagata's investigation focused on how the phonological and grammatical system of the Yonaguni language was altered by the spread of Standard Japanese. His empirical research relied on 72 informants between 11 and 89 years of age. With regard to phonological changes, Nagata found various examples in which Standard Japanese had begun to infiltrate the Yonaguni language. One of the most revealing results of his investigation centred on realization of the Yonaguni phoneme /ŋ/ which does not have phonemic status in Standard Japanese. Due to the phonemic status of the velar nasal /ŋ/ in Yonaguni, the word for 'east' /aŋai/ is thus never pronounced /agai/ by a fully proficient speaker. In his field studies, Nagata allocated each speaker three points for realization of the phoneme /ŋ/, one point for adherence to the phonological system of Standard Japanese, that is to say, pronunciation as /agai/, and two points for variation between /ŋ/ and /g/. Thus, a score of 3.0 indicates use of the Yonaguni phonological system, 1.0 denotes pronunciation of the word according to the phonological system of Standard Japanese, and any score between 1.0 and 2.0 indicates that a hybrid of Yonaguni and Standard Japanese pronunciation was observed. Nagata (2001: 440) obtained the following results.

As we can see from Table 7.1, speakers aged 40 or more distinguished /ŋ/ and /g/, but in younger informants the distinction was becoming weaker. Younger speakers instead tended to rely to a large extent on the phonological inventory of Standard Japanese. Nagata's study is a record of change not only in terms of one language replacing another, as with fragmentation. Rather, the infiltration of Standard Japanese phonology into the Yonaguni language is evidence of the subordinate status of Yonaguni relative to Standard Japanese being reproduced within the Yonaguni language system itself.

Table 7.1 Pronunciation of 'East' in the Yonaguni language

Age	Points allocated for pronunciation
10–19	1.83
20–29	2.14
30–39	2.56
40–49	3.0
50–59	2.92
60–69	3.0
70–79	2.94
80–89	3.0

Marginalization may also frequently be observed in the lexicon of the Ryukyuan languages, which is, as a consequence of a lack of adaptation to modernity (i.e. as a consequence of fragmentation), smaller than that of Standard Japanese. Furthermore, a process of relexification, replacing Yonaguni words by Japanese ones, is evident in all Ryukyuan languages. Adoption of Japanese words, in place of existing Ryukyuan alternatives, is an example of marginalization, in that the supposed superiority of status and corpus of Japanese is thereby reproduced, reaffirming the inequality between the two languages in contact. It is virtually impossible to conduct spoken activity in any Ryukyuan language today without inserting some Japanese expression, possibly with the exception of prayer and song (see Heinrich, 2008; Matsumori, 1995). The reason for the massive process of relexification is the restricted functional range of the Ryukyuan languages, which is, in turn, a consequence of fragmentation. Marginalization at the lexical level is not simply restricted to filling lexical gaps, however. There are also many instances in which existing Ryukyuan words were replaced by Japanese expressions. Nagata (2001: 450), for example, reports that speakers of 80 years of age or more exclusively refer to 'mushrooms' with the Yonaguni term *naba*, while younger speakers use the Japanese expression of *kinoko*.

Today, the effects of marginalization can be heard in almost every concrete utterance in every Ryukyuan language. The restriction of language use and structure resulting from fragmentation and marginalization forms the next stage of progressive erasure, and is known as sublimation. It is to this next phase in the deterioration of a language's utility, use and status that we shall turn now.

Sublimation

Sublimation is the process by which a language is decontextualized from its unmarked functions, whereby use of the dominated language becomes marked. Whereas Ryukyuan languages were spoken in all domains until 1879, their use became progressively more restricted once marginalized as a result of the spread of Japanese. Over time, the number of domains in which Ryukyuan languages were used as the usual medium of communication decreased, as did the number of speakers thereof, and consequently, their use slowly began to accumulate various connotations. In other words, deliberately choosing to use a local Ryukyuan language, rather than defaulting to Japanese, started to carry new significance. Today, very few domains remain in which the Ryukyuan languages are the default language choice, that is, the unmarked choice. Local music, festivals and religious rites are the most important of these domains, but even these are now shifting to Japanese.

A loss of proficiency in local languages among speakers born after 1950, one result of language shift expanding into the domain of the family and the neighbourhood, contributed much to the process of sublimation. To younger Ryukyuans, local languages serve only as a symbolic commodity of restricted nature. Use of Ryukyuan languages in public speaking has been sublimated to the extent that the artificial domains of specialized academic circles and speech contests must be created to provide a forum for the use of local languages. Although selected parts of Ryukyuan languages and customs have recently been incorporated into the new school subject of integrated study (*sōgōteki na gakushū*) (Gishi, 2001: 9–10), it is important to recognize that the local languages being taught in schools, after more than a century's absence from the curriculum, are fragmented, marginalized and sublimated. Note that although compulsory schooling was never established in the Ryukyu Kingdom, there existed about 200 schools in the Ryukyu Kingdom before Okinawa Prefecture was established (Morita, 1967: 123). Today, the local languages at school return marginalized and in short sequences, taking the form of songs and tales.

For an ever-greater percentage of the Ryukyuan population, local languages no longer offer a neutral means of communication. Today, local language use invariably signifies the adoption or inference of specific attitudes, connotations and experiences. This marking of local languages is contingent upon two main factors: domain of use and the age of speakers. It governs the language choices made in certain domains, and this makes it difficult to revitalize language use in those domains already lost to Japanese. While full speakers and so-called 'rusty speakers' continue to use local languages in informal settings, such as in their homes and neighbourhoods, the use of local languages by semi-speakers and monolinguals is usually marked. The infrequent insertion of elements of local language most often serves simply as a marker of identity (Heffernan, 2006), or is used to create a sense of informality (Sugita, 2007, 2010).

Subordination

Subordination is the final phase of progressive erasure, whereby it becomes impossible to develop a discourse of resistance against the dominant language and the ideologies that support it (Tsitsipis, 2003). Once this stage is reached, the progressive erasure of a language has advanced to such an extent that it is no longer possible to seriously challenge the dominance of that language in any domain. When faced with an ideologically mediated language shift, therefore, subordination is the point of no return.

Skutnabb-Kangas (2000: 426) has observed that the existence of 'a language' is often considered a prerequisite for laying claim to a sense of nationhood, and it is for this reason that so many languages are redefined as dialects in nation-state contexts. It is the fear of calls for greater self-determination and a reevaluation of the balance of power that drives this downgrading of languages, the same process by which the Ryukyuan languages were declared dialects after the islands officially became part of the Japanese nation-state (see Chapter 5). In spite of the long-standing, and little-challenged, conceptualization of local languages as dialects of the national language in Japan, resisting this appraisal is still possible. It requires, however, that speakers of the local language undermine the process of progressive erasure in its earlier stages (fragmentation and marginalization) by using local languages in contexts where to do so is to make a marked choice (Heinrich, 2011). Language loss, however, poses a threat to claims for more autonomy (see Kymlicka, 1995; May, 2001 for consideration of endangered languages as emancipatory tools), limiting the possibilities for developing discourses of resistance against the way in which the Ryukyu Islands are part of the Japanese state today. To lose these possibilities would effectively constitute subordination.

In an important contribution to our understanding of the workings of language ideology, Irvine and Gal write that erasure 'is the process in which ideology, in simplifying the sociolinguistic field, renders some persons or activities (or sociolinguistic phenomena) invisible. Facts that are inconsistent with the ideological scheme either go unnoticed or get explained away' (Irvine & Gal, 2000: 38). From our consideration of progressive erasure in the Ryukyuan languages, we can add to Gal and Irvine's observation that language use adapts to ideology. Languages and language uses which disagree with dominant language ideological views retreat, thereby increasing the likelihood that they will 'go unnoticed or get explained away'. This process adds authenticity to ideological claims, making them more realistic. Our examination of this process at work under modernist Japanese language ideology thus demands consideration of the loss of linguistic diversity in a state which claims to be linguistically homogenous.

Language Shifts among Indigenous Linguistic Minorities in Japan

Language shift refers to a change in patterns of language use within a multilingual setting. It most often results either from the introduction of a new language into a community, or else from outmigration to a different linguistic environment. In both cases, language shift leads to the increased use of one language, and a corresponding decrease in the use of another language. When this shift reaches the domain of the family, natural intergenerational language transmission of the weaker language is interrupted, and it thus becomes endangered (if only spoken by the community within which the shift is taking place). This is precisely what has happened with every autochthonous minority language in Japan, so much so that the last of these languages looks set to become extinct by the second half of the 21st century. In the following, we shall discuss in some detail the cases of the Ainu, the Ogasawara Islanders and the Ryukyuans. Let us start, however, by briefly pointing out to Hachijo and Japanese Sign Language, two languages which are often overlooked in discussions on Japanese linguistic diversity. As a consequence of such negligence, studies of language shift still await their structured and purposeful inauguration.

Hachijo and Japanese Sign Language

The local Hachijo language and Japanese Sign Language constitute further examples of autochthonous linguistic diversity in Japan. Hachijo is a definitely endangered language spoken on the islands of Hachijo and Aogashima, that is, the furthest outlying and isolated islands of the Izu Archipelago. The two islands are located 280 and 380 km south of Tokyo, respectively. Throughout the Edo period (1602–1868) Hachijo Island served as a place of exile, a use of the island which only ended with the Meiji restoration. Like the Ryukyuan languages, Hachijo retains linguistic forms that predate the first written sources of Japanese (see Kaneda, 2005; Naitō, 1979). Unfortunately, no sociolinguistic research into Hajijo language shift has been conducted so far. According to the UNESCO (2009) online atlas, the language is endangered in the same degree as Amami, Kunigami, Uchinaaguchi and Miyako in the Ryukyu Islands. That is to say, only the oldest generation is seen to be fully proficient in the language. In other words, the Hachijo language too appears to be set for extinction before 2050 if no counter-measures are taken.

Japanese Sign Language, or *nihon shuwa* in Japanese, is at present used by some 300,000 persons in Japan. Needless to say, it is a language in its own rights, and not a 'manual version' (*temane*) of spoken Japanese. Japanese Sign Language emerged around schools for the Deaf, the first of which was established in 1878 in Kyoto. Little is known about sign language structure, variety and use in Japan before that time. Japanese Sign Language subsequently spread under Japanese administration in colonial Korea and Taiwan. As an effect, Japanese, Taiwanese and Korean sign languages maintain many structural similarities until today (Fischer & Gong, 2010: 501). In recent years, the view of being deaf has shifted away from a definition of having hearing impairments towards a sociocultural view of the Deaf as users of Japanese Sign Language. Hence, Deaf people constitute a linguistic and cultural community and ought to be spelled with a capital D.

Until very recently, the aim of education for the Deaf was their integration into Japanese speaking and hearing society. In 1948, the objective of 'mainstreaming' Deaf children fully was institutionalized with their inclusion to compulsory education. Mainstreaming efforts were further intensified in the 1970s (Nakamura, 2002: 216). As an effect, lip-reading and mouthing with sounds were promoted and use of Japanese Sign Language in school was suppressed to various degrees. Until 2002, it was altogether banned from schools for the Deaf. However, Japanese Sign Language still awaits its inclusion and use in the school curriculum. The view of Japan being monolingual makes itself again felt in this context. Nakamura notes, 'Japanese is the only language recognized within Japanese schools, which means no approved curricula can be developed using sign languages' (Nakamura, 2002: 219). It is as if the state would want to punish all those Japanese children not speaking Japanese for being 'deviant' in order lay claims to the Japanese being a monolingual nation.

Even since the 1960s, the number of hearing-impaired children has been reduced due to various medical advances. Today, their number is about half of what it was in the 1960s. Also the number of children enrolled in schools for the Deaf has been dropping sharply. It currently amounts to about one third of the number of pupils in the 1960s. As a consequence, Japanese Sign Language is losing speakers, and this tendency is reinforced through linguistic mainstreaming, discouragement to acquire sign language, and its exclusion from the curricula. While sociolinguistic research into Japanese Sign Language endangerment is still lacking, it is regarded as being endangered by specialists today, although to a lesser degree than other Japanese allochthonous languages. In September 2009, Japanese Sign Language was the topic of a panel, organized by Matsuo Shin and myself on language endangerment and documentation at the *26th Conference of the Japanese Association of Sociolinguistics Sciences*. Deaf participants communicated their concern about the endangerment of Japanese Sign Language at this occasion, and they also stressed their dedication to transmit their heritage language to future generations. Their endeavours are likely to meet with some success as new social movements have sprung up in support of recognition and promotion of Deaf language and culture in the past two decades (see Nakamura, 2006). In this context, it is also a noteworthy fact that the issue of language rights is currently being spearheaded by Deaf activists in Japan (Kimura, 2011).

Ainu

We saw in Chapter 5 that Ainu is not a unified language, but rather comprises three unroofed *abstand* languages. Prior to their assimilation into the Meiji state, the Ainu lived in river-based communities (*petiwor*), each using their own regional language variety. Although no interregional Ainu language has ever existed, research into Ainu language shift has tended to treat Ainu as a unified language. It has thus failed to distinguish between language shift (changing patterns of language use) and language loss (loss of variation in language), essentially projecting modernist ideas of what language ought to be onto languages that were never modernized. As a result, little is known about language shift within the Sakhalin and Kurile Ainu languages, for these were included in the general category of 'Ainu language', and the fact that both are today extinct is effectively hidden. In fact, Sakhalin Ainu became extinct in 1994, when its last speaker Asai Take (1902–1994) passed away (Murasaki, 2001). Less is known for the loss of Kurile Ainu. The Kurile communities suffered greatly from diseases such as smallpox, measles, cholera, tuberculosis, transmitted via contact with Russians and Japanese, and also from enforced relocation. Kurile Ainu was thus the first Ainu language to become extinct, with Ainu reported as no longer being spoken on the Kurile Islands in 1963 (Tamura, 2000: 1). In the absence of evidence on the contrary, it is reasonable to assume that it became extinct around that time. Accordingly, the following discussion on language shift will be restricted to Hokkaido Ainu.

Language shift in Ainu communities occurred more slowly than in other ethnolinguistic communities in Japan, the beginning of the shift there predating Japanese modernization (Maher, 2001: 326). Some Ainu had already acquired a degree of proficiency in Japanese and Russian by the 17th century, and by the end of the 19th century, both Japanese and Russian was used for interregional communication between Ainu communities (DeChicchis, 1995: 109). As in the case of Japan's other ethnolinguistic minorities, the establishment of schools conducting classes in Japanese proved to have the greatest impact on Ainu (see Chapter 5 for details), resulting not only in Ainu children becoming proficient in Japanese, but also in their coming to view their heritage language and culture as inferior (Hanami, 1995; Siddle, 1995a). Having been told that theirs was an inferior race, the Ainu inevitably began to view their ethnicity, culture and language with negativity and subsequently stopped transmitting the Ainu language to their children.

Natural intergenerational language transmission was interrupted in the first two decades of the 20th century. In the few cases in which the Ainu language was transmitted after that time, grandparents, and not parents, passed it on (see e.g. Kayano, 1994: 5). The loss of that generation of grandparents, the last generation not to have been schooled in Japanese, represented thus the loss of the family domain to Japanese. This may be seen in the case of Hatozawa Fujino (Ainu name, Wateke, 1890–1961), who spoke Ainu at home until her grandmother passed away in 1905. The language of the home subsequently shifted to Japanese (Tamura, 2001: 7). Since the

1920s, when Ainu first became endangered, three generations of Ainu have lived with Japanese as their first language. Those domains of Ainu that have been maintained, revitalized or newly created are music, prayer, ceremony, academic circles and speech contests. This set of domains recalls what Fishman (1991) terms as folklorization (see Chapter 9).

The last Ainu speakers to have been consulted by linguists in recent times were for the most part born in the first decade of the 20th century, and are therefore either very elderly, or no longer with us. Oda Ito (1908–2000) and Shirasawa Nabe (1905–1993) were two well-known speakers of Ainu. The scholar and activist Chisato Dubreuil considers Kayano Shigeru (1926–2006) to have been the last Ainu speaker who actually used Ainu in daily life. Dubreuil writes,

> with the passing of Ainu writer, researcher, curator and Diet member Kayano Shigeru, I know of no other Ainu who is a fluent speaker. Even he stated that his Ainu language was not viable. The language he knew as a youth did not evolve. Indeed, it could not, for there were not enough people left to talk to. Many of the Ainu who knew the language chose not to speak it for fear of discrimination. (Dubreuil, 2007)

The mark of language ideology at work in the loss of Ainu is all to clear from Dubreuil's comments.

Ainu was spoken as a community language until the 1960s, when the last fully competent speakers of Ainu passed away (Bugaeva, 2004: 7), as confirmed by Ainu speakers themselves. The aforementioned Kayano Shigeru (1994: 106) reported that at an Ainu funeral in 1953, three Ainu men were heard discussing how their own funerals might be conducted in accordance with Ainu rituals. The discussion was brought about by the fact that they saw themselves as the last Ainu speakers capable of reciting the ritual speeches and prayers necessary for such funerals. The three men were Nitani Kunimatsu (Ainu name, Nisukrekkur, born 1888), Nitani Tarō (Uparette, born 1892) and Kayano's father, Kaizawa Seitarō (Arekaynu, born 1893), and following their passing, the next generation of Ainu speakers would perhaps best be defined as 'rusty', that is lacking specific knowledge of 'how to do things with language' due to the loss of specific domains of language use (see Sasse, 1992 for details).

The last of these rusty speakers have themselves largely passed away during the first decade of the 21st century. The few Ainu speakers who remain are semi-speakers, second language learners, or token speakers (see DeChicchis, 1995 for an important classification of Ainu speakers). None of them has ever used Ainu for everyday communication, and as a result, the

Ainu language we may encounter today is one that has undergone considerable language attrition and language loss over the last three generations. Tamura reports that

> the influence of Japanese on syntax and pronunciation has been strong, and the vocabulary has shrunk as well, to the extent that when the today's elders hear the stories told by those who passed away some 20 years ago, there are many words that they do not know. (Tamura, 2001: 1)

The language shift and language loss described above has led to the definition of (Hokkaido) Ainu by UNESCO (2009) as critically endangered, or one step away from extinction. Today, Hokkaido Ainu survives with linguists such as Chiba University's Nakagawa Hiroshi, or with second language learners of varying degrees of proficiency. The token use of Ainu continues in specific domains such as song or festival, but this is all that remains at present to keep the Ainu language from sliding beneath the waves of extinction.

Ogasawara

Geographically isolated in the midst of the Pacific Ocean more than 1000 km from Tokyo, the linguistic history of the Ogasawara Islands is more complex than in other parts of Japan, owing to the mixed ethnicities of the first colonizers, to subsequent migration movements, and to the presence of not one, but two dominant languages in the past 150 years, Japanese and English. Long (2007) and Ishihara (2007) provide detailed accounts of these matters. For our purposes, we need to only focus on the language shift from varieties of English to varieties of Japanese.

The settlement of the Ogasawara Islands began in 1830 with the arrival of American and European men and their Pacific Islander wives. Until the coming of the first Japanese settlers in 1876, the Japanese language was entirely alien to this community. The first male settlers spoke various European languages such as English, German, Portuguese and Italian, while their wives spoke various Polynesian and Micronesian languages. From this complex sociolinguistic environment evolved a community language known as Ogasawara Creole English. More specifically, a Creoloid emerged, that is, a quickly stabilizing Creole language supported by many native speakers of the dominant language (here English) which resulted in less simplification than in a (classical) Creole language. Long (2007: 15) estimates that the total number of speakers of one English language variety or another as a community language on Ogasawara has at no time been greater than one or two hundred.

In the 19th century, Ogasawara Creole English, Japanese, native English and other European languages, Pacific English-based *lingua franca*, Polynesian and Micronesian languages existed side by side, in what was by that time a highly multilingual community. When Ogasawara became part of the Meiji state in 1876, however, this changed quickly. Within less than two years of the arrival of the first Japanese settlers, the Creole English-speaking inhabitants became a minority, with the number of new settlers arriving each year from Japan outnumbering the total population of the original colony. Only Japanese nationals were permitted to settle on the Ogasawara Islands after 1876, curbing any influx of new languages to the islands, which were themselves subsequently renamed with Japanese names – Peel Island became Chichijima and Bailey Island Hahajima. By 1882, all of the original settlers and their descendants had been naturalized as Japanese citizens, while 1878 saw the establishment of Japanese language education. It is worth noting in this context that English was for a brief time included in the Japanese school syllabus (Ishihara, 2007: 351), and an English-medium mission school was also operated and attended both by descendants of the original settlers and by ethnic Japanese (Cholmondeley, 1915: 176). This school remained open until the outbreak of the Pacific War in 1937. In 1938, however, the use of English was banned completely in the public domain, and deliberate efforts were made to suppress its use in the private domain too (Long, 2007: 22). Furthermore, all non-Japanese family names were 'Japanized' at that time (Hasegawa, 1998).

As a result of receiving schooling in Japanese, and language contact and intermarriage with Japanese settlers, all descendants of the original English Creole-speaking community became bilingual in Japanese and Ogasawara Creole English. By the start of the Taishō period (1912–1926), everyone on the islands was proficient in Japanese. Japanese became the language used in all public domains except for the church. As well as at church, Ogasawara Creole English was spoken in the homes and among the descendants of the first settlers (Long, 2007: 91). However, no stable multilingual order such as diglossia emerged, and intermarriage with ethnic Japanese began to push Ogasawara Creole English out of the home as early as the second half of the Meiji period (1868–1912). By the 1920s, language shift within the family was largely complete. Long concludes that

> English appears to be the first language of youngsters at the turn of the century, while Japanese is the first language of people born in the 1920s. So the shift occurred during the first couple of decades of the twentieth century. (Long, 2007: 13)

Children born after that time continued to be exposed to Ogasawara Creole English, however, and they are probably best described as receptive bilinguals. What could not be foreseen at the time was that English, albeit a very different variety, would return to dominate Ogasawara language life two decades later.

In 1944, with the Pacific War well underway, the entire population of Ogasawara was evacuated. Following the Japanese defeat in World War II, the Ogasawara Islands became detached from the Japanese state, and only non-ethnic Japanese settlers and their ethnic Japanese spouses were allowed to return from 1946 onwards. The returning community numbered just 135 individuals, as compared to the 7000 inhabitants before 1944. The US Navy established a military base on the main island of Chichijima, and so the returnees came into regular contact with US English. Further decreolization took place, accompanied by the emergence of a new Japanese–English mixed language used for in-group communication (Long, 2007: 31). Decreolization was driven by contact with Navy personal, by English-medium school instruction and by the negative language ideological perception of Creole languages by the Americans. While the Japanese–English language mixing was used within the family and the local community, US English was now used at work, in church, at school and in contact situations with the 20 or so military personnel stationed on Chichijima (Long, 2007: 158). Ogasawara Creole English was thereby replaced by US English in the public domain and by the Japanese–English-mixed language in private.

Then, in June 1968, the Ogasawara Islands were returned to Japan, ending 23 years of isolation and opening the way for ethnic Japanese settlement of Ogasawara once more. Within a few years, the descendants and families of the first settlers were outnumbered by ethnic Japanese ten to one. The Japanese language was re-instated in its pre-war position, becoming the default language choice in the public domain once more. Mixed language use declined, to be replaced by a newly formed local dialect (*koiné*) resulting from mixing of the various regional dialects of Japanese spoken in Ogasawara (Abe, 2006). Today, the descendants of the first settlers are completely assimilated into Japanese society, and as Long reports,

> find it not only unnecessary to use mixed language to maintain their identity, but unnecessary to embrace a unique identity at all. There is little reason to be optimistic about the survival of the Ogasawara Mixed Language after speakers born in the mid-twentieth century are gone. (Long, 2007: 208)

Already lost is Ogasawara Creole English, while very few speakers even of US varieties of English remain. These speakers, however, having been in Ogasawara under US occupation, have a unique language repertoire including Japanese, English and Ogasawara mixed language. Note that this mixed language is not the result of incomplete language acquisition, as those speaking it are both fluent in Japanese and English. Rather, it serves a generation of Ogasawara inhabitants as a means of distinguishing themselves both from Americans and from ethnic Japanese.

Today, all language varieties but Standard Japanese look set to become extinct. The loss of English as a community language may seem ironic in this age of globalization. Such a development will come as no surprise to students of language ideology, however, who will recognize the familiar pattern of ideologically driven language shift whereby regional community languages are replaced by national languages. In global Japan, for example English use is limited to 'international settings', and is not used as a community language among Japanese. Thus, English is not found to be replacing community languages anywhere in Japan, nor in any other country of the world where English is not already an official language (Brenzinger, 2001). This leaves the present-day descendants of the first settlers lamenting the loss of English, in view of the fact that their children could potentially have profited greatly from being Japanese–English bilinguals in today's globalized world.

The Ryukyus

As we have already discussed language ideology in the Ryukyus in detail both above and in Chapter 5, we will focus our attention here specifically on language shifts in the islands (see Heinrich, 2010a for more detailed discussions).

Language shift in the Ryukyus began much later than with the Ainu and Ogasawara Islanders, and so the linguistic repertoire of Ryukyuans today varies significantly across different generations (Motonaga, 1994), the older islanders being proficient in the respective local languages, the middle generation possessing passive skills, and the youngest Ryukyuans being in the vast majority of cases monolingual in Japanese. In other words, local languages are essentially set to be lost in the span of just three generations. Language shift in public domains began in 1880, with Japanese becoming the default language within families and neighbourhoods from the late 1930s onwards. The precise dates and pace of language shift differ across the individual islands, however. According to UNESCO (2009), the Ryukyuan Archipelago is home to six local languages. These are, from north to south, Amami, Kunigami, Uchinaaguchi (Okinawan), Miyako, Yaeyama and Yonaguni. Quantitative research (Heinrich, 2010a) has shown that language shift in the private domain started earliest in Amami, Uchinaa and Yaeyama, with change being most rapid in Yaeyama. Language shift also involved mixing of local languages with Japanese (see Sugita, 2007, 2010, 2011), being most pronounced in Amami. The inhabitants of Miyako Island and Yonaguni Island shifted later than other Ryukyuan communities, with local language still being transmitted within families well into the 1960s. Of these two speech communities, language shift in Yonaguni was more widespread and occurred more quickly. Due to the early shift in Yaeyama and the low number of speakers of Yonaguni, these two languages are classified as 'severly endangered' in the latest edition of UNESCO's (2009) atlas of endangered languages. The atlas defines Amami, Uchinaa and Miyako 'definitely endangered'.

Today, local languages are most widely used in Yonaguni and in Miyako. On Yonaguni Island, however, this is mainly due to widespread emigration of the island's younger inhabitants in the last 50 years. Local language use has declined most notably on the Yaeyama island group, followed by Okinawa Island. These islands are also the places where Japanese is most often used in the private domain. Meanwhile, language mixing is most prevalent in Amami, then in Uchinaa. Overall, language mixing represents the second most common language choice across the entire Ryukyu Archipelago, the most common being Standard Japanese. Language mixing initially emerged as a result of contact between local languages and Standard Japanese, but differs considerably with regard to time and place (Takaesu, 2005). Once denounced as a 'misuse of Japanese' (e.g. Kuwae, 1954), such mixed language has today become a deliberate and socially significant language choice. Evidence of language shift is most easily found in the language choices made within the home and neighbourhood by those younger than 30. Local languages have fallen into complete disuse among the young people of Yonaguni and Yaeyama, on precisely those islands where language shift towards Standard Japanese has been most thorough. Of all the islands, it is on Miyako that local language use by young people is strongest.

In his study on language shift in Uchinaa, Anderson (2009) confirms the observations made above. On the basis of a text corpus of 15 consultants, Anderson distinguishes between four different categories of language repertoire and local language proficiency. These categories are (1) full speakers; (2) rusty speakers; (3) semi-speakers; and (4) non-speakers of Uchinaaguchi. Full speakers are those born before the mid-1930s, rusty speakers between the mid-1930s and the mid-1950s, semi-speakers between the mid-1950s and the 1980s and non-speakers from 1970 to the present day. The first two groups are productive bilinguals, able to carry out complete speech acts in their local language. The difference between the two is that rusty speakers have little or no linguistic competence in formal situations requiring use of polite language. This, again, is a result of the relatively early shift to Japanese in formal situations. Semi-speakers find it difficult to make contributions using local language, but are able to understand most of what they hear (see Osumi, 2001). Non-speakers are essentially monolinguals, who retain only limited fragments of local language, and cannot understand local language utterances (Sugita, 2011).

Based on these insights, Anderson (2009: 266) predicts that by 2025 the last full speaker of Uchinaaguchi will have passed away, by 2055 the last rusty speakers and by 2085 the last semi-speaker. From the data on local language use collected by Heinrich (2010a), we can see that the process of language shift is most advanced in Yaeyama and least advanced in Miyako. Note, too, that the dates identified by Anderson (2009) refer to exceptional speakers who shifted relatively late, and that these speakers will not only be of advanced age, but also very few in number. Regardless, if language shift is not reversed, Ryukyuan languages will be neither be spoken nor understood by the end of the 21st century.

Today, all of Japan's autochthonous minority languages are either endangered or already extinct, thus increasingly supporting the claim of language ideology that state, nation and language are congruent in Japan. We have seen how language ideology plays a crucial role in the reduction of linguistic diversity, thereby constituting a self-fulfilling prophecy. That said, we should remember that modernist language ideology does not exist to reduce linguistic diversity, for diversity as a concept was never even contemplated by most language ideology brokers. Rather, this ideology was created to empower the Japanese in their attempt to join the modern world, and to counter negative comparisons of non-western languages and civilizations with western ones.

Indeed, the Japanese language ideologues proved successful in their attempts to have Japanese join the ranks of modernized national languages. The view from the margin, however, reveals that this has come at a cost. This cost was ultimately borne by those at the margin, by all those who were never considered part of what modern Japan was imagined to be. It was this imagining of a modern Japan that undermined the utility of languages other than Japanese, the very concept of utility itself being anchored in language ideology. This chapter has shown that regardless of whether a language has a long history (Ainu) or a short one (Creole English), is part of the same language family as Japanese (Ryukyuan languages) or is not (Ainu, Creole English), had many speakers (Ryukyuan) or few (Creole English), was used for wider communication (Creole English in the Marianas under Japanese occupation) or was more restricted in its use (Ryukyuan, Ainu), or had a history of writing (Okinawan) or no written form (Ainu, Creole English), Japan's minority languages were consistently viewed as a problem, and their solution always to require the creation of a monolingual regime. No other option was considered viable, for none agreed with notions of progress as defined by dominant ideology. In present-day Japan, however, modernist ideology has been exposed as just one deliberate choice among many, and this kind of late-modern insight encourages reflection on the consequences of modernity, one of them being the way in which languages were regimented and a hierarchy imposed on them. Reflection on modernity brings challenge just as it brings change, and it is to this that we shall turn next.

8 Current Challenges to Modernist Language Ideology

Over the last 20 years, modernist language ideology in Japan has found itself undermined from two directions, migration movements and reflection on modernity, both challenging the modernist idea of nation, state and language as an inseparable trinity. This led to doubts about the validity of the claims made by modernist ideology. It also led to emancipation efforts from all those who are not considered to be a constitutive part of what Japan is imagined to be. This not withstanding, language ideology is not easily to be displaced, as we shall see in this chapter.

Modernist ideology's claims have never accurately reflected the complexities of Japan's sociolinguistic situation, and while ideology as a self-fulfilling prophecy has done much to close this gap (see Chapter 7), the number of people aware that such a gap exists is on the rise. At the same time as modernity and its impact on language and society are being reflected upon, migration is reintroducing linguistic diversity to Japan in the form of immigrant languages. A new awareness and recognition of linguistic diversity within Japan is the effect. This increases the possibility of clashes between the ideology of linguistic homogeneity and the multilingualism on the ground. Such growing awareness of linguistic diversity gives rise to contradictions, between belief and self-image on the one hand, and the linguistic experiences of daily life on the other, and these contradictions must to be understood as harbingers of change (Coulmas, 2005).

Somewhat ironically perhaps, the review of immigration control legislation carried out in 1990 represents something of a watershed in the ideological perception of linguistic and cultural diversity in Japan. At the time, Japan attempted to tackle a shortfall in its labour force by granting the descendants of Japanese emigrants to South America (*nikkeijin*) unrestricted entry to Japan, only to find that the *nikkeijin* posed a significant threat to deeply entrenched ideologies of Japanese identity. *Nikkeijin* lack of or shortcomings in Japanese language proficiency were one such aspect (Kajita, 1994). The arrival of these so-called newcomer (*nyūkamā*) immigrants effectively created a new minority within Japanese society, rather than being the homecoming of 'majority Japanese' as the makers of new migration legislation imagined it would be. The arrival of these newcomers made it clear that no policy, no concepts and no ideology of how to deal with linguistic diversity within Japan existed. It did not exist because diversity within Japan in the form of autochthonous minorities had been ignored.

The Case of Autochthonous Minorities

Challenges to modernist language ideology from Japan's autochthonous minorities are certainly not unheard of. Throughout history, there have been examples of individuals able to see through ideology and point out its lack of connection to the more complex sociolinguistic reality (see Clarke, 1997; Siddle, 1999 for past accounts). In the words of John Maher (2001: 343), 'advocacy of cultural and linguistic pluralism in Japan is not a postmodern phenomenon but advocacy has a heritage'. What is different today, however, is the widespread popularity of such views and the increased support for ideologies and linguistic practices that run counter to modernist ideology. It is no longer possible to hide or explain away linguistic diversity with language ideology. Let us consider this with regard to the Ainu first.

The Ainu

As we saw in Chapter 5, the Ainu were found to be so different that they could only be portrayed as a 'dying people' once the idea of a Japanese language nation was introduced to Japan at the end of the 19th century. It became generally accepted for much of the 20th century that, as such, the best way to deal with their presence was to have them somehow dissolve into the Japanese nation. While their linguistic and cultural differences from ethnic Japanese led to widespread discrimination of the Ainu, these differences also made it easy for them to distance themselves from the ideological claim that they are ethnically Japanese. In 2008, the Ainu were formally recognized as an indigenous minority in Japan. In the following, we will briefly review the events that led up to this official recognition, and consider its impact both on Ainu language and on modernist language ideology.

In 1986, former Prime Minister Nakasone stated categorically that Japan was monoethnic and monolingual. His remark sparked a resurgence in Ainu activisim. One year later, in 1987, the Japanese government reported to a UN request that Ainu indeed existed in Japan, but that they did not constitute an ethnic minority as they were only individuals. In 1991, the Japanese government acknowledged at another UN request that the Ainu were an ethnic minority. From this, the Ainu found support, first in the international arena and then closer to home, for their efforts to free themselves from the ideologies and policies that had for so long denied their existence. Their emancipation was aided greatly by the United Nation's Year of Indigenous People in 1993, which was followed by the Decade of the World's Indigenous People. The 1990s saw the establishment of Ainu conversation classes (Komatsu, 2000), Ainu speech contests (DeChicchis, 1995) and Ainu newspapers, textbooks and radio programmes (Maher, 2001). While these activies were relatively few in number and of limited scope, they nevertheless marked a concerted effort to maintain the Ainu language and seek its recognition as one of Japan's languages. In 1994, Kayano Shigeru became the first Ainu to be elected to the National Diet, delivering his inauguration speech first in Ainu and then in Japanese. Kayano was well aware that language shift and the cultural loss that accompanies it are neither quasi-natural nor an inevitable consequence of modernity. Like many Ainu activists, Kayano (1994: 154) believed such loss to have been deliberately orchestrated, and in the same year as his election to the Diet he commented that it was the assimilation and suppression policies of the state which were responsible for the decline of the Ainu language and culture.

Ainu activists pushed for more than a decade for the repeal of the discriminatory Hokkaido Former Aborigines Protection Act of 1899, and in 1997 it was replaced by the Law for the Promotion of Ainu Culture and the Dissemination and Advocacy for the Traditions of the Ainu and the Ainu Culture (*Ainu bunka no shinkō narabi ni Ainu dentō nado ni kansuru chishiki no fukyū oyobi keihatsu ni kansuru hōritsu*). However, the Ainu wanted the new law to contain:

(1) A declaration of basic human rights to eliminate discrimination.
(2) Assurances regarding the protection of human rights.
(3) The establishment of a fund to promote Ainu self-reliance.
(4) The establishment of consultative bodies on Ainu policies.
(5) Consideration of the promotion of Ainu culture. (Dubreuil, 2007)

Only the last of these demands found its way into the final draft, and as a result, the struggle for Ainu emancipation continues today. In order to promote Ainu culture in accordance with the new law, the Foundation for Research and Promotion of Ainu Culture (*Ainu bunka shinkō kenkyū suishin kikō*) was established in June 1997. Among its various activities, the foundation offers Ainu language classes and language teacher training (see FRPAC, 2007).

A further step towards recognition of the Ainu as an indigenous minority of Japan was made during Hokkaido's hosting of the G8 summit in 2008, with the presentation of a petition, signed by more than 6600 people, requesting that Prime Minister Fukuda grant the Ainu *senjūmin* (indigenous) status. Finally, on 6 June 2008, both Houses of the Diet passed the Resolution Calling for the Recognition of the Ainu People as an Indigenous People of Japan (*Ainu minzoku o senjūminzoku to suru koto o mitomeru kokkai ketsugi*). Crucial to this surprisingly sudden shift in policy was Japan's signing in 2007 of the UN Declaration on the Rights of Indigenous Peoples (see Lewallen, 2008 for details). Japan's subsequent recognition of the Ainu's indigenous status was accompanied by the establishment of a comprehensive policy to deal with Ainu issues, and contained the following statement:

> In the course of Japan's modernization, many Ainu were discriminated against, despite being equal national citizens by law. We must solemnly react to the historical fact that [the Ainu] have been driven into great poverty. That the honour and dignity of all indigenous people be protected, and their culture and pride transmitted to subsequent generations is [in accordance] with the development of an international society. (Shūgi'in, 2008)

Although the direction of future Ainu policy is currently under discussion, concrete measures are yet to be agreed upon and implemented (see Winchester, 2009). At the present time, no form of ethnic education has been accommodated into mainstream Japanese education, and Ainu language instruction remains limited to those courses offered by the various Ainu associations.

John Maher (2001: 344) observed 10 years ago that reversing language shift requires political struggle. Today, political struggle in the name of greater autonomy for the Ainu is well underway, and language issues are fully incorporated into the agenda (Kimura, 2011), with bodies such as The Expert Council on the Current State of Ainu Policy (*Ainu seisaku no arikata ni kansuru yūshikisha kondankai*), which released its first report in July 2009, of particular importance in pursuing the goals of Ainu language activism in the political arena. Needless to say, a language brought so close to the brink of extinction as Hokkaido Ainu is difficult to maintain and revitalize. A report by the Ainu language expert, Nakagawa Hiroshi, covers therefore a wide range of topics relating to language status, corpus and prestige language planning, but perhaps of most relevance to this book, Nakagawa cites negative language ideological associations with regard to Ainu as one of the fundamental obstacles to language revitalization. In his consideration of the future of Ainu language education, Nakagawa warns that

> while it is of course important to view the incorporation of Ainu language education into mainstream public education (at elementary school level, for example) as a future ideal, it is also important to be aware of the dangers inherent in such a move, at least at this time. This is due to the fact that sufficient knowledge and concern about this subject on the part of teachers is currently lacking. The introduction of a subject to the education system by people who lack knowledge thereof, [...] would, due to the general tendency of Japanese society to reject people who are different, be highly likely to result in discrimination. (Nakagawa, 2009: 7)

The need to change standing ideologies on minorities and, more crucially, on the assumed homogeneity of Japanese nationals, which is the very base for rejecting what is singled out to be different, is clearly evident in Nakagawa's assessment.

Also in 2009, a Comprehensive Ainu Policy Office was established within the Cabinet Secretariat. While the institutions, meetings and declarations detailed above are important manifestations of a re-evaluation of Ainu language and culture, it remains to be seen whether these will be accompanied by an ideological departure from modernist language ideological beliefs. The question of whether the Ainu language receives the support and recognition it does today because it no longer poses a threat to the perception of Japan as monolingual is a difficult one to answer, for the linguistic reality of Ainu can only be described as dire (see Chapter 7). For this reason, some Ainu activists see little benefit in focusing resources on a language that has already lost the last of its speakers to use that language for daily communication. As Chisato Dubreuil comments,

> We have to face the fact that the Japanese language is the language of Japan. The Ainu language will never again be the 'spoken' language of the Ainu people, and to now throw money at us for Ainu language study is hypocritical! (Dubreuil, 2007)

Whether Dubreuil is correct to assume that the Ainu language will never be the spoken language of the Ainu again is still open to conjecture. What is certain, however, is that fostering Ainu as a minority language within a state that proclaims itself to be monolingual is a decidedly futile exercise, and therefore of little benefit to any future speakers of Ainu. To what extent ideological views about minority languages in Japan are undergoing change may be further explored in the case of the Ryukyuan languages and efforts to maintain them.

The Ryukyuans

The Ryukyuan languages are less endangered than Hokkaido Ainu (UNESCO, 2009), making it easier for their speakers to resist the ideological claim that Japan is monolingual and that, by logical extension, all Japanese can be defined via one historically shared national language. On the other hand, of course, the principal justification for the assimilation of Ryukyuans into the Japanese nation was the claim that their languages constitute 'greater dialects' of Japan's national language.

It is clear by now that language ideology cannot be in place if it is contradicted and a more meaningful ideology is offered in its place. At present, however, no such viable alternative exists, and while the perception of modernist language ideology as a simplification of the sociolinguistic field is increasingly acknowledged, modernist ideology continues to dominate language life in the Ryukyus. Evidence of this may be found in the fact that the vast majority of both Ryukyuans and Japanese continue to refer to Ryukyuan languages as *hōgen*, meaning dialect. Such conceptualization of the Ryukyuan languages also manifests in popular use and in the media (see Sugita, 2011), as well as in linguistic research (see Fija *et al.*, 2009 for a discussion). In other words, for most Japanese, the language varieties spoken in the Ryukyu Islands do not constitute a contradiction to the ideological claim that all Japanese can be defined by their sharing a common national language. This is perhaps the greatest difference between this situation and that in Ainu Mosir.

The reason for the Ryukyuan languages not being considered languages in their own right has its roots deep within a language ideology that negates the possibility of languages other than national language existing in Japan. To the modernist mind, the Ainu languages did not represent a significant challenge, for dominant ideology claimed that they would soon retreat, and so they did, thereby fulfilling the prophecy. With the Ryukyuan language varieties, however, Heinrich (2010b) has argued that there exist today four possible ways of conceptualizing them in relation to Japanese. The first is to claim that language and dialect cannot be distinguished. The second, that the Ryukyuan language varieties are simultaneously both languages and dialects. The third possibility is that regional languages are dialects of national language, while the fourth views them as languages in their own right. These four conclusions stem from quite different and even contradictory language ideological views. Those claiming that no distinction between language and dialect can be made view language as detached from its speakers, despite considerable evidence to the contrary (see Coulmas, 2009). Their stance deems the structures and system of a language to be autonomous from its speakers (see e.g. Uemura, 2003). Since language and dialect cannot be distinguished according to such stance, they most often uphold the dominating view, that is, claim that the Ryukyuan languages are dialects. Proponents of the view that the Ryukyuan varieties are both language and dialect at the same time are on the other hand highly aware of the influence of power on ontology and thus content themselves with deconstructing the relationship between ontology and power (see e.g. Maher, 1997). Those claiming that the Ryukyuan varieties are dialects of Japanese base everything on the premise that there is only one language in Japan, giving no justification for what they consider to be a logical and common-sense approach (see e.g. Kokuritsu Kokugo Kenkyūjo, 1963). Finally, those claiming that Ryukyuan varieties constitute languages in their own right value linguistic diversity and see minority languages and their speakers as worthy of protection and support (see e.g. Gottlieb, 2005; Osumi, 2001). It is worth noting here that linguistics is not detached from language ideology, but is an important part thereof (see Heinrich, 2002; Koyama, 2003 for the case of Japan). Having considered these four possible conceptualizations of Ryukyuan languages, we shall restrict the following discussion to the last of these, for only this stance represents a challenge to modernist language ideology in Japan, while outside Japan this is how these languages are generally perceived (see e.g. Grimes, 2000; Herbermann, 1997; Klose, 1987; Ruhlen, 1987; UNESCO, 2009; Voegelin, 1977).

Efforts to maintain the Ryukyuan languages have become far more prominent in the last 20 years (see Hara, 2005 for an overview). The most organized efforts to maintain local languages to date have been made by the *Uchinaaguchi fukyū kyōgikai* (Society for Uchinaaguchi Revitalization). Founded in the year 2000 (Ryūkyū Shinpō, 2000) as the *Okinawa hōgen fukyū kyōgikai* (The Society for Okinawan Dialect Revitalization), the society renamed itself in 2006. Amongst other things, it has tasked itself with orthographic development, textbook compilation and local language teacher training (see Miyara, 2010a). Its vice president, linguistics professor Miyara Shinshō, has repeatedly argued in favour of the Ryukyuan language varieties being treated as languages in their own right, and has supported his arguments with detailed accounts of Ryukyuan phonetics, lexicon and morphosyntax (e.g. Miyara, 2008, 2010b). Among the most significant achievements of the *Uchinaaguchi fukyū kyōgikai* have been the creation of Community Language Day (*shimakutuba no hi*) and the successful lobbying of Okinawa

Prefecture to establish a Community Language Deliberation Committee (*Shimakutuba Kentō I'inkai*).

The first *shimakutuba no hi*, or Community Language Day, was held at the Central Community Centre in Naha on 18 September 2005 (see Ishihara, 2010 for a discussion), and has been held annually since. In Uchinaaguchi (Okinawan), September 18 may be read *ku-tu-ba* (9, 10, 8), meaning language. The first event was reported in the local newspapers, and included a podium discussion on language maintenance, questions to the panellists from the audience, and performances of local music and dance. It lasted for two hours and was attended by around a hundred people, and it closed with the endorsement of a Community Language Day Declaration (*shimakutuba no hi sengen*) demanding greater language rights for four speech communities identified within Okinawa Prefecture. The declaration stated:

> On the occasion of this first 'Community Language Day' of 18 September 2005 [...], and taking the importance of community language into consideration, we adopt the following declaration. In accordance with the Universal Declaration of Linguistics Rights recognized as an international convention by the United Nations, we, the present assembly, request of the state and the prefecture that [the demands of] this declaration be swiftly implemented.
> (1) Recognition of the Okinawa language (on Okinawa Island and neighbouring islands), Miyako language (in Miyako District), Yaeyama language (in Yaeyama District excluding Yonaguni Island) and Yonaguni language as native speech communities on the basis of the Universal Declaration of Linguistics Rights [drafted] in Barcelona on 6 June 1996. [...]
> (2) The individual members of the aforementioned speech communities be afforded the inviolable rights stated below:
>   (a) The right to use these languages in private and in public.
>   (b) The right to receive training and education to [attain] proficiency of expression of these native local languages.
>   (c) The right to be received in these languages at official and public facilities.
> (3) The speech communities identified above be afforded the right to [receive] funds and institutional support necessary to enable the future transmission of these native local languages. (SHSJI, 2005)

The above demands are as yet to be met. However, in a discussion on language rights in Japan, Kimura (2011) identifies the Community Language Day Declaration as being part of a greater discourse on language rights currently taking place in Japan. Following Utada (2008), Kimura sees this discourse as having a series of cyclical stages, sequentially addressing (1) the question of why language rights are necessary in the first place; (2) what kind of language rights should be granted to whom and why; and (3) how demands for greater language rights can be implemented through policy. The demands of the Society for Uchinaaguchi Revitalization are part of the second circle, but are somewhat detached from the academic discussions of the first, which deals with the question of why language rights are necessary at all (see e.g. Gengoken Kenkyū-kai, 1999). Following Kimura's (2011) discussion on the Community Language Day Declaration, we must now wait to see how scholars, policy makers and education experts will react to the demands for language rights.

The first Community Language Day, which I attended almost by accident while conducting research in Uchinaa, was a rather modest affair, with little to suggest that it might one day be significant to many more than just the members and supporters of the Society for Uchinaaguchi Revitalization. However, the event gained immediate, and rather unexpected, support by a visit of Peruvian-born descendents of Okinawan migrants to their ancestral homeland in early 2006. Their visit was part of the centennial commemoration of Okinawan migration to South America, and many local people were surprised to learn that these Peruvian visitors had maintained Uchinaaguchi far more successfully than they themselves had. The Society for Uchinaaguchi Revitalization was at the time in discussions with the prefectural administration over language maintenance, and Community Language Day became more widely known among prefectural administrators and politicians as a result. Following these discussions and the show of support from the Peruvian visitors, a resolution demanding prefectural support for Community Language Day was submitted and approved by the Prefectural Assembly in March 2006 (Okinawa Taimusu, 2006). Law No. 35 of the resolution contains the following in reference to Community Language Day:

Paragraph 1

Community language, the intergenerational transmission of which has been interrupted in all regions of the prefecture, is the cultural basis of this prefecture and in view of the necessity to transmit community language to the following generations, to increase interest in and knowledge of prefectural citizens towards community language, and in order to promote the spread of community language, Community Language Day is to be established.

Paragraph 2

Community Language Day is set as 18 September.

Paragraph 3

(3.1) Centred on this specific day, the prefecture supports endeavours of raising public awareness on Community Language Day and of carrying out projects aimed at proliferating community language.

(3.2) The prefecture supports requests by municipalities and related organizations for projects aimed at proliferating community language.
(Quoted from Ishihara, 2010: 140–141)

At the time of writing, Community Language Day has been held five times, and is today well known throughout the prefecture and widely reported in the local media, which also organizes special coverage related to Ryukyuan languages on this day. Fija and Heinrich (2007) have commented on this legislation that prefectural 'support for *shimakutuba no hi* in 2006 [...] must be seen as an important symbolic contribution to Okinawan language revitalisation since, for the first time ever, Okinawa Prefecture was acting in support of the local languages'.

Closely related to the legislative support received by Community Language Day was the establishment of a Community Language Investigation Committee (*Shimakutuba Kentō I'inkai*) in October 2008. The committee is attached to the prefectural government's Division of Cultural Affairs. It was created with the aim of (Shimakutuba Kentō I'inkai, 2008: 7) 'planning affairs relevant to successfully maintaining and transmitting community language', and is made up of 'persons experienced in academic fields related to community language'. After regularly meeting for one year, the committee issued its first report in September 2009.

Let us consider what the report has to say with regard to issues relating to language ideology. In the second section of the report (Shimakutuba Kentō I'inkai, 2009), the committee refers to the 2009 UNESCO *Atlas of the World's Languages in Danger of Disappearing*, which lists all Ryukyuan languages either as severely or definitely endangered. While UNESCO recognizes the Ryukyuan languages as languages in their own right, however, the committee's report is somewhat less assertive, using both the terms community language (*shimakutuba*) and dialect (*hōgen*). This is perhaps less surprising when we learn that six of the seven committee members were in fact national language dialectologists, that is, scholars who have published extensively on the Ryukyuan languages while framing them as dialects. In other words, these committee members represent the very language ideology brokers responsible for disseminating and promoting modernist language ideology. Thus, only one committee member remained to argue the case for recognition of the Ryukyuan languages as languages in their own right, Miyara

Shinshō. Miyara, vice president of the Society for Uchinaaguchi Revitalization, was the driving force behind the creation of Community Language Day, as well as negotiating the establishment of the committee with prefectural governor Nakaima Hirokazu. This notwithstanding, the appointment of 'persons experienced in academic fields related to community language' to the committee Miyara had helped found led to his being sidelined within it.

The third section of the report contains a brief historical summary of the oppression of the local languages, mentioning the Movement for the Enforcement of Standard Language (*Hyōjungo reikō undō*), the use of dialect tags (*hōgen fuda*) and the interruption of natural intergenerational language transmission. The ideology behind these measures is not addressed, however, nor is the question of which language ideological views must be tackled in order to successfully maintain and revitalize the Ryukyuan languages. The fourth and final section of the report, meanwhile, details the importance of promoting documentation and transmission of language. In a passage describing the importance of school education for local language maintenance, the committee writes:

> The Ministry of Education specifies in its 2008 Outline for Guidance of School Education (*Gakkō kyōiku shidō yōryō*) that 'studies are undertaken on matters relating to regional livelihood, tradition and culture etc., or on regional and other specific characteristics of the school'. Accordingly, we believe that efforts should be made to [include] community language as [part of] traditional culture in school education. (Shimakutuba Kentō I'inkai, 2009: 4)

What cannot be ignored is that this proposal to include local languages in the Japanese school curriculum accepts as equal all regional cultures within Japan, ignoring the idea that certain regions within Japan possess regional languages and cultures that differ from the dominant one, and might therefore be treated differently. In other words, the ideology of a linguistically and culturally unified Japan is here being reproduced, even in a call for community language education by an expert committee on community languages in Okinawa Prefecture.

The meta-language of the report also warrants attention. The preference for the term *shimakutuba* – with *shima* referring to local community and *kutuba* to language – over Japanese terms such as *Okinawago* (Okinawa language), *chi'iki gengo* (local language) or *shōsū gengo* (minority language) serves to downplay the shift from existing language ideology by which there can be no other language in Japan but Japanese. While this strategy has proven quite successful for shifting ideology with as uncontroversially as possible, some have criticized use of this term, *shimakutuba*, as unscientific, citing the more scientific equivalent as *hōgen* (dialect) (Nohara, 2009).

Attempting to reverse language shift by politicizing the issue, as the Ainu have done, is largely avoided by Ryukyuans, for the very reason that nation, state and citizenship are seen as congruent in Japan. Pushing the interests of an endangered minority language on such an ideological basis would exclude all those who speak or possess a heritage language other than Japanese from the Japanese nation, and exclusion is a price too high to pay even for those seeking to maintain the endangered Ryukyuan languages. As I have written elsewhere,

> membership to the Japanese nation is tantamount to Japanese ethnicity, which is in turn defined by national language, i.e. (Standard) Japanese. Re-conceptualizing Ryukyuan languages as languages in their own right thus raises the question of ethnicity and, what is more, of nationality. [...] The idea of the Japanese nation having built the Japanese state, gives nation precedence over state. Under such conditions, ethnicity is the prerequisite for membership to the state. (Heinrich, 2011: 47)

Most people are not fully aware of these complex relationships, however, and for this reason, although ultimately the dominant modernist language ideology may well find itself under attack in the Ryukyus, for the time being at least it remains firmly in place. How else could there be such a prominent lack of understanding of the deliberate oppression of Ryukyuan languages through ideology and the negative perceptions it creates? And how else could the very foundation of that ideology, the claim that the Ryukyuan languages are in fact Japanese, go effectively unchallenged, even in the face of considerable evidence to the contrary? Indeed, many Ryukyuan language specialists themselves rationalize and reinforce these modernist concepts, most of them unaware that they are doing so, clinging steadfastly to their academic standards and the ideological perspectives that accompany them. Let us see, whether and to what extent migrant languages undermine these seemingly ineffaceable language ideological assumptions. Assumptions which, to repeat, emerged only in the Meiji-period (1868–1912).

The Case of Allochthonous Minorities

We shall consider the case of Japan's allochthonous minorities first by taking into account the historical background, demographic developments and educational experiences of migrant language communities, and then by assessing the consequences thereof for the dominant language ideology. With regard to migrant communities in Japan, a distinction is commonly made between the so-called newcomers (in Japanese, *nyūkamā*) and oldcomers (*orudokamā*). For the sake of convenience I will use both terms in the following. The oldcomers are mainly those migrants of Korean or Chinese descent. This includes those groups known in Japanese as *zainichi kankokujin* (literally, Resident South Koreans), *zainichi chōsenjin* (Resident Koreans), *zainichi chūgokujin* (Resident Chinese) and *kakyō* (Overseas Chinese). In 2007, the number of Chinese nationals residing in Japan surpassed that of Korean nationals for the first time, with a total of 606,889 Chinese registered, as compared with 593,489 Koreans (Statistics Bureau, 2008). Overall, Koreans and Chinese amount for half of Japan's 2.2 million foreign residents, and with about 10,000 Koreans newly naturalized as Japanese nationals every year, and with more than 80% of Korean marriages in Japan being mixed, the number of Koreans resident in Japan is set to decrease further still. This demographic development of oldcomer communities is even more remarkable when one learns that the 1980 census listed 664,536 Koreans as registered in Japan, but only 52,896 Chinese (Wetherall, 1987: 313). Comparison with the 2008 census gives some idea of the extent of the influx of Chinese newcomer migration that began in the 1980s, and includes significant numbers of repatriated war orphans, as well as a large number of students who entered the Japanese workforce after graduation (see Beech, 2008).

The newcomers may be broadly divided into working-class immigrants and the so-called Chinese war orphans and their families. The term war orphans is a generic term used to describe both Japanese children (*zanryū koji*, literally stranded orphans) and women (*zanryū fujin*, meaning stranded women) abandoned in China during the hasty and chaotic retreat of the Japanese Army at the end of the Pacific War. As such, they are of Japanese decent, but Chinese by nationality. The number of war orphans and their families repatriated with the financial support of the Japanese government was around 5000 in 1994 (Maher, 1995a: 127), but rose sharply to 17,093 by 1997 (Tomozawa, 2001: 133). The working-class immigrants, on the other hand, consist mainly of *nikkeijin*, the descendents of Japanese emigrants. The majority of these are Brazilian *nikkeijin*, amounting to 316,000 in 2008. Together with the second largest contingent, the Peruvian *nikkeijin*, this number totals 376,663 immigrants, again a dramatic increase on earlier figures. In 1989, for example, Brazilian and Peruvian *nikkeijin* totalled just 18,649 (Tanaka, 1995: 218).

Another immigrant group to have seen rapid growth in the last years consists of university students and professionals, whose educational and economic backgrounds place them in a relatively elite class. Unlike the other communities we have looked at in the previous chapters, in this group, bilingualism is viewed not as a burden but as an indication of skill and talent (see Kanno, 2008). Hence, bilingualism within this group is accepted accordingly, something that is clearly not the case with other bilinguals in Japan. Similarly, the oldcomer and newcomer experiences differ considerably, and we shall examine this in more detail below, beginning with the oldcomers.

The Oldcomers

Oldcomers reside mainly in urban areas, with a third of those of Korean descent living in Osaka. Today, more than 90% of Koreans listed as resident in Japan were born and raised there (Ryang, 1997: 3). Long-established Chinatowns are to be found in Yokohama, Nagasaki and Kobe, though due to newcomer migration, most Chinese in Japan live today in the greater Tokyo area.

Japan, China and Korea have been in contact throughout history, and Korean and Chinese communities have always existed in Japan as a result. Until the Meiji period (1868–1912), however, these communities remained fairly small. With the colonization of Taiwan in 1895, and Korea in 1910, these residents became imperial subjects of Japan, and by the early Shōwa period (1926–1989), their numbers had grown considerably, in part due to the practice of indentured labour. By the end of the Pacific War, about half of the Koreans living in Japan were there against their own will, often forced to live and work in harsh and degrading conditions (see Sakhaee Kashani, 2006; Weiner, 1989 for detailed accounts). It is of little surprise, therefore, that many Koreans chose to return to their homeland after the war, and of 2.1 million Koreans registered as living in Japan in 1945, by March of the following year only 650,000 remained. In December 1946, the Japanese government announced that its repatriation of Koreans was at an end. This was accompanied by a resolution stating that all children of the remaining Koreans resident in Japan would be expected to enroll in state education forthwith (see Hanami, 1995). The case of the Chinese community is both less drastic and involved less people. After almost two years of uncertainty about their status in Japan, almost one million Chinese and Korean residents became legally classifies as aliens in accordance with the newly enacted Alien Registration Law (*Gaikokujin tōrokurei*) of 1947. They nevertheless retained Japanese nationality until the San Francisco Peace Treaty of 1952 ended the Allied Occupation of Japan and restored Japanese sovereignty. Thereafter, they were granted resident status on condition that they adopt either Korean or Chinese nationality.

Many of these residents set up schools reflecting their own cultural values. Chinese ethnic schools have a long history in Japan, stretching back to the late-19th century. In 1897, the Datong School opened in Yokohama, to be rebuilt and renamed on several occasions before its present-day incarnation, the Yokohama Yamate Chinese School. The Overseas Chinese School in Nagasaki closed in 1988, but other such schools are to be found in Kobe, Osaka and Tokyo. These schools serve both oldcomer and newcomer Chinese, the ratio of these in Yokohama being approximately 2:1, respectively. In other cities, particularly Tokyo and Osaka, the percentage of newcomers has notably risen steadily in recent years. These Chinese ethnic schools all have dual Japanese and Chinese language programmes (see Kanno, 2008: 59–82), which Maher (1995a: 136) identifies as providing 'a model for bilingual education in Japan'.

Koreans residents, too, set about establishing ethnic schools in the years following World War II, largely in an effort to help maintain the Korean language as an integral part of their identity. Their number was far greater than that of the Chinese schools, however, with more than 500 in existence in the immediate post-war years, when Korean parents sought to prepare their children for the possibility of returning to their ancestral homeland. Attending a Korean school was the only alternative to Japanese-medium education for these children, for Japan's language education policy-makers never considered providing bilingual education for its non-Japanese residents (Fujita-Round & Maher, 2008: 398).

Japan's Korean residents were not unaffected by the division of the Korean Peninsula following World War II, being forced to pledge their allegiances either to the north or to the south. Accordingly, two separate Korean resident organizations were formed, the Korean Resident Union (commonly referred to as *Mindan*) being affiliated to South Korea, and the General Association of Korean Residents in Japan (or *Chongryon*) to North Korea (see Ryang, 1997: 77–129 for details). Both organizations operate their own schools, but *Chongryon* has been the more proactive in this respect, at one time managing more than 200 ethnic schools. This number has dropped to about 60 in recent years, however, largely as a result of changing attitudes towards North Korea in general, as well as to the perceived importance of maintaining Korean as a community language in Japan. *Mindan*, meanwhile, operates just two Korean ethnic schools in Osaka, one in Tokyo and a fourth in Kyoto. The vast majority of these ethnic Koreans today consider Japan their home (Ryang, 2009), and because of this the future of Korean ethnic schools is somewhat uncertain. The number of students enrolled therein has declined sharply, from over 46,000 in the early 1970s to just 15,000 today (McBride, 2008), with the majority of Korean school children, around 86%, enrolled in Japanese schools today (Maher & Kawanishi, 1995: 89). The curriculum of the ethnic schools has been revised several times in response to this decline in students, with Japanese language now featuring more heavily than ever before in the mixed Japanese–Korean language programme employed today at all Korean ethic schools.

The existence of these Korean and Chinese communities does not directly contradict modernist language ideology's claim to a linguistically homogenous Japan, nor does it invalidate that ideology either. Rather, such questions go largely ignored, pushed aside by state institutions wishing to avoid such controversial topics, and thereby effectively outsourcing them to parallel institutions not supported by the state. Like Japan's autochthonous language minorities, the Korean and Chinese communities, too, are experiencing language shift (Kanno, 2008; Maher, 1995a, 1995b; Vasishth, 1997). Just as with autochthonous minority language shift, however, this serves to reinforce the modernist claim of linguistic homogeneity. The ideological context within which these communities make their language choices offers them two options. The first is to accept assimilation under the pretence of being 'like everyone else', but with the ever-present threat of exclusion on ethnic, linguistic and cultural grounds. The second, meanwhile, is to assert one's difference, thereby accepting exclusion and seeking to establish parallel institutions such as schools and labour markets. Neither option presents a challenge to modernist language ideology, because both have as an inevitable consequence that ethnic minority groups in Japan remain ideologically invisible.

The invisibility of minorities includes their institutions, with neither *Chongryon* nor *Mindan* schools ever being officially accredited by the Ministry of Education. Consequently, these schools have received little in the way of government subsidies, while their students have faced discrimination when attempting to enrol in Japanese educational institutions, or to enter the Japanese labour market. It is almost as if the Japanese state were attempting to punish all those not falling in line with the myth of cultural and linguistic homogeneity. Cary thus aptly comments that by 'refusing to confer fullfledged school status to Korean ethnic schools and to recognise and support the existence of a well-developed Korean-language school system operating throughout Japan, the government reinforces the view that diversity is not valued in Japanese society' (Cary, 2001: 106). It is not valued precisely because it contradicts and diverges from Japan's monolingual self-image, John Maher therefore concluding that for Koreans

> to even suggest the possibility of government-sponsored bilingual education for the Korean community is unthinkable. [...] The guiding concept of cultural pluralism which positively welcomes ethnic and linguistic diversity hardly exists in Japan. The absence of a social consensus which

may support Korean bilingualism may be attributed to two sets of factors: firstly the systematic attempt on the part of the Japanese during the colonial era, both in Japan and in Korea, to eliminate the Korean language and culture; and secondly a still prevalent obsession with racial homogeneity, uniqueness and racial purity, and a fear that ethnic diversity will upset the social order. (Maher, 1995b: 169)

In other words, language ideology claiming homogeneity overrides the existence of genuine linguistic diversity in the case of oldcomer minorities. Let us consider now the case of newcomers, and see to what extent their existence has challenged dominant language ideology.

The Newcomers

In view of commonly held beliefs about Japanese society, it is not hard to see how the presence of immigrants could be seen as problematic by institutions of all kinds. Migration to Japan has proved a controversial issue since it began to feature heavily in public debate from the end of the 1980s onwards. At that time, the need to compensate for labour shortages led companies to pressure politicians to allow unskilled foreign workers into Japan, and the government was forced to decide whether or not Japan should open its doors to immigration. This was no easy decision, and both available options were believed to have substantial drawbacks. On one hand, there was concern that the presence of immigrant communities within Japanese society would fundamentally change its character, and was therefore an idea many were opposed to. On the other hand, a shortage of unskilled workers to fill the so-called 3D jobs – dirty, dangerous and demeaning (which could equally be identified in Japanese as 3K jobs – *kitanai*, *kiken* and *kitsui*) – called for an immediate solution. Faced with an obvious dilemma, the government opted for a compromise, increasing the opportunities for skilled workers to enter Japan, and allowing the descendants of Japanese emigrants, down to the third generation, unrestricted entry to Japan. Japan thereby met the shortage of unskilled workers without actually changing its policy of not allowing unskilled foreigners entry (Hirataka *et al.*, 2001: 165). It was assumed that, owing to their Japanese ancestry, the *nikkeijin* descendants would understand at least a degree of Japanese, and, on this basis, that they would reintegrate readily into Japanese society. Today, there is a great deal of evidence to the contrary, and this assumption now seems to have been rather naive (see e.g. de Carvalho, 2003; Shikama, 2008).

The years following the June 1990 revision of the Immigration Control and Refugee Recognition Act (*Shutsunyūkoku kanri oyobi nanmin ninteihō*) saw a dramatic increase in the numbers of South American *nikkeijin* migrating to Japan. This gave rise to a range of unforeseen social problems, many relating to the fact that these immigrants, though sharing the 'Japanese blood' of their emigrant ancestors, were often not able to re-enter Japanese society as smoothly as had been expected due to the language barrier. Multilingual information and services had to be established quickly in those areas where the *nikkeijin* were most heavily concentrated (Takahashi & Vaipae, 1996), for example, industrial cities like Hamamatsu in Shizuoka Prefecture, Ota in Gunma Prefecture and Toyota in Aichi Prefecture (see GSTK, 2006 for details).

For regions faced with a sudden influx of such newcomers, one of the greatest challenges has been to effectively accommodate the children of foreign nationals in Japanese schools. By 2004, 120,417 such children between the ages of 6 and 14 were registered in Japan, of whom 70,345 attended Japanese public schools (Kanno, 2008: 13–14). The Japanese Ministry of Education has reacted, albeit slowly, to the problems caused by having foreign language-speaking pupils enrolled in an education system established on the basis that every pupil within that system speaks Japanese as their first language and, moreover, will have received all of their education within that system (Galan, 2005, 2011). Since 1999, the Ministry of Education has begun collecting data on those foreign children in need of additional Japanese language instruction, defining them as follows:

> Necessity of additional Japanese language instruction refers to [...] pupils whose Japanese is insufficient for daily conversation, as well as pupils whose Japanese is sufficient for daily conversation but whose academic vocabulary for their respective grade is insufficient and therefore represents an obstacle to their participation in study activities. (MEXT, 2008)

The 2008 survey identified 28,575 children in need of additional Japanese language instruction – a notable increase from the 18,585 pupils identified in the first survey in 1999. According to the more recent survey, 10,206 of these pupils had Portuguese as their first language, 5978 had Chinese, 3634 Spanish and 7724 spoke other languages (MEXT, 2008). In view of the rather obscure criteria by which these pupils are identified, Kawakami (2006) assumes that the actual number of foreign children experiencing language problems within Japanese schools is likely to be somewhat greater, and this is supported by the fact that 11% of foreign national children in compulsory school education age (6–15 years) are estimated to not visit school, or to no longer visit it (Ōta & Tsuboya, 2005).

It is important to remember, of course, that children with foreign nationality are not obliged to comply with the same laws regarding compulsory school education as their Japanese peers. There are no local government initiatives to ensure that such children receive school education, and while most schools accept such pupils, they see this as 'doing them a favour', perceiving the prime task of the Japanese school system to foster Japanese citizens (Fujita-Round & Maher, 2008: 394). In an important ethnographic survey of Japanese schooling, Kanno provides evidence to suggest that the regularity with which foreign-born children drop out of the education system is largely due to the difficulties of integrating them successfully into the existing system:

> According to one survey report recently issued by Midori Town Board of Education, 38.7 percent of school-age foreign national children (grade 1–9) who reside in this town are not attending any full-time school. [...] In the same way, 70 percent of junior high school-age students who are not attending full-time school have attended elementary schools, suggesting that at some point, Japanese schools failed them. (Kanno, 2008: 141)

Kanno's doubts may be further substantiated when one considers the demographics of those foreign-born children identified as being in need of additional instruction in Japanese. According to the Ministry of Education, 18,142 elementary school students, 7576 middle-school students and 1365 high-school students (MEXT, 2008) are identified as in need of such supplementary tuition. One prominent solution to the problems of having foreign nationality pupils in the Japanese school system is thus to having them gradually excluded from the Japanese school.

In a study of ideology at work within the Japanese education system, Christian Galan concludes that the

> inability to handle cases such as *kikokushijo* (repatriate children), *kaigaishijo* (overseas children) or immigrant children (*nikkeijin* and others) is as much a consequence as a symptom of the Japanese school system. It has always externalised the 'problem' by creating special schools or leaving the 'management' of these children to municipal and extracurricular structures or NGOs. No other industrialised country, to my knowledge, has done this with its repatriate children or immigrant children whose time in special schools or classrooms is generally temporary and transitional, enabling them to be quickly integrated into 'normal' classrooms [...]. Not so in Japan. (Galan, 2011: 86)

Galan thus perceived the problem to be a structural one, in that the Japanese school was never ideologically prepared to deal with the kind of linguistic and cultural diversity represented by the children of newcomer immigrants (see Kojima, 2006; Onai, 2003 for detailed studies). Academia's response to this can be seen in the sudden flurry of new publications dealing with the problems faced not only by Japanese educational establishments, but also by local and regional administrative bodies, teaching staff and foreign-born students themselves (see e.g. Bunkachō Bunkabu Kokugoka, 1997; Hibiya & Hirataka, 2005; Kawakami, 2006; Kojima, 2006; Nuibe, 1999, 2002; OJNSK, 2008; Tajiri et al., 2004). To what extent, and how quickly, such important research can influence current educational practices and the ideologies that underpin them remains to be seen, but certain changes can be predicted with relative certainty (see Chapter 9).

Much of the opposition to plans to restructure the education system is rooted in the ideological claim of linguistic and cultural homogeneity. In that sense, the educational experiences of foreign students urge us to reevaluate the ideologies in question. Sellek makes the point that the presence of newcomer migrants

> also provides an opportunity to reconsider what it means to be 'Japanese'. It also raises questions about the ideological boundary which separates the Japanese from certain national minorities within Japan [...]. The common-sense definition of 'Japaneseness' encompasses both culture and pseudobiological notions of Japanese 'race'. Although *nikkeijin* are descendants of Japanese emigrants and therefore share the same lineage as the Japanese, their languages and culture, customs and behaviour derive from South America. (Sellek, 1997: 201)

Sellek's argument is further strengthened by the fact that the so-called Chinese war-orphans are of Japanese decent, though they speak Chinese as their first language and in most cases choose to keep their Chinese nationality. At the same time, they have little or no connection to the old-comer Overseas Chinese community in Japan because they are not ethnically Chinese (Tomozawa, 2001: 137). Clearly, the Japanese–foreigner dichotomy is just another ideological simplification demanding closer examination by researchers and language education policy makers (Gottlieb, 2007: 38–39; Tai, 2007).

When studying modernist language ideology, we must always remain mindful of the fact that both nation and national language are ideological constructs in dialectic relationship (Silverstein, 2000). Not only foreign nationals, but all those who find themselves between the foreign versus Japanese dichotomy must bridge the gap between the idea of Japan and the realities of Japan. There are already many Japanese of mixed ethnic, cultural and linguistic heritage, and their numbers are growing year on year, today including war-orphans, returnees, the children of mixed marriages, naturalized Japanese, the Deaf, Ainu, Ryukyuans, and Ogasawara and Hachijo Islanders. Because such identities are contradictory within a nation that imagines itself to be homogenous, however, these other forms of 'Japaneseness' are never directly addressed (Heinrich, 2011). Their multilingualism and multiculturalism disturb the idea of Japan, and so efforts are made to accommodate them within the monolingual and monocultural frame. For newcomer migrants this means little, if anything, is done to accommodate their respective first languages, and the same applies for the heritage languages of oldcomers and autochthonous minorities. School education continues to focus on teaching Japanese (national language), reminding us that Japan has never offered Japanese nationals and residents anything but Japanese-medium schooling on the grounds that all pupils are imagined to be linguistically alike (Hirataka *et al.*, 2001; Nakamura, 2006). Inevitably, the only orientation available of how to deal with pupils diverging from dominant language ideology is linguistic mainstreaming.

We have by now seen many times throughout this book that the way in which Japan has been linguistically imagined has never been an accurate reflection of the sociolinguistic situation. We have come to understand, too, that ideology is not necessarily about being right or wrong, but about empowerment, and the legitimization of certain practices, which is why ideology must 'make sense' to be successful. Language ideology is also capable of shaping sociolinguistic realities, and in Japan, speakers of minority languages have shifted to Japanese to such a degree that all the autochthonous languages of Japan other than Japanese are endangered today. Ethnic Chinese and Koreans, too, are shifting to using Japanese in a number of domains, including the family. At the same time, the newcomer immigrants present a new challenge to modernist language ideology in Japan. The difference now is that, while similar efforts are made to mainstream newcomers into the monolingual language regime, the gap between ideology and reality is now more clearly visible today than it was in the past.

Both immigrant and autochthonous minorities in Japan have for a long time accepted the dominant ideology as legitimate and have adjusted their language attitudes and choices accordingly. In so doing, they have been complicit in their own subjugation. Not only has the vitality of community languages decreased as a result, but also minorities have found themselves silenced, and their ability to decide their own fate diminished, too. Dominated in this way, the interests of minority groups have been underrepresented and their life choices restricted – those already lacking power have thus been further disempowered, and the only way out being offered to them has been to fall into line with dominant monolingual and monocultural ideology and practices. As we have seen, this is precisely the route taken by many linguistic minorities throughout the 20th century in Japan.

There are clear signs of change in how language in Japan is imagined ideologically today, however, and various emancipatory movements are to be found striving for the maintenance of their heritage and community languages. The call for greater language rights is the most direct manifestation of political struggle for ideological change, but there are others too. Examination of the modernist language order, of its negative impacts and discrepancies, has gained in its intensity over the last 20 years, undermining the credibility and legitimacy of the dominant ideology, thereby drawing that dominance into question. Counter-ideologies that value linguistic diversity in Japan and seek to support it, rather than eradicating it in the name of progress, may be found too, and so a new connection between minority languages and non-linguistic issues is today in the process of being forged. This new way of framing minority languages ideologically finds reflection in meta-language, where terminological shifts from vanishing language to heritage language, from dialect to language, from foreign language to Japanese community language, and so on, may be seen. As language ideology is not a body of fixed ideas that may be falsified and then displaced, however, but is rather a generative principle forever capable of adapting to generate new meaning in its defence, the challenges we witnessed in the present chapter will not suffice to undo modernist language ideology. Those who wish to see it displaced must be able to provide an alternative means of making sense of language in present-day Japan. In order to do so, they must strengthen their arguments, and possess the kind of power needed to draw others to their cause and to sharing their perspective on language in Japan. In the final chapter of this book, we will assess their prospects, and the future of linguistic diversity in 21st-century Japan.

9 Language Ideology in 21st-century Japan

We began this book with a consideration of how the way we speak is regulated by language ideology, and over the course of the chapters that followed we looked at how the dominant language ideology which accompanied Japanese modernity thereby led to specific language choices. Indeed, we may reasonably assert that it is impossible to speak or write without being influenced by modernist ideologies of what language ought to be. In the course of this book, we discussed the fundamental ideological entities of national language in Japan, their evolution and impact on language and society. Let us first provide a summary of our findings before turning our attention to the prospects for language ideology in 21st-century Japan.

The Fundamental Ideological Entities of *Kokugo*

Language becomes ideologically loaded by the linking of language with non-linguistic matters, some of the most important of these links being concerned with history and society. Of the historical connections, there exists the idea that all Japanese speak Japanese and that they always have done. Another such belief asserts that Japanese is and has always been the first language of all Japanese, and also that it is the only language of Japan. Thus, Japanese constitutes a common bond between all Japanese since time immemorial, as well as a barrier between Japanese and non-Japanese. One more idea holds that Japanese has always been the unitary language it appears to be today, accompanied by an imagined sense of linguistic unity in which regional varieties exist in the form of *hōgen* (dialect), but has no linguistic variation corresponding to social class, milieu or educational background. Such ideology would have us believe that all Japanese nationals have equal access to this uniform national language, and should therefore be equally proficient in its use. Hence, linguistic attitudes and use deviating from this sense of homogeneity should be blamed on the shortcomings of individuals. In this way, the national language is both represented by and may be equated with written Standard Japanese, and the correctness of spoken language may be judged on the basis of written Japanese. All these ideas are parts of that ideology within which Japanese is the national language of Japan and the Japanese constitute a homogenous language nation.

For the purposes of this study, it is in fact irrelevant whether these ideas about language in Japan are right or wrong. The fact that some of them are quite clearly wrong serves only as a reminder that they are ideological, and that they exist to serve a specific purpose. One such purpose is to make sense of the way language is regimented, while another is to foster pride and cohesion among Japanese nationals. Thus, the statements above may be true and ideological as they may be wrong and ideological, and this is perhaps not such a surprise. Rather than being concerned with right and wrong, these ideas were meant to align the Japanese people to the prospect of the Japanese nation. Now let us consider how these ideas, some of which are wrong for this specific reason, have evolved.

How Language Ideological Entities Evolved

The ideological beliefs about language we have encountered in this study were not always seen as common sense, of course, they were made to be so. It must be remembered that what may appear indisputable fact to many today was at one time controversial and open to conjecture. The idea of Japanese being fit for the role of national language, the possibility of finding unity in spoken and written language, the congruence of language, nation and state territory, and the idea of language as transcending social class are all examples of this. These views were either established or became dominant only during the process of modernization. Such modernist language ideology was shaped by members of a counter-elite who came to prominence during the Meiji period, and took inspiration for their own schemes of Japanese (language) modernization from the experiences of their western counterparts. The shift in power from the old premodern elite towards the young counter-elite was an essential precondition to the process of rendering novel views about language and society as common sense.

We understand, thus, that in this way national language is defined in part by the experiences of its speech community. Ideological assertions, therefore, are founded on specific perspectives and experiences, and so two important factors must be taken into consideration when studying Japanese language ideology: the specific circumstances of Japanese modernization, and the specific reactions of Japanese language modernizers to those circumstances. The latter of these is deeply intertwined with issues of power, for it was modernist ideologies which promoted the values, views and behaviour regarding language to be adequate which were closest to those of the dominant language ideology brokers. Many of these brokers owed their status to the positions they held in influential institutions, and their exalted position within Japanese society was crucial to the credibility their arguments attained. Such brokers are empowered to judge and regulate the linguistic behaviour of others, and in order to promote ideology, they need to have access to certain institutions. Most important among these are state institutions, in particular schools and the civil service, for these are the means by which ideas of adequate linguistic behaviour are disseminated, popularized and reinforced.

That some fundamental claims of language ideology are not backed by empirical evidence is not really a problem, because language ideology typically functions by denigrating criticism directed against it. This is due to the fact that ideologies are only accepted where they have become normalized to such an extent that it becomes difficult, if not impossible, to hold an opposing view. As a consequence, the ideological nature of what are seen as common-sense facts is hidden, and so it becomes unnecessary, and therefore unusual, to draw explicit attention to the authority of the dominant ideology. Accordingly, ideologies give rise to the existence of a binary opposition, whereby the self and the familiar are assigned a positive value, while the other and the new are seen as negative. Deviance to and criticism on standing ideology is part of the negative pole. This, then, is the part of ideology which influences linguistic behaviour. Let us thus consider the impact of language ideology on language and society in more detail.

The Impact of Modernist Language Ideology

Modernist language ideology hides the existing sociolinguistic reality. The many consequences of this are far reaching, and of these, three deserve particular attention: the way in which language ideology hides or denigrates language problems, how it affects language attitudes and language choices, and how it influences linguistic research. Let us examine these in detail:

Language ideology hides or denigrates language problems

Language ideology has succeeded in hiding many of the language problems faced in modern Japanese society, and even in rendering some completely irrelevant. This is due to modernist language ideology strengthening and promoting the centre while neglecting the margin which has ethnic, geographical, social and linguistic aspects. What may be considered common sense in terms of language in modern Japan may not necessarily be evident at the linguistic margin, and this results in language problems. Since the margin is expected to behave as part of a uniform and homogenous language nation, however, and because those within it still subscribe to dominant language ideology, the deviations from imagined linguistic homogeneity that are to be found at the margin remain hidden. Language problems are thereby rendered invisible, for where they may be found, they are a potential source of embarrassment, for according to ideological beliefs such problems are evidence of individual shortcomings.

Language ideology affects language attitudes and language choices

Despite its successful modernization, the Japanese language has attracted a great degree of scepticism. While the question of whether Japanese is a good or a meagre language has been settled by its becoming a modern, standardized language, lingering doubts over its merits remain. In times of crisis, therefore, these doubts about the suitability of Japanese for use as a modern language inevitably resurface. Likewise, the idea that Japanese is superior to other languages has also been resurgent in the periods between those times of crisis (see Miller, 1982 for a review). Despite the presence of the dominant language ideology, wild praise of Japanese and crushing doubts about its qualities are in fact less contradictory than they might at first appear, both having their origins in the formative period of modernist language ideology. Expressions of doubt echo the attitudes against which language ideology brokers first reacted when they created an ideology that allowed the Japanese people to take pride in their national language and, by extension, their nation. Language ideology thus has two sides, an oppressive or negative view which is then defended in an emancipative discourse. In the case of Japanese, the former originated in the western views on non-western languages of the 18th and 19th century, while the latter was first produced in defense of Japanese by language modernizers. The former view emerges in times of crisis, while the second gains currency in times of national exuberance. Thus, both sides of the equation are part of modernist language ideology, and it is relatively easy to predict when one view or the other will dominate popular opinion.

Attitudes towards language may also be manipulated to make the linguistic reality agree more closely with the ideological blueprint of what language ought to be. Ever since linguistic homogeneity was deemed to be a critical component of the Japanese nation-state, loss of linguistic diversity has occurred. Value was given to homogeneity and uniformity of language, while diversity and deviation from homogeneity were disparaged, and viewed as a problem. Accordingly, the creation and spread of modern Japanese has resulted in suppression and stigmatization of linguistic diversity in the form of both local languages and of local and social language varieties. At the same time, language ideology offered marginalized groups the chance to raise their status by subscribing to the dominant ideology and behaving according to the values it promoted, with further homogenization being the inevitable outcome. In short, language ideology shapes linguistic reality which, feeding back into the cycle of self-fulfilment, confirms the validity of language ideology. By this process, language and its ideological double become one.

Language ideology affects linguistic research

Speech communities are often unaware of the extent to which language ideology mediates ideas about language and constrains linguistic behaviour, and linguists are by no means immune to this themselves. In general terms, attempts to differentiate between language ideology, on the one hand, and the more complex sociolinguistic field, on the other, are all too often avoided. To put it more bluntly still, vast amounts of linguistic research deal with language, the ideology. Linguistics thus plays a central role in perpetuating the confusion between language ideology and language use across time and space, and as a result, linguistic meta-language is loaded with language ideology, which facilitates the reinforcement of language ideology through linguistic research (see Harris, 1980). This is one of the problems, and a major one at that, which stand in the way of changing existing language ideologies.

Of course, ideologies are more than the sum of their parts. That is to say that what may be stated in a descriptive account of the fundamental entities of a specific ideology can never be the whole picture, for an ideology is not simply a body of ideas. Rather, ideologies are dispositions developed and internalized over time, which provide their subscribers with a blueprint for action. They are responsive and adaptable, not fixed modes of conviction. Thus, ideology constantly generates meaningful interpretations of the world around us, even when faced with challenge, change and contradiction. That said, it is clear that language ideologies cannot be deliberately replaced, but can only be transformed through examination of their component parts and the way in which they affect society and language by impacting on language behaviour. Let us therefore consider those forces most likely to generate such examination in 21st-century Japan, as well as some of the language practices and policies informed and guided thereby.

Examining the Linguistic Consequences of Modernity

Ideology must make sense of existing orders and practices, and it is for this reason that contradictions to ideology do not simply result in their undoing. On the contrary, such challenges invariably provide the impetus for tightening up of regulation along embattled ideological lines. Together with that other fundamental quality of ideology, adaptability in the face of change, modernist language ideology in Japan actively engages such change for its own defence. Evidence of a diversification of language use, for example, is viewed by those seeking to promote linguistic homogeneity as a warning to reaffirm the modernist order, diversity being an indication of the inadequacy of the efforts to create such order so far. This reaction of language ideology under pressure has been noted in previous research. Fujita-Round and Maher (2008: 396) note that policies aimed at internationalization (*kokusaika*) reproduce modernist ideas of projecting diversity on the outside, while assuming or inferring homogeneity within Japan. According to such logic, the homogenous Japanese people must prepare themselves to deal with the entirely novel experience of diversity which the global age brings with it. Of such a view of internationalization, Brian McVeigh (2002: 150) aptly observes that 'instead of being a time to learn a foreign language, [English class] becomes an opportunity to experience one's Japaneseness', while Ann Cary (2001: 105) concludes that the 'emphasis placed on internationalisation (*kokusaika*) in Japan since the 1980s has done little to include other national groups within Japan. *Kokusaika* does not necessarily imply an increase in understanding and valuing which is culturally diverse within Japan' (Cary, 2001: 105). I have commented elsewhere on this contradiction (Heinrich, 2009: 24), that 'a state and its inhabitants not valuing the linguistic and cultural plurality within the confines of its own state borders cannot convincingly claim to be doing just that with regard to international languages'. In other words, rather than undoing the modernist dichotomy of 'Japanese versus foreign', and the notion that being Japanese implies homogeneity, discourse on multicultural education and policies in the *kokusaika* mould reproduces, if not deepens, the ideological boundaries between Japanese and foreign nationals.

As we have seen in the course of this study, modernist language ideology is regularly contradicted in present-day Japan, but it is yet to be successfully transformed. Therefore, we should not simply expect that the challenges to modernist language ideology we are seeing today will ultimately result in the creation of a new, post-modern language ideology. To begin with, transforming language ideology demands an understanding of how it works, of the discrepancies in what it claims, and what it fails to achieve. The sense-making mechanism of language ideology needs first to be exposed, for it is this mechanism that is at the heart of its ability to function.

One of the fundamental principles of modernist language ideology is its claim to be egalitarian. All Japanese, for example, are believed to be linguistically homogenous (=equal). But we have seen that they are in fact equal only through the looking-glass of ideology. What is more, the monolingual language regime founded on these ideological beliefs privileges Japanese monolinguals, and inhibits the maintenance of the community and heritage languages of multilingual speakers, for by definition they deviate from what modernist language ideology dictates Japanese people should be. This contradiction, between claiming equality while practising inequality, owes itself to two closely related features of language ideology. Firstly, linguistic homogeneity is the objective of language ideology and not, as it is claimed, the basis from which it departs, and secondly, language ideology exists to settle power struggles. Not only does it require power to successfully disseminate specific ideologies, but ideologies also sustain and reinforce the existing distribution of power and the language practices associated with the powerful. This is the very mechanism by which the empowerment of those who conform to modernist ideology is assured, and which urges those who deviate from the dominant language ideology to subscribe to it, even though it undermines their own linguistic practices and heritages. This mechanism must be made visible before the ideology it supports can be undone and thereby transformed. This is easier said than done, of course, for successful ideologies nullify attempts to challenge their dominance by making them seem unrealistic or meaningless.

Changing Japan's modernist language ideology will require more than a newfound appreciation of diversity. Transforming it, and creating more freedom of linguistic choice, will require a shift in ontology to redefine what Japan is seen to represent, and what role language has to play in that. While we are seeing efforts to value linguistic diversity in contemporary Japan, this still takes place largely within a modernist framework that stresses homogeneity. Such discourse reduces diversity either to the level of the individual, or else takes place only within the ontological framework of a homogenous nation, for example, by re-evaluing the place and future of autochthonous languages, albeit as dialects. The present situation is effectively a deadlock, with Japan unable to move beyond the ideologies created in the course of its modernisation. What, then, is the future of modernist language ideology in 21st-century Japan, and what impact will this have on issues of parity and inequality?

The Difference between Claiming and Practising Equality

Most Japanese nationals still believe in what modernist ideology claims. What has changed is that this ideology no longer functions as smoothly as it once did. Thus, the question might be recast what the relationship between Japanese nationals and the Japanese language is. Without doubt, any new answers to that question are far from being unanimously accepted by the Japanese people themselves. In other words, there exists no new ideology capable of rationalizing the relationship between Japanese nationals and the Japanese language. Lack of ideological consensus over these issues does not necessarily imply that nothing has changed, much less that any future change is impossible to predict, however.

Modernism's attempts to force the existing sociolinguistic field to reflect the claims of dominant language ideologies have so far failed, and there is little to suggest that this might change in the future. Quite the opposite, in fact, for three things would stand in the way of any potential reversal of fortunes for modernist ideology in Japan. To begin with, internationalization in Japan has brought with it a new wave of diversification, and this can only be expected to increase. Further, ideological attempts to stigmatize diversity have lost much of their power, and are less effective now than at any time in the 20th century, as illustrated, for example, by the popularity and spread of efforts to maintain community and heritage languages. Finally, in some domains, diversity has become highly desirable, most notably among young, urban Japanese. In an important contribution to our understanding of how cultural and linguistic attitudes have changed in contemporary Japan, John Maher (2005) observes playful involvements with cultural and linguistic diversity employed in the construction of what he calls metroethnic identities. The active construction of such ethnicity by design encompasses both minorities and the majority. Although at present the construction of metroethnic identities is restricted to specific areas like food, fashion, festivals and music, for example, and is largely devoid of political involvement and therefore principally aesthetic in its orientation, Heinrich and Galan (2011b: 10) have commented that already 'the very existence of aesthetic multiculturalism demonstrates that orders other than those that value only uniformity, monotony and clarity are possible'.

While aesthetic multiculturalism cannot be directly employed in the political quest to transform language ideology, practices and policies (Katsuragi, 2011), however, it is capable of undermining the credibility and range of modernist ideology. Along with diversification through migration and via the maintenance of community and heritage languages in Japan, therefore, aesthetic multiculturalism represents yet another challenge to existing ideologies, helping in raising the profile and appeal of linguistic diversity in present-day Japan. Japanese cities in particular are increasingly multicultural and multilingual (see e.g. Backhaus, 2007), and the central government will ultimately be forced to acknowledge this through the enactment of policies respectful of diversity. At a local level, the issue of diversification can no longer be sidestepped. Evidence of local communities acknowledging their multilingual and multicultural makeup and transcending modernist ideologies can already be found throughout Japan, in the actions of town councils, educational committees, volunteer language classrooms, NPOs and various grassroots movements. It is just this kind of civil action from which change and challenge to modernist ideology evolves, and research into these local institutions and the ideologies that guide their activities is therefore of key importance to the future study of language ideology in Japan.

Above all, successfully transforming modernist language ideology will require all to depart from the view that Japan is multilingual and multicultural. Many Japanese are still to be convinced of this, however, among them are education policy-makers. Even as the argument against modernist language ideology gathers strength, as acceptance of diversity in certain spheres and communities grow, and as more and more Japanese find themselves pushed to the margin as a by-product of neoliberal reforms and a shrinking middle class, the balance has not yet tipped in favour of new language choices and orders. When it does, thereby breaching the boundaries of modernist language ideology, it will force consideration of a whole new range of options for the creation and maintenance of the ideological connection between language and society (Heinrich & Galan, 2011). No longer will the point of departure be a call for equal treatment of all, for the inhabitants of Japan have never been culturally and linguistically homogenous, nor will they ever be. The result of an ideologically claimed homogeneity as equality will finally be revealed: that to attempt to treat all alike due to their alleged homogeneity in fact creates inequality. Rather, the search for a truly inclusive equality requires the acknowledgement and acceptance of difference, and of differentiated treatment.

To conclude this study, let us consider the role of academia in such transformations of language ideology and the linguistic choices resulting thereof. Already in Chapter 1, we argued that scholastic research would be well advised not to take part in ideological struggles, by way of preserving its own credibility. At the same time, merely descriptive accounts that seek to avoid influencing their subject matter do nothing to combat the negative effects of modernist language ideology. The oppressive aspects of dominant ideology – the dark side of modernity as it were – will remain in place while no alternative is on offer.

The current sociolinguistic situation in Japan is crucially shaped by power relations, and large parts of linguistics are oblivious of this fact. What is more, linguists are crucially involved in supporting and defending the present sociolinguistic situation and, in doing so, the power-inequalities which support them. To be sure, such a position is not neutral. Such a position sacrifices the interests of minorities for the benefit of the majority. As we have seen in the course of this book, such attitudes are the hallmark of modernism. Pierre Bourdieu (1991: 43) has a point in writing that the 'the illusion of linguistic communism', that is, the idea of linguistic uniformity, 'haunts all linguistic theory'. Social sciences and humanities are prone to adopt and support such a stance because these disciplines were both established in support of modernist attitudes, and because these disciplines are concerned with the study of modern institutions (Giddens, 1990: 40). This book has also shown that we should have some reservations about notions of language, because language is usually associated with modernity. Such bias encompasses more than simply the outlook on and assessment of language. Modernist ideology influences the research agendas, research theories and methodologies.

Overcoming the limitations of modernist ideologies on linguistics requires a two-fold strategy. To start, we need to question the obvious and self-evident, and include in research what has been excluded or has been dismissed as irrelevant. Ultimately, we need to stop treating ideologically mediated self-evidence as proof for its appropriateness. A good point of departure is to free linguistic research of the most obvious modernist features, that is, ideas reproducing evolutionism, teleology and the privileged position and experiences of the west (Giddens, 1990: 52–53). This is not sufficient, though. A position rooted in a critique of modernism and power-inequality remains modernist at its heart. Treating powerless communities as if they were powerful will not contribute much to changing their fate. Hence, Sinfree Makoni and Pedzisai Mashiri appropriately noted that '[p]eople's social-economic status will not necessarily improve because the status of their languages has been changed' (Makoni & Mashiri, 2006: 64). This is not really surprising. Replacing institutionally supported inequalities by claims of ideological equality leave the basis of inequalities in place.

What is urgently needed is an ideological anchoring of linguistics beyond the limitations of modernist ideologies, that is, an anchoring in something else but power and inequality. Needless to say, the conclusion of this book is not the place to comprehensively lay down the basis for such new research practices, nor am I sufficiently qualified to engage in such an outline. Nevertheless, two directions in which such research should be developed may be indicated here. The first such direction is the idea of cultural liberty. Cultural liberty differs from cultural diversity in stressing that diversity should be the result of liberty. Diversity should be the result of the exercise of individual freedom and choice, and not one of heritage or other imposed restrictions on choice or encouragement of conformism (Sen, 2006: 116–117). In other words, not diversity as such should be valorized, but the freedom to make choices also in support for diversity. Anything else remains modernist at its core, and results in parallel monoculturalism and multilingualism. The second basis on which to ground a study of language transcending modernist ideologies is the idea of solidarity. Truly multicultural and multilingual societies can only emerge and be sustained in cases in which there exist mutual care, concern and responsibility. Only such communities allow for cultural liberty. Solidarity, Zygmunt Bauman (1992: xxi, emphasis in the original) writes, 'acknowledges not just the *otherness* of the other, but the legitimacy of the other's interests and the other's right to have such interests respected and, if possible, gratified'. That is to say, tolerance of diversity is not enough. Engaging with the other's interests distinguishes solidarity from tolerance. To be sure, we do not yet widely practice such attitudes – even the very idea may be unfamiliar to many today. However, with diversity on the increase through migration and the emancipatory struggles of autochthonous minorities, we will need to learn living with difference. Enjoying or benefitting from such difference, to quote Bauman once more, 'does not come easily, and certainly not under its own impetus. This ability is an art which, like all arts, requires study and exercise' (Bauman, 2000: 106).

We thus need to probe ourselves and clarify our own ideological positions. No doubt, there is also nothing neutral in ignoring the power-inequalities which sustain the modernist orders. *Laissez-faire* is to engage in the perpetuation of these orders. This book has shown that there are alternatives. Denying, erasing or downplaying these alternatives means complicity with powerful actors and communities. Language and society cannot be studied in non-ideological ways. There is no neutral position. If linguistics cannot be neutral but only engaged, I suggest it should engage in something other than the support of power-inequalities through its acceptance of dominant language ideologies and negligence of how these ideologies came about. Linguistics prime task may rather be to ensure that choices for language and diversity are as unrestricted as possible, and remain to be so, in societies not built upon an ideology of linguistic homogeneity, but on the valorization of diversity rooted in ideologies of cultural liberty and solidarity.

References

Abe, H. (2000) *Speaking of Power. Japanese Professional Women and their Speeches*. München: Lincom.
Abe, S. (2006) *Ogasawara shotō ni okeru nihongo no hōgen sesshoku [Dialect Contact on the Ogasawara Islands]*. Kagoshima: Nanpō Shinsha.
Agawa, H. (1994) *Shiga Naoya [Shiga Naoya]*. Tokyo: Iwanami.
Ahagon, C. (1980) *Okinawa-ken no senzen ni okeru shihan gakkō o chūshin to suru kyōin yōsei ni tsuite no jisshō-teki kenkyū [A Documenting Study of Pre-War Okinawa Concerning the Employment of Teaching Staff with Particular Consideration of the Normal Higher Schools]*. Naha: Okinawa Kyōiku Yōsei-shi Kenkyū-kai.
Aitchison, J. (2001) *Language Change. Progress or Decay* (3rd edn). Cambridge: Cambridge University Press.
Albrow, M. (1996) *The Global Age*. Cambridge: Polity Press.
Ammon, U. (1995) On the social forces that determine what is standard in a language and on conditions of successful implementation. In U. Ammon (ed.) *Sociolinguistica. International Yearbook of European Sociolinguistics* (pp. 1–10). Berlin: de Gruyter.
Anderson, B. (1991) *Imagined Communities. Reflection on the Origin and Spread of Nationalism* (rev. edn). London: Verso.
Anderson, M. (2009) Emergent language shift in Okinawa. PhD thesis, Sydney University.
Anezaki, S. (1889) Genbun itchi-ron ni tsuite [On the debate on genbun itchi]. *Bun [Letters]* 2, 740–741.
Anhalt, G. (1991) *Okinawa zwischen Washington und Tokyo*. Marburg: Marburger Japan Reihe.
Baba, T. (1873) *An Elementary Grammar of the Japanese Language. With Easy and Progressive Exercise*. London: Trübner.
Backhaus, P. (2007) *Linguistic Landscapes. A Comparative Study of Urban Multilingualism in Tokyo*. Clevedon: Multilingual Matters.
Barbour, S. (2000) Germany, Austria, Switzerland, Luxembourg. The total coincidence of nations and speech communities. In S. Barbour and C. Carmichael (eds) *Language and Nationalism in Europe* (pp. 151–167). Cambridge: Cambridge University Press.
Bauman, Z. (1992) *Intimations of Postmodernity*. London: Routledge.
Bauman, Z. (1997) *Postmodernity and Its Discontent*. London: Routledge.
Bauman, Z. (2000) *Liquid Modernity*. Cambridge: Polity Press.
Bedell, G.D. (1968) Kokugaku grammatical theory. PhD thesis, MIT.
Beech, H. (2008) Chasing the Japanese dream. *Time Magazine* (6 December 2008) – Online document: http://www.time.com/time/magazine/article/0,9171,1691615-4,00.html. Accessed 27.9.11.
Blommaert, J. (ed.) (1999) *Language Ideological Debates*. Berlin: de Gruyter.
Blommaert, J. and Verschueren, J. (1991) The pragmatics of minority politics in Belgium. *Language in Society* 20, 503–531.

Boudon, R. (1988) *Ideologie. Geschichte und Kritik eines Begriffs*. Hamburg: Rowohlt.
Bourdieu, P. (1977) *Outline of a Theory of Practice*. Cambridge: Cambridge University Press.
Bourdieu, P. (1991) *Language and Symbolic Power*. Cambridge: Polity Press.
Bradley, D. and Bradley, M. (eds) (2002) *Language Endangerment and Language Maintenance*. London: RoutledgeCurzon.
Braisted, W. (1976) *Meiroku Zasshi. Journal of Japanese Enlightenment*. Tokyo: Tokyo University Press.
Brenzinger, M. (2001) Language endangerment through marginalization and globalization. In O. Sakiyama (ed.) *Lectures on Endangered Languages* (Vol. II, pp. 91–121). Kyoto: ELPR.
Brenzinger, M. (ed.) (2007) *Language Diversity Endangered*. Berlin: Mouton de Gruyter.
Briggs, C. (1998) You're a liar – You're just like a woman! Constructing dominant ideologies of language in Warao men's gossip. In B.B. Schieffelin, K.A. Woolard and P.V. Kroskrity (eds) *Language Ideologies. Practice and Theory* (pp. 229–255). Oxford: Oxford University Press.
Bugaeva, A. (2004) *Grammar and Folklore Texts of the Chitose Dialect of Ainu*. Kyoto: ELPR.
Bunkachō Bunkabu Kokugoka (1997) *Chūgoku kikokusha no tame no nihongo kyōiku Q&A [Japanese Language Education for Chinese Returnees Q&A]*. Tokyo: Bunkachō Bunkabu Kokugoka.
Burns, S. (2003) *Before the Nation. Kokugaku and the Imagining of Community in Early Modern Japan*. Durham: Duke University.
Cameron, D. (1995) *Verbal Hygiene*. London: Routledge.
Carroll, T. (2001) *Language Planning and Language Change in Japan*. Richmond: Curzon.
Cary, A.B. (2001) Affiliation, not assimilation. Resident Koreans and ethnic education. In M. Goebel Noguchi and S. Fotos (eds) *Studies in Japanese Bilingualism* (pp. 98–132). Clevedon: Multilingual Matters.
Chamberlain, B.H. (1999) *Essay in Aid of a Grammar and Dictionary of the Luchuan Language*. Tokyo: Yumani Shobō.
Cholmondeley, L.B. (1915) *The History of the Bonin Islands from the Year 1827 to the Year 1876*. London: Constable.
Clark, P.H. (2002) The Kokugo Revolution. Ueda Kazutoshi, language reform and language education in Meiji Japan. PhD thesis, University of Pittsburgh.
Clarke, H. (1997) The great dialect debate. The state and language policy in Okinawa. In E.K. Tipton (ed.) *Society and the State in Interwar Japan* (pp. 193–217). London: Routledge.
Coulmas, F. (1985) *Sprache und Staat*. Berlin: de Gruyter.
Coulmas, F. (1991) Vorwort des Übersetzers. In A. Yanabu (ed.) *Modernisierung der Sprache. Eine kulturhistorische Studie über westliche Begriffe im japanischen Wortschatz* (pp. 7–17). München: Iudicium.
Coulmas, F. (1997) Germanness. Language and nation. In P. Stevenson (ed.) *The German Language and the Real World* (pp. 55–68). Oxford: Clarendon Press.
Coulmas, F. (2003) *Writing Systems. An Introduction to their Linguistic Analysis*. Cambridge: Cambridge University Press.
Coulmas, F. (2005) Changing language regimes in globalizing environments. *International Journal of the Sociology of Language* 175/176, 3–15.
Coulmas, F. (2009) Democracy and the crisis of normative linguistics. In F. Coulmas (ed.) *Language Adaption* (pp. 177–193). Cambridge: Cambridge University Press.
Coyaud, M. (1983) La réforme de la langue au Japon. In I. Fodor (ed.) *Language Reform* (Vol. I, pp. 441–454). Hamburg: Buske.

Craig, A.M. (1968) Fukuzawa Yukichi. The philosophical foundations of Meiji nationalism. In R. Ward (ed.) *Political Development in Modern Japan* (pp. 99–148). Princeton: Princeton University Press.
De Carvalho, D. (2003) *Migrants and Identity in Japan and Brazil*. London: RoutledgeCurzon.
DeChicchis, J. (1995) The current state of the Ainu language. In J.C. Maher and K. Yashiro (eds) *Multilingual Japan* (pp. 103–124). Clevedon: Multilingual Matters.
Doi, T. (1977) *The Study of Language in Japan*. Tokyo: Shinosaki Shorin.
Dubreuil, C.O. (2007) The Ainu and their culture. A critical twenty-first century assessment. *Japan Focus* – Online document: http://japanfocus.org/-Chisato_Kitty_Dubreuil/2589. Accessed 27.9.11.
Duchêne, A. and Heller, M. (eds) (2007) *Discourses of Endangerment. Ideology and Interest in the Defence of Languages*. London: Continuum.
Eagleton, T. (1991) *Ideology. An Introduction*. London: Verso.
Edwards, J. (1985) *Language, Society and Identity*. Oxford: Blackwell.
Errington, J. (1998) Indonesian('s) authority. On the state of a language state. In B.B. Schieffelin, K.A. Woolard and P.V. Kroskrity (eds) *Language Ideologies. Practice and Theory* (pp. 271–284). Oxford: Oxford University Press.
Errington, J. (2000) Indonesian('s) authority. In P.V. Kroskrity (ed.) *Regimes of Language* (pp. 205–227). Santa Fe: School of American Research Press.
Eschbach-Szabo, V. (1997) Ueda Kazutoshi und die moderne japanische Sprachwissenschaft. In D. Naguschewski and J. Trabant (eds) *Was heißt hier fremd? Studien zu Sprache und Fremdheit* (pp. 253–265). Berlin: Akademie Verlag.
Fair, J.K. (1996) Japanese women's language and the ideology of Japanese uniqueness. PhD thesis, Illinois University.
Fairclough, N. (2001) *Langue and Power*. Harlow: Pearson.
Ferguson, C. (1959) Diglossia. *Word* 15, 325–340.
Fija, B., Brenzinger, M. and Heinrich, P. (2009) The Ryukyu's and Japan's new, but endangered, languages. *The Asia Pacific Journal* – Online document: http://japanfocus.org/-Fija-Bairon/3138. Accessed 27.9.11.
Fija, B. and Heinrich, P. (2007) Wanee Uchinaanchu – I am Okinawan. Japan, the US and Okinawa's endangered languages. *Japan Focus* – Online document: http://japanfocus.org/products/details/2586. Accessed 27.9.11.
Fisch, A.G. (1988) *Military Government in the Ryukyu Islands 1945–1950*. Washington, DC: Center of Military History United States Army.
Fischer, S. and Gong, Q. (2010) Variation in East Asian sign language structures. In D. Brentari (ed.) *Sign Languages* (pp. 499–518). Cambridge: Cambridge University Press.
Fishman, J.A. (1991) *Reversing Language Shift*. Clevedon: Multilingual Matters.
Formigaria, L. (1999) Idealism and idealistic trends in linguistics and in the philosophy of language. In P. Schmitter (ed.) *Geschichte der Sprachtheorie* (Vol. IV, pp. 230–253). Tübingen: Gunter Narr.
FRPAC (The Foundation for Research and Promotion of Ainu Culture) (2007) Ainu bunka shinkō, kenkyū suishin kikō [Foundation for Research and Promotion of Ainu Culture] – Online document: http://www.frpac.or.jp/. Accessed 27.9.11.
Fujisawa, K. (2000) *Kindai Okinawa kyōiku-shi no shikaku [A Viewpoint of Modern Okinawan History of Education]*. Tokyo: Shakai Hyōronsha.
Fujita-Round, S. and Maher, J.C. (2008) Language education policy in Japan. In S. May and N.H. Hornberger (eds) *Encyclopedia of Language and Education* (2nd edn, Vol. I, pp. 393–404). NY: Springer.

Fujiyama, Y. (1889) Bunshō-ron ni tsuite Kojima-kun oyobi Bimyōshi-kun ni tsuku [On the debate on writing, Kojima and Bimyō]. *Bun [Letters]* 2, 609–610.
GSTK (Gaikokujin Shūjū Toshi Kaigi) (2006) *Kai'in toshi oyobi dēta [Member Cities and Data]* – Online document: http://homepage2.nifty.com/shujutoshi/. Accessed 27.9.11.
Gal, S. (1992) Multiplicity and contention among ideologies. *Pragmatics* 2, 445–450.
Galan, C. (2001) *L'enseignement de la lecture au Japon*. Toulouse: Presses Universitaire du Mirail.
Galan, C. (2005) Learning to read and write in Japanese (kokugo and nihongo). A barrier to multilingualism. *International Journal of the Sociology of Language* 175/176, 249–269.
Galan, C. (2011) Out of this world, in this world, or both? The Japanese school at a threshold. In P. Heinrich and C. Galan (eds) *Language Life in Japan. Transformations and Prospects* (pp. 77–93). London: Routledge.
Garvin, P.L. (1993) A conceptual framework for the study of language standardization. *International Journal of the Sociology of Language* 100/101, 37–54.
Gengoken Kenkyū-kai (1999) *Kotoba e no kenri. Gengoken to wa nanika [Rights to Language. What Are Language Rights]*. Tokyo: Sangensha.
Geuss, R. (1981) *The Idea of a Critical Theory. Habermas and the Frankfurt School*. Cambridge: Cambridge University Press.
Gishi, M. (2001) *Aka kāra to basājin to B gunhyō [Bright Red, Okinawan Kimono and B Type Yen]*. Okinawa: Yui Shuppan.
Giddens, A. (1990) *The Consequences of Modernity*. Stanford: Stanford University Press.
Gluck, C. (1985) *Japan's Modern Myths*. Princeton: Princeton University Presss.
GOH (Gekidō no Okinawa Hyakunen) (1981) Geidō no Okinawa hyakunen [One-Hundred Years of Agitated Okinawa]. Naha: Gekkan Okinawa-sha.
Gottlieb, N. (1995) *Kanji Politics. Language Policy and Japanese Script*. London: Kegan Paul.
Gottlieb, N. (2005) *Language and Society in Japan*. Cambridge: Cambridge University Press.
Gottlieb, N. (2007) Challenges for language policy in today's Japan. In F. Coulmas (ed.) *Language Regimes in Transformation. Future Prospects for German and Japanese in Science, Economy and Politics* (pp. 33–52). Berlin: Mouton de Gruyter.
Grimes, B.F. (2000) *Ethnologue* (14th edn). Dallas: International Academic Bookstore.
Haarmann, H. (1990) Language planning in the light of a general theory of language. A methodological framework. *International Journal of the Sociology of Language* 86, 103–126.
Hagège, C. (1993) *The Language Builder. An Essay on the Human Signature in Linguistic Morphogenesis*. Amsterdam: Benjamins.
Hagenauer, C. (1952) Le japonais. In A. Meillet (ed.) *Les langues du monde* (Vol. I, pp. 447–574). Geneva: Slatkine.
Hall, I.P. (1972) Hoitonii ate shokan ni tsuite [On the letter addressed to Whitney]. In T. Ōkubo (ed.) *Mori Arinori zenshū [Collected Works of Mori Arinori]* (Vol. I, pp. 93–95). Tokyo: Senbundō Shoten.
Hall, I.P. (1973) *Mori Arinori*. Cambridge: Harvard University Press.
Hanami, M. (1995) Minority dynamics in Japan. Towards a society of sharing. In J.C. Maher and G. Macdonald (eds) *Diversity in Japanese Culture and Language* (pp. 121–146). London: Kegan Paul International.
Hara, K. (2005) Regional dialect and cultural development in Japan and Europe. *International Journal of the Sociology of Language* 175/176, 193–211.
Harris, R. (1980) *The Language Makers*. London: Duckworth.

Hasegawa, Y. (1998) Chichijima no gengo kyōiku kankyō ni kansuru shiron [Essay on the language education environment on Chichijima]. *Nihongo kenkyū sentā hōkoku [Report of the Japanese Research Centre]* 6, 161–174.

Hattori, S. (1932) Ryūkyūgo to kokugo to no on'in hōsoku [Sound laws between Ryukyuan and Japanese]. *Hōgen [Dialect]* 2, 1–16.

Hattori, S. (1954) Gengo nendaigaku sunawachi goi tōkeigaku no hōhō ni tsuite [Concerning the method of glottochronology and lexicostatistics]. *Gengo kenkyū [Journal of the Linguistic Society of Japan]* 26/27, 29–77.

Hattori, S. (ed.) (1964) *Ainugo hōgen jiten [Dictionary of Ainu Dialects]*. Tokyo: Iwanami.

Heath, S.B. (1989) Language ideology. In E. Barnouw (ed.) *International Encyclopedia of Communications* (Vol. II, pp. 393–435). Oxford: Oxford University Press.

Heath, S.B. (1991) Women in conversation. Covert models in American language ideology. In R.L. Cooper and B. Spolsky (eds) *The Influence of Language on Culture and Thought* (pp. 199–218). Berlin: de Gruyter.

Heffernan, K. (2006) Prosodic levelling during language shift. Okinawan approximations of Japanese pitch accent. *Journal of Sociolinguistics* 10, 641–666.

Heinrich, P. (2002) *Die Rezeption der westlichen Linguistik im modernen Japan bis Ende der Shōwa-Zeit*. München: Iudicium.

Heinrich, P. (2008) Reappreciating Okinawa's languages, while there's still time. *Japan Times* – Online document: http://search.japantimes.co.jp/cgi-bin/ek20081104a1.html. Accessed 27.9.11.

Heinrich, P. (2009) The Ryukyuan languages in the 21st century global society. In M. Nakahodo, K. Yamazato and M. Ishihara (eds) *Human Migration and the 21st Century Global Society* (pp. 16–27). Okinawa: University of the Ryukyus.

Heinrich, P. (2010a) Ryūkyū shotō ni okeru gengo shifuto [Language shift in the Ryukyu Islands]. In P. Heinrich and S. Matsuo (eds) *Higashi ajia ni okeru gengo fukkō [Language Revitalization in East Asia]* (pp. 147–173). Tokyo: Sangensha.

Heinrich, P. (2010b) Ryūkyū shogo wa 'hōgen' de wa nai [The Ryukyuan languages are not 'dialects'] In P. Heinrich and M. Shimoji (eds) *Ryūkyū shogo kiroku hozon no kiso [Essentials in Ryukyuan Language Documentation]* (pp. 1–11). Tokyo: Tokyo University of Foreign Studies.

Heinrich, P. (2011) Difficulties of establishing heritage language education in Uchinaa. In P. Heinrich and C. Galan (eds) *Language Life in Japan. Transformations and Prospects* (pp. 34–49). London: Routledge.

Heinrich, P and Galan, C. (eds) (2011a) *Language Life in Japan. Transformations and Prospects*. London: Routledge.

Heinrich, P. and Galan, C. (2011b) Modern and late modern perspectives on language life in Japan. In P. Heinrich and C. Galan (eds) *Language Life in Japan. Transformations and Prospects* (pp. 1–13). London: Routledge.

Herbermann, C.P. (1997) *Sprache & Sprechen*. Wiesbaden: Harrasowitz.

Hibiya, J. and Hirataka, F. (2005) *Tabunka shakai to gaikokujin no gakushū shien [Multicultural Society and Learning Support for Foreigners]*. Tokyo: Keiō Gijuku Daigaku Shuppan.

Higashionna, K. (1940) Okinawa kenmin no tachiba yori [From the viewpoint of the people of Okinawa Prefecture]. *Gekkan mingei [Monthly Folk Art]* 1940. Reprinted in K. Tanigawa (ed.) (1970) *Waga Okinawa [Our Okinawa]* (Vol. II, pp. 41–51). Tokyo: Mokujisha.

Hijiya-Kirschnereit, I. (1981) *Selbstentblößungsrituale. Zur Theorie und Geschichte der autobiographischen Gattung 'shisōsetsu' in der modernen japanischen Literatur*. Wiesbaden: Steiner.

Hill, J. (1998) Today there is no respect. Nostalgia, respect and oppositional discourse in Mexicano (Nahuatl) language ideology. In B.B. Schieffelin, K.A. Woolard and P.V. Kroskrity (eds) *Language Ideologies. Practice and Theory* (pp. 263–280). Oxford: Oxford University Press.

Hill, J. and Hill, K.C. (1986) *Speaking Mexicano. Dynamics of Syncretic Language in Central Mexico.* Tucson: University of Arizona Press.

Hirai, M. (1998[1948]) *Kokugo kokuji mondai no rekishi [History of Problems of the National Language and Script].* Tokyo: Sangensha.

Hirataka, F., Koishi, A. and Kato, Y. (2001) On the language environment of Brazilian immigrants in Fujisawa City. In M. Goebel Noguchi and S. Fotos (eds) *Studies in Japanese Bilingualism* (pp. 164–183). Clevedon: Multilingual Matters.

Hokama, S. (1971) *Okinawa no gengo-shi [Language History of Okinawa].* Tokyo: Hōsei Daigaku Shuppan.

Hōryoku, C. (2002) Ueda Kazutoshi no gengo-kan ni tsuite [On Ueda Kazutoshi's view on language]. *Kyōiku shisō [Philosophy of Education]* 29, 19–27.

Hoshina, K. (1902) Kokugo Chōsa I'inkai ketsugi jikō ni tsuite [On decisions taken by the National Language Research Council]. *Gengogaku zasshi [Journal of Linguistics]* 3, 70–86.

Hoshina, K. (1936) *Kokugo to nihon seishin [National Language and the Spirit of Japan].* Tokyo: Jitsugyō no Nihonsha.

Hutton, C. (2001) Cultural and conceptual relativism – Universalism and the politics of linguistics. Dilemmas of a would-be progressive linguistics. In R. Dirven, R. Frank and C. Ilie (eds) *Language and Ideology* (Vol. I, pp. 277–296). Amsterdam: Benjamins.

Hyōtan, S. (1889a) Kojima sensei to Yoshimi sensei e [To Professor Kojima and Professor Yoshimi]. *Bun [Letters]* 2, 397–398.

Hyōtan, S. (1889b) Kojima sensei e [To Professor Kojima]. *Bun [Letters]* 2, 531–532.

Ide, S. (1999) Gengo ideorogii to washa no aidentitii [Language ideology and speaker identity]. In H. Shoji (ed.) *Kotoba no nijū seiki [The Twentieth Century of Language]* (pp. 218–234). Tokyo: Domesu Shuppan.

Iha, F. (1916) *Ryūkyūgo binran [Ryukyuan Handbook].* Tokyo: Tōgyō Kenkyū-kai Shuppan.

Iha, F. (1940) Hōgen wa muyami ni dan'atsu subekarazu. Shizen ni shōmetsu sase [Do not excessively suppress the dialect. Let it vanish naturally]. *Ōsaka kyūyō shinpō [Osaka Kyūyō News]* (1 November 1940).

Iha, F. (1975) Ryūkyū to yamatoguchi [Ryukyu and Japanese]. In S. Hattori, S. Nakasone and S. Hokama (eds) *Iha Fuyū zenshū [Collected Works of Iha Fuyū]*, (Vol. VIII, pp. 457–459). Tokyo: Heibonsha.

Inamura, T. (ed.) (1987) *Ueda Kazutoshi, Okamoto Kanoko, Kitahara Hakushō, Shimazuki Tōson, Izumi Kyōka [Ueda Kazutoshi, Okamoto Kanoko, Kitahara Hakushō, Shimazuki Tōson, Izumi Kyōka].* Tokyo: Yumami Shobō.

Inoue, K. (1991) *MacArthur's Japanese Constitution. A Linguistic and Cultural Study of its Making.* Chicago: Chicago University Press.

Inoue, M. (1996) The political economy of gender and language in Japan. PhD thesis, Washington University.

Inoue, M. (2003) Speech without a speaking body. 'Japanese women's language' in translation. *Language and Communication* 23, 315–330.

Inoue, M. (2006) *Vicarious Language. Gender and Linguistic Modernity in Japan.* Berkeley: University of California Press.

Irvine, J.T. (1989) When talk isn't cheap. Language and political economy. *American Ethnologist* 16, 248–267.

Irvine, J.T. and Gal, S. (2000) Language ideology and linguistic differentiation. In P.V. Kroskrity (ed.) *Regimes of Language* (pp. 35–83). Santa Fe: School of American Research Press.
Ishihara, M. (2010) Ryūkyūgo no sonzokusei to kikido. Gyakkōteki gengo shifuto wa kanōka [Ryukyuan language vitality and endangerment. Is reversing language shift possible]. In P. Heinrich and S. Matsuo (eds) *Higashi ajia no gengo fukkō [Language Revitalization in East Asia]* (pp. 111–178). Tokyo: Sangensha.
Ishihara, S. (2007) *Kindai nihon to Ogasawara shotō [Modern Japan and the Ogasawara Islands]*. Tokyo: Heibonsha.
Ising, E. (1987) Nationalsprache/Nationalitätensprache. In U. Ammon (ed.) *Sociolinguistics. Handbücher zur Sprach- und Kommunikationswissenschaft* (Vol. III, pp. 335–343). Berlin: de Gruyter.
Itani, Y. (2006) *Okinawa no hōgen fuda [The dialect tag in Okinawa]*. Naha: Bōdāinku.
Japan Weekly Mail (1873a) English in Japan. *Japan Weekly Mail* (1 May 1873).
Japan Weekly Mail (1873b) Language reform. *Japan Weekly Mail* (19 July 1873).
Japan Weekly Mail (1873c) Foreign education in Japan. *Japan Weekly Mail* (2 August 1873).
Jernudd, B. and Neustupný, J.V. (1987) Language planning. For whom? In L. Laforge (ed.) *Proceedings of the International Colloquium on Language Planning* (pp. 69–84). Québec: Les Presses de l'Université Laval.
Jones, M., Jones, R. and Woods, M. (2006) *Introduction to Political Geography*. London: Routledge.
Joseph, J.E. and Taylor, T.J. (eds) (1990) *Ideologies of Language*. London: Routledge.
Kajita, T. (1994) *Gaikokujin rōdōsha to nihon [Foreign Workers and Japan]*. Tokyo: Nihon Hōsō Shuppan Kyōkai.
Kamegawa, S. (1972) *Okinawa no eigaku [Okinawan English Studies]*. Tokyo: Kenkyūsha.
Kamusella, T. (2009) *The Politics of Language and Nationalism in Modern Central Europe*. Basingstoke: Palgrave Macmillan.
Kaneda, A. (2005) The tense-aspect system and evidentiality in the Hachijo dialect. *Lingua Posnaniensis* 47, 75–86.
Kanno, Y. (2008) *Language and Education in Japan. Unequal Access to Bilingualism*. Basingstoke: Palgrave Macmillan.
Karatani, K. (1993) *Origins of the Modern Japanese Literature*. Durham: Duke University Press.
Karimata, S. (2001) 'Fumarete mo fumarete mo' to watashi no 'ima' ['Trampled down' and 'present' me]. *Edge* 12, 36–42.
Katsuragi, T. (2011) Prospects and prerequisites for a third way language policy in Japan. In P. Heinrich and C. Galan (eds) *Language Life in Japan. Transformations and Prospects* (pp. 202–217). London: Routledge.
Kawakami, I. (2006) *Idō suru kodomotachi to nihongo kyōiku [Moving Children and Japanese Language Education]*. Tokyo: Akashi.
Kawamura, M. (1994) *Umi o watatta nihongo [Japanese which Crossed the Sea]*. Tokyo: Seidosha.
Kayano, S. (1994) *Our Land was a Forest. An Ainu Memoir*. Boulder: Westview Press.
KCIIK (Kokugo Chōsa I'inkai) (1904) *Hōgen saishū-bo [Dialect Survey Handbook]*. Tokyo: Nihon Shoseki.
KCIIK (Kokugo Chōsa I'inkai) (2000) *Kōgohō [A Grammar of Spoken Language]*. Tokyo: Bensei Shuppan.
KCIIK (Kokugo Chōsa I'inkai) (1980) *Kōgohō bekki [Supplement to the Grammar of Spoken Language]*. Tokyo: Bensei Shuppan.

Kerr, G.H. (1958) *Okinawa. The History of an Island People*. Rutland: Charles E. Tuttle.
Kimura, G.C. (2011) Language rights in Japan. What are they good for? In P. Heinrich and C. Galan (eds) *Language Life in Japan. Transformations and Prospects* (pp. 14–33). London: Routledge.
Kindaichi, H. (1957) *Nihongo* [Japanese]. Tokyo: Iwanami.
Kindaichi, H. (1978) *The Japanese Language* (translated and annotated by Hirano Umeyo). Rutland: Charles E. Tuttle.
King, K.A. (2001) *Language Revitalization Processes and Prospects*. Clevedon: Multilingual Matters.
Kinjō, C. (1944) *Naha hōgen gaisetsu [Outline of the Naha Dialect]*. Tokyo: Sanshōdō.
Kizaki, A. (1889) Shigen [A wise saying] *Bun [Letters]* 2, 743–745.
Klose, A. (1987) *Sprachen der Welt*. München: Saur.
Kloss, H. (1967) Abstand languages and Ausbau languages. *Anthropological Linguistics* 9, 29–41.
Kobayashi, T. (2001) Mori Arinori no 'datsua nyūō chōō' gengo shisō no shosō 1 [Aspects of Mori Arinori's 'De-Asianization, Europanization, surpassing Europe' language ideology 1]. *Seijō bungei [Seijō Arts and Literature]* 176, 39–131.
Kobayashi, T. (2002) Mori Arinori no 'datsua nyūō chōō' gengo shisō no shosō 2 [Aspects of Mori Arinori's 'De-Asianization, Europanization, surpassing Europe' language ideology 2]. *Seijō bungei [Seijō Arts and Literature]* 178, 35–77.
Koerner, E.F.K. (1993) The natural science background to the development of historical-comparative linguistics. In H. Aertens and R.J. Jeffers (eds) *Historical Linguistics. Papers from the 9th International Conference on Historical Linguistics* (pp. 1–24). Amsterdam: Benjamins.
Koerner, E.F.K. (2001) Linguistics and ideology in the 19th and 20th centuries studies of language. In R. Dirven, R. Frank and C. Ilie (eds) *Language and Ideology* (Vol. I, pp. 253–276). Amsterdam: Benjamins.
Kojima, A. (2006) *Nyūkamā no kodomo to gakkō bunka [Newcomer Children and School Culture]*. Tokyo: Keisō Shobō.
Kojima, K. (1889a) Bunshō-ron [Debate on writing]. *Bun [Letters]* 2, 346–351.
Kojima, K. (1889b) Futatabi bunshō o ronji Bimyō-shi ni shimesu [Debating once more on writing and instructions for Bimyō]. *Bun [Letters]* 2, 483–487.
Kojima, K. (1889c) Futatabi ni bunshō o ron zu [Debating once more on writing]. *Bun [Letters]* 2, 538–540.
Kojima, K. (1889d) Genbun itchi o ronji Bimyō-sai shuji no kōgeki ni kotau [Debating genbun itchi and answering to Bimyō's rhetorical refutation]. *Bun [Letters]* 2, 600–605.
Kojima, K. (1889e) Bimyō-shi ni nanji awasete Hyōtan Sei oyobi Fujiyama Yutaka-shi ni mōsu [Remarks to Hyotan Sei and Fujiyama Yutaka joining Bimyō in rebellion]. *Bun [Letters]* 3, 208–301.
Kokugo Gakkai (1980) *Kokugogaku daijiten [Comprehensive Encyclopaedia of the National Language Studies]*. Tokyo: Tokyodō.
Kokuritsu Kokugo Kenkyūjo (1963) *Okinawago jiten [Okinawa Language Dictionary]*. Tokyo: Ōkurashō Insatsukyoku.
Komai, C. (1889a) Genbun itchi-ron ni tsuite [On the debate on genbun itchi]. *Bun [Letters]* 2, 605–607.
Komatsu, K. (2000) Samani Ainugo kyōshitsu no genjō to kadai [The situation and tasks of the Ainu classes in Samani]. In M. Yamamoto (ed.) *Nihon no bairingaru kyōiku [Bilingual Education in Japan]* (pp. 47–84). Tokyo: Akashi.

Kondo, D. (1990) *Crafting Selves. Power, Gender, and Discourses of Identity in a Japanese Workplace*. Chicago: Chicago University Press.
Kondō, K. (1997) Kokka sōdōin taiseika no Okinawa ni okeru hyōjungo reikō undō [The movement to enforce the standard language in Okinawa in its correlation with the national mobilization campaign]. *Nantō shigaku [Historical Studies of the Southern Islands]* 49, 28–47.
Kondō, K. (1999) Kindai Okinawa ni okeru hōgen fuda 1 [The dialect tag in modern Okinawa 1]. *Aichi kenritsu daigaku bungakubu ronshū [Collected Papers of the Faculty of Letters of Aichi National University]* 47, 27–50.
Kondō, K. (2000) Kindai Okinawa ni okeru hōgen fuda 2 [The dialect tag in modern Okinawa 2]. *Aichi kenritsu daigaku bungakubu ronshū [Collected Papers of the Faculty of Letters of Aichi National University]* 48, 29–52.
Kondō, K. (2006) *Kindai Okinawa ni okeru kyōiku to kokumin tōgō [Education and National Mobilization in Modern Okinawa]*. Sapporo: Hokkaido University Press.
Koshida, K. (1993) From a 'perishing people' to self-determination. *Ampo Japan-Asia Quarterly Review* 24, 2–6.
Koyama, W. (2003) Language and its Double. A Critical History of Metalanguages in Japan. PhD thesis, University of Chicago.
Kroskrity, P.V. (1998) Arizona Tewa Kiva speech as a manifestation of a dominant language ideology. In B.B. Schieffelin, K.A. Woolard and P.V. Kroskrity (eds) *Language Ideologies. Practice and Theory* (pp. 103–122). Oxford: Oxford University Press.
Kroskrity, P.V. (2000) Regimenting languages. Language ideological perspectives. In P.V. Kroskrity (ed.) *Regimes of Language* (pp. 1–34). Santa Fe: School of American Research Press.
Kurashima, N. (2002) *Kokugo 100 nen. 20 seiki nihongo wa dono michi o ayunde kita-ka [100 Years National Language. Which Course Did Japanese Take in the Twentieth Century]*. Tokyo: Shōgakkan.
Kuroda, Y. (2002) Nihongo kyōiku no rekishi 1. Meiji Taishō-ki no Ainu minzoku no kēsu o tsūshite [History of Japanese language education 1. Approached from the case of the Ainu in the Meiji and Taishō period]. *Yokohama kokudai kokugo kenkyū [Yokohama Kokudai National Language Studies]* 20, 12–19.
Kuwae, Y. (1954) *Hyōjungo taishō Okinawago no kenkyū [A Contrastive Study of Okinawan and the Standard Language]*. Naha: Aoyama Shoten.
Kymlicka, W. (1995) *Multicultural Citizenship*. Oxford: Oxford University Press.
Ladefoged, P. (1992) Another view of endangered languages. In *Languages* 68, 809–811.
Lee, R. (2002) *Chōsen genron tōsei-shi [History of the Regulation of Korean Press]*. Tokyo: Shinzansha Shuppan.
Lee, Y. (1990) Mori Arinori to Baba Tatsui no nihongo-ron [Discourse on Japanese Between Mori Arinori and Baba Tatsui]. *Shisō [Ideology]* 9, 49–64.
Lee, Y. (1996) *'Kokugo' to iu shisō* [An Ideology Called 'Kokugo'] Tokyo: Iwanami. (Maki Hirano Hubbard, trans., 2009). *The Ideology of Kokugo*. Honolulu: University of Hawai'i Press.
Lewallen, A.E. (2008) Indigenous at last! Ainu grassroots organizing and the indigenous peoples summit in Ainu Mosir. *Japan Focus* – Online document: http://www.japan focus.org.articles/print_article/2971. Accessed 27.9.11.
Lewin, B. (1979) Demokratisierungsprozesse in der modernen Sprachentwicklung. In K. Kracht (ed.) *Japan nach 1945* (pp. 87–101). Wiesbaden: Harrassowitz.
Lewin, B. (1982) *Sprachbetrachtung und Sprachwissenschaft im vormodernen Japan*. Opladen: Westdeutscher Verlag.

Lewis, M.P. (ed.) (2009) *Ethnologue. Languages of the World* (16th edn). Dallas: SIL International.
Long, D. (2007) *English on the Bonin (Ogasawara) Islands*. Durham: Duke University Press.
Maher, J.C. (1995a) The Kakyo. Chinese in Japan. In J.C. Maher and K. Yashiro (eds) *Multilingual Japan* (pp. 135–138). Clevedon: Multilingual Matters.
Maher, J.C. (1995b) Maintaining culture and language. Koreans in Osaka. In J.C. Maher and G. Macdonald (eds) *Diversity in Japanese Culture and Language* (pp. 160–177). London: Kegan Paul International.
Maher, J.C. (1997) Linguistic minorities and education in Japan. *Educational Review* 49, 115–127.
Maher, J.C. (2001) Akor Itak – Our language, your language. Ainu in Japan. In J.A. Fishman (ed.) *Can Threatened Languages be Saved* (pp. 323–349). Clevedon: Multilingual Matters.
Maher, J.C. (2005) Metroethnicity, language, and the principle of Cool. *International Journal of the Sociology of Language* 175/176, 83–102.
Maher, J.C. and Kawanishi, Y. (1995) On being there. Koreans in Japan. In J.C. Maher and K. Yashiro (eds) *Multilingual Japan* (pp. 87–101). Clevedon: Multilingual Matters.
Maher, J.C. and Yashiro, K. (eds) (1995) *Multilingual Japan*. Clevedon: Multilingual Matters.
Makoni, S. and Pedzisai, M. (2006) Critical historiography. Does language planning in Africa need a construct of language as a part of its theoretical apparatus? In S. Makoni and A. Pennycook (eds) *Disinventing and Reconstituting Languages* (pp. 62–89). Clevedon: Multilingual Matters.
Masiko, H. (1997) *Ideorogii to shite no 'nihon'. 'Kokugo' 'nihonshi' no chishiki shakaigaku ['Japan' as an Ideology. The Sociology of Knowledge of the 'National Language' and the 'History of Japanese']*. Tokyo: Sangensha.
Matsumori, A. (1995) Ryūkyuan. Past, present, and future. In J.C. Maher and K. Yashiro (eds) *Multilingual Japan* (pp. 19–44). Clevedon: Multilingual Matters.
Matsumoto, I. (1889b) Meiji bungaku no ni daigimon [The two major problems of Meiji literature]. *Bun [Letters]* 2, 610–611.
Matsumura, A. (1956) Kokugogaku [National language study]. In Kokuritsu Kokugo Kenkyūjo (eds) *Kokugo nenkan. Shōwa 31 nenhan [Yearbook of National Language. 1956 Edition]* (pp. 14–17). Tokyo: Dainihon Tosho.
Matsunaga, N. (2002) *Nihon gunsei-ka no maraya ni okeru nihongo kyōiku [Japanese Language Education in Malaysia under Japanese Military Administration]*. Tokyo: Kazama Shobō.
Matsushita, T. (1960a) Genbun itchi-ron to sono hantai-ron [Comments in favour of genbun itchi and against it]. *Kokugo kokubun [National Language National Literature]* 29, 39–56.
Matsushita, T. (1960b) Yamada Bimyō no genbun itchi shisō [Yamada Bimyō's ideas on genbun itchi]. *Kokugo kokubun [National Language National Literature]* 29, 16–29.
May, S. (2001) *Language and Minority Rights. Ethnicity, Nationalism and the Politics of Language*. Harlow: Longman.
McBride, B. (2008) Young 'Zainichi' Koreans look beyond Chongryon ideology. *Japan Times* (12 December 2008) – Online document: http://search.japantimes.co.jp/cgi-bin/fl20081216zg.html. Accessed 27.9.11.
McVeigh, B.J. (2002) Self-orientalism through occidentalism. How 'English' and 'foreigners' nationalize Japanese students. In B.J. McVeigh (ed.) *Japanese Higher Education as Myth* (pp. 148–179). Armonk: Sharpe.

MEXT (Ministry of Education, Culture, Sports, Science and Technology) (2008) 'Nihongo shidō ga hitsuyō na gaikoku jidō seito no ukiire jōkyō ni kansuru chōsa (Heisei 2008 nendo)' no kekka ni tsuite [Results of 2008 'Survey on the Situation of the Acceptance of Pupils in Need of Japanese Language Guidance'] – Online document: http://www.mext.go.jp/b_menu/toukei/001/index32.htm. Accessed 27.9.11.
Miller, R.A. (1975) The Far East. In T. Sebeok (ed.) *Current Trends in Linguistics* (Vol. XIII, pp. 1213–1264). Den Haag: Mouton de Gruyter.
Miller, R.A. (1982) *Japan's Modern Myth. The Language and Beyond*. NY: Weatherhill.
Miller, R.A. (1986) *Nihongo. In Defense of Japanese*. London: Athlone Press.
Milroy, J. (2001) Language ideologies and the consequences of standardization. *Journal of Sociolinguistics* 5, 530–555.
Milroy, J. and Milroy, L. (1985) *Authority in Language. Investigating Language Prescription and Standardisation*. London: Routledge.
Miyara, S. (2008) 'Uchiaaguchi' to wa Okinawago? Okinawa hōgen? [Is 'Uchinaaguchi' Okinawa language or Okinawa dialect] In Ryūkyū Daigaku-hen (eds) *Yawarakai minami no gaku to shisō [Peaceful Studies and Thought of the South]* (pp. 150–165). Naha: Okinawa Taimusu.
Miyara, S. (2010a) Okinawago kōshi no yōsei ni tsuite [Training teachers of Okinawan]. In P. Heinrich and S. Matsuo (eds) *Higashi ajia ni okeru gengo fukkō [Language Revitalization in East Asia]* (pp. 179–202). Tokyo: Sangensha.
Miyara, S. (2010b) Japonikku gozoku no naka no Ryūkyū goha [The Ryukyuan language branch in the Japonic language family]. In P. Heinrich and M. Shimoji (eds) *Ryūkyū shogo kiroku hozon ni kiso [Essentials in Ryukyuan Language Documentation]* (pp. 12–41). Tokyo: Tokyo University of Foreign Studies.
Mizutami, A. (1996) Meiji-ki nihon no kokugo seisaku to chishikijin-tachi no kokugo-kan [Japan's language planning and intellectuals' views on national language in the Meiji period]. *Kokusai kankei-gaku kenkyū [Studies in International Relations]* 23, 19–32.
MKK (Monbushō Kyōkashokyoku Kokugoka) (1949) *Kokugo chōsa enkaku shiryō [Material on the History of National Language Research]*. Tokyo: Monbushō Kyōkashokyoku Kokugoka.
Morioka, K. (1985) Genbun itchi-tai seiritsu shiron [Essay on the formation of genbun itchi style]. *Kokugo to kokubungaku [Studies in National Language and National Literature]* 1985, 78–92.
Morita, T. (1967) *Amerika no Okinawa kyōiku seisaku [American Education Policy for Okinawa]*. Tokyo: Meiji Tosho Shuppan.
Motonaga, M. (1994) *Ryūkyūken seikatsugo no kenkyū [Studies on the Daily Language of the Ryukyus]*. Tokyo: Shunjūsha.
Mufwene, S. (2003) Language endangerment. What have pride and prestige got to do with it. In B.D. Joseph (ed.) *When Languages Collide. Perspectives on Language Conflict, Language Competition and Language Coexistence* (pp. 324–345). Columbus: Ohio State University.
Mühlhäusler, P. (1996) *Linguistic Ecology. Language Change and Linguistic Imperialism in the Pacific Region*. London: Routledge.
Munzinger, C. (1894) Die Psychologie der japanischen Sprache. *Mittheilungen der Deutschen Gesellschaft für Natur- und Völkerkunde* 53, 103–142.
Murasaki, K. (2001) *Arai Take mukashibansi zenshū [Tuytah Collection by Asai Take]*. Kyoto: ELPR.

Nagata, T. (2001) Yonaguni no gengo henka [Language change in Yonaguni]. In F. Inoue, K. Shinozaki, T. Kobayashi and T. Ōnishi (eds) *Ryūkyū hōgen-kō [Considerations about the Ryukyu Dialects]* (Vol. VII, pp. 439–451). Tokyo: Yumani Shobō.
Naitō, S. (1979) *Hachijō no hōgen [The dialect of Hachijo]*. Tokyo: Kuraun kōbō.
Nakagawa, H. (2009) *Ainugo gakushū no mirai ni mukete [Towards the Future of Ainu Language Learning]* – Online document: http://www.kantei.go.jp/jp/singi/ainu/dai5/5siryou. pdf. Accessed 27.9.11.
Nakamura, Ka. (2002) U-turn, Deaf shock, and hard of hearing. In L. Monaghan, C. Schmaling, K. Nakamura and G. Turner (eds) *Many Ways to be Deaf* (pp. 211–229). Washington, DC: Gallaudet University Press.
Nakamura, Ka. (2006) *Deaf in Japan*. Ithaca: Cornell University Press.
Nakamura, Ke. (2000) Funabashi Yōchi, Shiga Nayoa soshite Mori Arinori. Seiyō no daigengo to kōkoku gengo no hazama de [Funabashi Yōchi, Shiga Naoya and Mori Arinori. At the gap between big western languages and languages of small countries]. *Seijō bungei [Seijō Arts and Literature]* 170, 1–32.
Nakamura, T. (1987) Meiji-ki ni okeru kokumin kokka no keisei to kokugo kokuji-ron no sōkoku. Kokugogakusha Ueda Kazutoshi no rekishiteki isō [Conflicts between nation building, state formation and discussions on the national language in the Meiji period. The historical significance of Ueda Kazutoshi]. *Tōkyō daigaku kyōikugakubu kiyō [Bulletin of the Faculty of Education of Tokyo University]* 27, 207–216.
Nakamatsu, T. (1996) *Ryūkyū gogaku [Ryukyu Language Studies]*. Naha: Okinawa Gengo Bunka Kenkyūjo.
Narita, Y. (2001) Okinawa no gengo seikatsu [The language life of Okinawa]. In F. Inoue, K. Shinozaki, T. Kobayashi and T. Ōnishi (eds) *Ryūkyū hōgen-kō [Considerations about the Ryukyu Dialects]* (Vol. III, pp. 245–261). Tokyo: Yumani Shobō.
Neustupný, J.V. (1974) The modernization of the Japanese system of communication. *Language and Society* 3, 33–50.
Neustupný, J.V. (1995) Gengo kanri to Mori Arinori. Kindai izen kara kindai zenki e no idō [Language management and Mori Arinori. Transition from pre-modern to early modern]. *Edo no shisō [Edo Ideology]* 2, 122–131.
Nishi, M. (1889) Genbun itchi-ron [Debate on genbun itchi]. *Bun [Letters]* 2, 736–740.
Nohara, M. (2009) A language to be held dearly. *The Okinawan* 2, 18.
Nuibe, Y. (1999) *Nyūkoku jidō no tame no nihongo kyōiku [Japanese Language Education for Immigrant Children]*. Tokyo: Suriiēnettowāku.
Nuibe, Y. (2002) *Tabunka kyōsei jidai no nihongo kyōiku [Japanese Language Education for the Period of Multicultural Symbiosis]*. Tokyo: Rekirekisha.
OCNO (Office of the Chief of Naval Operations) (1944) *Civil Affairs Handbook. Ryukyu (Loochoo) Islands*. Washington, DC: Office of the Chief of Naval Operations.
ODJKJ (Okinawa Dai-hyakka Jiten Kankō Jimukyoku) (1983) *Okinawa dai-hyakka jiten [Encyclopaedia of Okinawa]*. Naha: Okinawa Taimusu.
Oguma, E. (1998) *'Nihonjin' no kyōkai [The Boundaries of 'the Japanese']*. Tokyo: Shinyōsha.
Oguma, E. (2001) Shiryō kaidai [Material notes]. *Edge* 12, 38–95.
Oguma, E. (2002) *A Genealogy of 'Japanese' Self-Images*. Melbourne: Trans Pacific Press.
Ohara, Y. (1999) Ideology of language and gender. A critical discourse analysis of Japanese prescriptive texts. In J. Verschueren (ed.) *Language and Ideology. Selected Papers from the 6th International Pragmatics Conference* (pp. 422–432). Antwerp: International Pragmatics Association.
OJNSK (Ochanomizu Joshidaigakuin Ningen-bunka Sōsei Kagaku-kenkyūka) (2008) *Kyōsei nihongo kyōiku no kyōin yōsei ni kansuru kenkyū [Research on Symbiosis Japanese*

Language Teacher Training]. Tokyo: Ochanomizu Joshidaigakuin Ningen-bunka Sōsei Kagaku-kenkyūka.
Okamoto, S. (1995) 'Tasteless' Japanese. Less 'feminine' language among young Japanese women. In K. Hall and M. Bucholz (eds) *Gender Articulated. Language and the Socially Constructed Self* (pp. 297–325). NY: Routledge.
OKGB (Okinawa-ken Gakumubu) (1940a) Aete kenmin ni utaeru mingei undō ni mayowana [Daring to not be perplexed by the Folk Craft Movement's appeal to the people of the prefecture]. *Ryūkyū shinpō [Ryukyu News]* (11 January 1940).
OKGB (Okinawa-ken Gakumubu) (1940b) Futatabi hyōjungo mondai ni tsuite I [Once more concerning the standard language I]. *Ryūkyū shinpō [Ryukyu News]* (25 June 1940).
OKGB (Okinawa-ken Gakumubu) (1940c) Futatabi hyōjungo mondai ni tsuite II [Once more concerning the standard language II]. *Ryūkyū shinpō [Ryukyu News]* (16 June 2004).
Okinawa Kyōiku I'inkai (1965–1977) *Okinawa kenshi [History of Okinawa Prefecture]*. Tokyo: Kokusho Kankō-kai.
Okinawa Taimusu (2006) Hanasu koto o tanoshimō [Lets enjoy talking]. *Okinawa taimusu [Okinawa Times]* (18 September 2006).
Ōkubo, T. (1972) *Mori Arinori zenshū [Collected Works of Mori Arinori]*. Tokyo: Senbundō Shoten.
Onai, T. (2003) *Zainichi burajirujin no kyōiku to hoiku [School Education and Day Nursery of Brazilian Residents]*. Tokyo: Akashi.
Ōno, S. (1976) Nihongo no kenkyū no rekishi 2. Meiji ikō [The history of the study of Japanese 2. From Meiji onwards]. In T. Sibata and S. Ōno (eds) *Iwanami kōza nihongo [Iwanami's Course on Japanese]* (Vol. I, pp. 231–274). Tokyo: Iwanami.
Ōno, S. (1983) *Nihongo no sekai [The World of Japanese]*. Tokyo: Chūō Kōron.
Osa, S. (1992) Nisshin sensō ni okeru kanji mondai no kaiten [The turning point in Chinese character problems during the Sino-Japanese War]. *Hisutoria [Historia]* 136, 1–22.
Osa, S. (1998) *Kindai nihon to kokugo nashonarizumu [Modern Japan and National Language Nationalism]*. Tokyo: Kikawakō Bunkan.
Osumi, M. (2001) Language and identity in Okinawa today. In M. Goebel Noguchi and S. Fotos (eds) *Studies in Japanese Bilingualism* (pp. 68–97). Clevedon: Multilingual Matters.
Ōta, H. and Tsuboya, M. (2005) Gakkō ni kayowanai kodomotachi [Children not attending school]. In T. Miyajima and H. Ōta (eds) *Gaikokujin no kodomo to nihon no kyōiku [Foreign Children and Education in Japan]* (pp. 17–36). Tokyo: Tokyo Daigaku Shuppan-kai.
Ota, M. (2000) *Essays on Okinawa Problems*. Okinawa: Yui Publishing.
Oyafuso, K. (1986) Yanagi Muneyoshi no Chōsen-kan to Okinawa-kan [Yanagi Muneyoshi's Views on Korea and Okinawa]. *Kokusai kankeigaku kenkyū [Studies of International Relations]* 12, 27–45.
Peng, F. and Geiser, P. (1977) *The Ainu. Past and Present*. Hiroshima: Bunka Hyoron.
Phillips, S.U. (2000) Constructing a Tongan nation-state through language ideology in the courtroom. In P.V. Kroskrity (ed.) *Regimes of Language* (pp. 229–257). Santa Fe: School of American Research Press.
Pyle, K.B. (1969) *The New Generation in Meiji-Japan. Problems of Cultural Identity 1885–1895*. Stanford: Stanford University Press.
Rampton, B. (2006) *Language in Late Modernity. Interaction in an Urban School*. Cambridge: Cambridge University Press.

Ramsey, R.S. (2004) The Japanese language and the making of tradition. *Japanese Language and Literature* 38, 81–110.
Ruhlen, M. (1987) *A Guide to the World's Languages*. Palo Alto: Stanford University Press.
Rustow, D. (1968) Language, modernization, and nationhood. An attempt at typology. In J.A. Fishman, C.A. Ferguson and J. Das Gupta (eds) *Language Problems of Developing Nations* (pp. 27–35). NY: Wiley.
Ryan, M.G. (1965) *Japan's First Modern Novel. Ukigumo*. NY: Columbia University Press.
Ryang, S. (1997) *North Koreans in Japan*. Boulder: Westview Press.
Ryang, S. (2009) *Diaspora without Homeland. Koreans in Japan*. Berkeley: Berkeley University Press.
Ryūkyū Shinpō (2000) Uchinaaguchi gakkō de mo jidai keishō mokuteki ni fukyū kyōgikai setsuritsu [Revitalization society established aiming at transmitting Uchinaaguchi to the following generation also at school]. *Ryūkyū shinpō [Ryukyu News]* (22 October 2000).
Said, E.S. (1978) *Orientalism*. London: Routledge and Kegan Paul.
Sakhaee Kashani, S. (2006) Colonial migration to the 'Manchester of the Orient'. The origins of the Korean community in Osaka, Japan, 1920–1945. In S.I. Lee, S. Murphy-Shigematsu and H. Befu (eds) *Japan's Diversity Dilemmas. Ethnicity, Citizenship, and Education* (pp. 168–189). NY: iUniverse.
Sanada, S. (1987) *Hyōjungo no seiritsu jijō [The Circumstances of Standard Language Formation]*. Tokyo: PHP
Sasse, H.J. (1992) Theory of language death. In M. Brenzinger (ed.) *Language Death. Factual and Theoretical Explorations with Special Reference to East Africa* (pp. 7–30). Berlin: Mouton de Gruyter.
Sayce, A.H. (1880) *Introduction to the Science of Language*. London: Kegan Paul.
Seeley, C. (1991) *A History of Writing in Japan*. Leiden: E.J. Brill.
Sellek, Y. (1997) Nikkeijin. The phenomenon of return migration. In M. Weiner (ed.) *Japan's Minorities. The Illusion of Homogeneity* (pp. 178–210). London: Routledge.
Sen, A. (2006) *Identity and Violence*. NY: Norton.
Shi, G. (1993) *Shokuminchi shihai to nihongo [Management of the Colonies and Japanese]*. Tokyo: Sangensha.
Shibatani, M. (1990) *The Languages of Japan*. Cambridge: Cambridge University Press.
Shiga, N. (1946) Kokugo mondai [The national language problem]. *Kaizō [Reconstruction]* 4, 94–97.
Shikama, A. (2008) Integration policy towards migrants in Japan with a focus on language. In P. Heinrich and Y. Sugita (eds) *Japanese as Foreign Language in the Age of Globalization* (pp. 51–64). München: Iudicium.
Shimakutuba Kentō I'inkai (2008) *Shimakutuba Kentō I'inkai setchi yōkō [Outlines for the Community Language Investigation Committee]*. Naha: Shimakutuba Kentō I'inkai.
Shimakutuba Kentō I'inkai (2009) *Shimakutuba Kentō I'inkai hōkokusho [Report of the Community Language Investigation Committee]*. Naha: Shimakutuba Kentō I'inkai.
Shimizu, Y. (1990) Kindai 'kokugo'-shi kenkyū no shiten [A historical viewpoint on the study of 'national language' in modernity]. *Kokubungaku kaishaku to kanshō [Interpretation and Appreciation of National Literature]* 55, 121–126.
Shimizu, Y. (2002) Kokugo kara kokugogaku e [From national language to national linguistics]. In K. Noyama (ed.) *Gengo bunka kenkyū [Studies in Language Culture]* (Vol. I, pp. 146–158). Tokyo: Hosō Daigaku Daigakuin Kyōzai.
Shinzato, K. (2001) Okinawa ni okeru hyōjungo seisaku no kōzai [The merits and demerits of standard language policy in Okinawa]. In F. Inoue, K. Shinozaki, T. Kobayashi

and T. Ōnishi (eds) *Ryūkyū hōgen-kō [Considerations on the Ryukyu Dialects]* (Vol. III, pp. 238–244). Tokyo: Yumani Shobō.
SHSJI (Shimakutuba no Hi Seitei Jikkō I'inkai) (2005) *2005 nen 'shimakutuba nu hi' sengen [Declaration of 'Community Language Day' 2005]*. Naha: Shimakutuba no Hi Seitei Jikkō I'inkai.
Shūgi'in (2008) *Ketsugi dai 169 kai kokkai 1, Ainu minzoku o senjūminzoku to suru koto o motomeru ketsugian [Resolution no. 1, 169th Diet, Resolution Calling for the Recognition of the Ainu People as an Indigenous People]* – Online document: http://www.shugiin.go.jp/itdb_gian.nsf/html/gian/honbun/ketsugian/g16913001.htm. Accessed 27.9.11.
Sibata, T. (1977) Hyōjungo, kyōtsūgo, hōgen [Standard language, common language, dialect]. In Bunkachō (ed.) *Hyōjungo to hōgen [Standard Language and Dialect]* (pp. 22–32). Tokyo: Bunkachō.
Siddle, R. (1995a) The Ainu. Construction of an image. In J.C. Maher and G. Macdonald (eds) *Diversity in Japanese Culture and Language* (pp. 73–94). London: Kegan Paul International.
Siddle, R. (1995b) Deprivation and resistance. Ainu movements in modern Japan (with K. Kitara, My heritage of pride and struggle). In J.C. Maher and G. Macdonald (eds) *Diversity in Japanese Culture and Language* (pp. 147–159). London: Kegan Paul International.
Siddle, R. (1999) *Race, Resistance and the Ainu of Japan*. London: Routledge.
Silverstein, M. (1976) Shifters, linguistic categories, and cultural description. In K.H. Basso and H.A. Selby (eds) *Meaning and Anthropology* (pp. 11–55). Albuquerque: University of New Mexico Press.
Silverstein, M. (1979) Language structure and linguistic ideology. In P.R. Clyne, W.F. Hanks and C.L. Hofbauer (eds) *The Elements. A Parasession on Linguistic Units and Levels* (pp. 193–247). Chicago: Chicago Linguistics Society.
Silverstein, M. (1985) Language and the culture of gender. At the intersection of structure, usage and ideology. In E. Mertz and R.J. Parmentier (eds) *Semiotic Mediation* (pp. 219–259). Orlando: Academic Press.
Silverstein, M. (1993) Metapragmatic discourse and metapragmatic function. In J.A. Lucy (ed.) *Reflexive Language. Reported Speech and Metapragmatics* (pp. 33–58). Cambridge: Cambridge University Press.
Silverstein, M. (2000) Whorfianism and the linguistic imagination of nationality. In P.V. Kroskrity (ed.) *Regimes of Language* (pp. 85–138). Santa Fe: SAR Press.
Skutnabb-Kangas, T. (2000) *Linguistic Genocide in Education or Worldwide Diversity and Human Rights*. Mahwah: Lawrence Erlbaum Associates.
Smits, G. (1999) *Visions of Ryukyu. Identity and Ideology in Early-Modern Thought and Politics*. Honolulu: University of Hawai'i Press.
Soviak, E. (1963) The case of Baba Tatsui. Western enlightenment, social change and the early Meiji intellectual. *Monumenta Nipponica* 18, 191–235.
Statistics Bureau (2008) *Japan Statistical Yearbook 2010* – Online document: http://www.stat.go.jp/english/data/nenkan/index.htm. Accessed 27.9.11.
Steele, W.M. (1995) Nationalism and cultural pluralism in modern Japan. Sōetsu Yanagi and the Mingei Movement. In J.C. Maher and G. Macdonald (eds) *Diversity in Japanese Culture and Language* (pp. 27–48). London: Kegan Paul.
Sugita, Y. (2007) Language revitalization or language fossilization. Some suggestions for language documentation from the viewpoint of interactional linguistics. In P.K. Austin, O. Bond and D. Nathan (eds) *Proceedings of Conference on Language Documentation and Linguistic Theory* (pp. 243–250). London: SOAS.

Sugita, Y. (2010) Jissen to shite no gengo no kiroku hozon. Uchinaa no tagengo shakai saisei e mukete [Documentation of language as practice. Towards a regeneration of bilingual Uchinaa society]. In P. Heinrich and S. Matsuo (eds) *Higashi ajia ni okeru gengo fukkō [Language Revitalization in East Asia]* (pp. 203–232). Tokyo: Sangensha.

Sugita, Y. (2011) The emerging borderless community in the local radio in Uchinaa. In P. Heinrich and C. Galan (eds) *Language Life in Japan. Transformations and Prospects* (pp. 50–76). London: Routledge.

Sugito, S. (2009) Lexical aspects of the modernization of Japanese. In F. Coulmas (ed.) *Language Adaptation* (pp. 116–126). Cambridge: Cambridge University Press.

Sugiyama, H. (1940a) Ryūkyū no hyōjungo [The standard language of Ryukyu]. *Tokyo asahi shinbun [Tokyo Asahi Newspaper]* (22 May 1940).

Sugiyama, H. (1940b) Bungei jihyō [Comments on current literature]. *Kaizō [Reconstruction]* 22, 288–299.

Sugiyama, H. (1940c) Bungei jihyō [Comments on current literature]. *Kaizō [Reconstruction]* 22, 262–273.

Sugiyama, H. and Tanaka, T. (1941) Okinawa ronsō shūketsu ni tsuite [Concerning the termination of the dialect debate]. *Gekkan mingei [Monthly Folk Art]* 1941. Reprinted in K. Tanigawa (ed.) (1970) *Waga Okinawa [Our Okinawa]*. Tokyo: Mokujisha: 156–167.

Suzuki, H. (1994) Ueda Kazutoshi to W.D. Hoittonii [Ueda Kazutoshi and W.D. Whitney]. *Kokugogaku [Studies in the Japanese Language]* 176, 1–13.

Suzuki, T. (1996) *Narrating the Self. Fictions of Japanese Modernity*. Stanford: Stanford University Press.

Swale, A. (2000) *The Political Thought of Mori Arinori. A Study in Meiji Conservatism*. Richmond: Japan Library.

Tai, E. (2007) Multicultural education in Japan. *Japan Focus* – Online document: http://www.japanfocus.org/-Eika-Tai¿2618. Accessed 27.9.11.

Taira, K. (1997) Troubled national identity. The Ryukyuans/Okinawans. In M. Weiner (ed.) *Japan's Minorities. The Illusion of Homogeneity* (pp. 140–177). London: Routledge.

Tajiri, E., Tanaka, H., Yoshino, T., Yamanishi, Y. and Yamada, I. (2004) *Gaikokujin no teijū to nihongo kyōiku [Foreign Residence and Japanese Language Education]*. Tokyo: Hituzi Syobō.

Takaesu, Y. (2005) Uchinaa Yamatuguchi [Uchinaa Japanese]. In S. Sanada and H. Shōji (eds) *Jiten. Nihon no tagengo shakai [Encyclopaedia of Japan's Multilingual Society]* (pp. 265–268). Tokyo: Iwanami.

Takahashi, M. and Vaipae, S.S. (1996) *'Gaijin' seito ga yatte kita ['Foreign' Pupils Have Turned Up]*. Tokyo: Taishūkan.

Takamatsu, K. (1900) *Meiji bungaku. Genbun itchi [Meiji Literature. Genbun Itchi]*. Tokyo: Taiheiyō Bungakusha.

Takebe, Y. (1977) Kokugo kokuji mondai no yūrai [Origins of national language and script problems]. In S. Ōno and T. Sibata (eds) *Iwanami kōza nihongo [Iwanami's Course on Japanese]* (Vol. III, pp. 259–308). Tokyo: Iwanami.

Tamura, S. (2000) *The Ainu Language*. Tokyo: Sanseido.

Tamura, S. (2001) *Ainugo Saru hōgen no onsei shiryō 1 [Ainu Language. Audio Recordings of the Saru Dialect 1]*. Kyoto: ELPR.

Tanaka, A. (1983) *Tokyogo. Sono seiritsu to tenkai [Tokyo Language. Formation and Development]*. Tokyo: Meiji Shoin.

Tanaka, A. (1999) *Nihongo no isō to isōsa [Japanese Registers and Register Variation]*. Tokyo: Meiji Shoin.

Tanaka, A. (2001) *Kindai nihongo no bunpō to hyōgen [Modern Japanese Grammar and its Usage]*. Tokyo: Meiji shoin.

Tanaka, H. (1995) *Zainichi gaikokujin. Hō no kabe, kokoro no mizo [Foreign Residents. Legal Barriers and Psychological Gaps]*. Tokyo: Iwanami.
Tanaka, K. (1978) *Gengo kara mita minzoku to kokka [Nation and State from the Perspective of Language]*. Tokyo: Iwanami.
Tanaka, K. (ed.) (1997) *Gengo, kokka, soshite kenryoku [Language, State and Authority]*. Tokyo: Shinyōsha.
Tanaka, K. (1989) *Kokkago o koete [Beyond Nation-State Language]*. Tokyo: Chikuma Shobō.
Tanaka, K. (2000) Kōyōgo to wa nanika [What is official language]. *Gekkan gengo [Monthly Language]* 29, 40–46.
Tanaka, L. (2004) *Gender, Language and Culture. A Study of Japanese Television Interview Discourse*. Amsterdam: John Benjamins.
Tanaka, Y. (2001) Kyōshū no 'nihon' [Nostalgic 'Japan']. *Edge* 12, 12–15.
Tani, Y. (2000) *Dai-tōa kyōeiken to nihongo [Greater East Asia Co-Prosperity Sphere and Japanese]*. Tokyo: Keisō Shobō.
Tanigawa, K. (ed.) (1970) *Waga Okinawa [Our Okinawa]*. Tokyo: Mokujisha.
Thompson, E.P. (1984) *Studies in the Theory of Ideology*. Berkeley: University of California Press.
Thompson, E.P. (1990) *Ideology and Modern Culture. Critical Social Theory in the Era of Mass Communication*. Cambridge: Polity Press.
Tōjō, M. (1927) *Dai-nihon hōgen chizu [Dialect Map of Greater Japan]*. Tokyo: Ikuei Shoin.
Tōjō, M. (1938) *Hōgen to hōgengaku [Dialect and Dialectology]*. Tokyo: Shun'yōdō Shoten.
Tōjō, M. (1940) Kokugogaku to nantō hōgen kenkyū [National linguistics and the study of the dialects of the Southern Islands]. *Gekkan mingei [Monthly Folk Art]* 1940, 61–65.
Tokieda, M. (1940) *Kokugogaku-shi [History of National Linguistics]*. Tokyo: Iwanami.
Tokieda, M. (1962) *Kokugo mondai no tame ni [For the Sake of National Language Problems]*. Tokyo: Tōkyō Daigaku Shuppan.
Tomozawa, A. (2001) Japan's hidden bilinguals. The languages of 'war orphans' and their families after repatriation from China. In M. Goebel Noguchi and S. Fotos (eds) *Studies in Japanese Bilingualism* (pp. 133–163). Clevedon: Multilingual Matters.
Townson, M. (1992) *Mother-Tongue and Fatherland. Language and Politics in German*. Manchester: Manchester University Press.
Tsitsipis, L.D. (1998) *A Linguistic Anthropology of Praxis and Language Shift*. Oxford: Clarendon Press.
Tsitsipis, L.D. (2003) Implicit linguistic ideology and the erasure of Arvanitika (Greek-Albanian) discourse. *Journal of Pragmatics* 35, 539–558.
Twine, N. (1978) The genbunitchi movement. Its origin, development, and conclusion. *Monumenta Nipponica* 33, 333–356.
Twine, N. (1988) Standardizing written Japanese. A factor in modernization. *Monumenta Nipponica* 43, 429–454.
Twine, N. (1991) *Language and the Modern State. The Reform of Written Japanese*. London: Routledge.
Ueda, K. (1895a) Kokugo to kokka to [National Language and the State]. In K. Ueda (ed.) *Kokugo no tame [For the National Language]* (pp. 1–28). Tokyo: Fusanbō.
Ueda, K. (1895b) Kokugo kenkyū ni tsuite [On the study of the national language]. In K. Ueda *Kokugo no tame [For the National Language]* (pp. 29–50). Tokyo: Fusanbō.
Ueda, K. (1895c) Hyōjungo ni tsuite [On the standard language]. In K. Ueda *Kokugo no tame [For the National Language]* (pp. 51–66). Tokyo: Fusanbō.
Ueda, K. (1895d) Kokugo kaigi ni tsuite [On a national language conference]. In K. Ueda *Kokugo no tame [For the National Language]* (pp. 282–298). Tokyo: Fusanbō.

Ueda, K. (1903) Kokugo ni tsuite nihon kokumin no toraerubeki san dai-hōshin [On the three main directions on national language Japanese nationals should follow]. In K. Ueda *Kokugo no tame dai-ni [For the National Language Part Two]* (pp. 96–100). Tokyo: Fusanbō.
Ueda, M. (1976) *Modern Japanese Writers*. Stanford: Stanford University Press.
Uemura, Y. (2003) *The Ryukyuan Language*. Kyoto: ELPR.
UNESCO (2009) *Interactive Atlas of the World's Languages in Danger* – Online document: http://www.unesco.org/culture/ich/index.php?pg=00206. Accessed 27.9.11.
Unger, J.M. (1996) *Literacy and Script Reform in Occupied Japan. Reading between the Lines*. Oxford: Oxford University Press.
Utada, H. (2008) Shohyō [Book review]. K. Shibuya and I. Kojima (eds) (2007) Gengoken no riron to jissen [Theory and Practice of Language Rights]. *Shakai gengogaku [Sociolinguistics]* 8, 145–56.
Vasishth, A. (1997) A model minority. The Chinese community in Japan. In M. Weiner (ed.) *Japan's Minorities. The Illusion of Homogeneity* (pp. 108–139). London: Routledge.
Voegelin, C.F. (1977) *Classification and Index of the World's Languages*. NY: Elsevier.
Walker, B.L. (2006) *The Conquest of Ainu Lands*. Berkeley: University of California Press.
Weiner, M. (1989) *The Origins of the Korean Community in Japan, 1910–1923*. Manchester: Manchester University Press.
Weinreich, M. (1945) Der YIVO un di problemen fun undzer tsayt. *YIVO Bletter* 1, 3–18.
Wetherall, W. (1987) Foreigners in Japan. In Kodansha (eds) *Encyclopedia of Japan* (Vol. II, pp. 313–314). Tokyo: Kodansha.
Wetzel, P.J. (2004) *Keigo in Modern Japan. Polite Language from Meiji to Present*. Honolulu: University of Hawai'i Press.
Winchester, M. (2009) On the dawn of a new national Ainu policy. The 'Ainu as a situation' today. *The Asia-Pacific Journal* 41-3-09 – Online document: http://www.japanfocus.org/-Mark-Winchester/3234. Accessed 27.9.11.
Woolard, K.A. (1985) Language variation and cultural hegemony. Towards an integration of sociolinguistics and social theory. *American Ethnologist* 16, 268–278.
Woolard, K.A. (1998) Introduction. Language ideology as a field of inquiry. In B.B. Schieffelin, K.A. Woolard and P.V. Kroskrity (eds) *Language Ideologies. Practice and Theory* (pp. 3–47). Oxford: Oxford University Press.
Wright, S. (2007) The right to speak one's own language. Reflections on theory and practice. *Language Policy* 6, 203–224.
Yamada, B. (1889a) Genbun itchi kogoto [Nagging about genbun itchi]. *Bun [Letters]* 2, 394–397.
Yamada, B. (1889b) Genbun itchi-ron ni tsuki Kojima Kenkichi-shi no bakugeki ni kotae [On the debate on genbun itchi and answering to Kojima Kenkichi's refutation]. *Bun [Letters]* 2, 532–538.
Yamada, B. (1889c) Kojima Kenkichi-shi no futatabi bunshō o ron zu o yonde [Re-reading Kojima Kenkichi's debating on writing]. *Bun [Letters]* 2, 599–600.
Yamada, B. (1889d) Genbun itchi-ron aru toi [Certain questions about the debate on genbun itchi]. *Bun [Letters]* 2, 607–609.
Yamada, B. (1889e) Kojima Kenkichi-shi oyobi sono hoka no hi-genbun itchi ronsha soshi e [To Kojima Kenkichi and the other obstructing critics of genbun itchi]. *Bun [Letters]* 2, 663–667.
Yamada, B. (1889f) Kojima Kenkichi-shi oyobi sono hoka no hi-genbun itchi ronsha soshi e [To Kojima Kenkichi and the other obstructing critics of genbun itchi]. *Bun [Letters]* 2, 732–736.
Yamada, Y. (1935) *Kokugogaku shiyō [Main History of National Linguistics]*. Tokyo: Iwanami.

Yamamoto, M. (1981) *Genbun itchi no rekishi ronkō [A Study of the History of Genbun Itchi].* Tokyo: Ōfūsha.
Yanagi, M. (1940a) Kokugo mondai ni kanshi Okinawa-ken gakumubu ni kotaeru no sho [A note answering to the Department for Educational Affairs of Okinawa Prefecture on the problem of the national language]. *Ryūkyū shinpō [Ryukyu News]* (15 January 1940).
Yanagi, M. (1940b) Okinawajin ni utaeru no sho [A note of appeal to the people of Okinawa]. *Gekkan mingei [Monthly Folk Art]* 1940, 64–70.
Yanagi, M. (1940c) Okinawago no mondai [The problem of Okinawan]. *Tōkyō asahi shinbun [Tokyo Asahi Newspaper]* (1 June 1940).
Yanagi, M. (1940d) Aete gakumubu no sekinin o tou I [Daring to question the responsibility of the Department of Educational Affairs I]. *Ryūkyū shinpō [Ryukyu News]* (2 August 1940).
Yanagi, M. (1940e) Aete gakumubu no sekinin o tou II [Daring to question the responsibility of the Department for Educational Affairs II]. *Ryūkyū shinpō [Ryukyu News]* (3 August 1940).
Yanagita, K. (1940) Okinawa-ken no hyōjungo kyōiku [Standard language education in Okinawa Prefecture]. *Gekkan mingei [Monthly Folk Art]* 1940. Reprinted in K. Tanigawa (ed.) (1970) *Waga Okinawa [Our Okinawa]* (pp. 51–55). Tokyo: Mokujisha.
Yasuda, T. (1997a) *Shokuminchi no naka no 'kokugogaku' ['National Linguistics' in the Colonies].* Tokyo: Sangensha.
Yasuda, T. (1997b) *Teikoku nihon no gengo hensei [Language Regimentation in Imperial Japan].* Tokyo: Seishiki Shobō.
Yasuda, T. (1999a) *'Kokugo' to 'hōgen' no aida [Between 'National Language' and 'Dialect'].* Tokyo: Jinbun Shoin.
Yasuda, T. (1999b) *'Gengo' no kōchiku [The Construction of 'Language'].* Tokyo: Sangensha.
Yasuda, T. (2000a) *Kindai nihon gengo-shi saikō [Reconsidering the History of Modern Japanese].* Tokyo: Sangensha.
Yasuda, T. (2000b) 'Gengo seisaku' no hassei. Gengo mondai isshiki no keipu [The dawn of 'language planning'. A genealogy of language problem awareness]. *Jinbun gakuhō [Humanities Academic Report]* 83, 143–183.
Yoshida, S. (1940a) Aigan-ken [Treasured prefecture]. In *Okinawa asahi shinbun [Okinawa Asahi Newspaper]* (10 January 1940).
Yoshida, S. (1940b) Yanagi ni ataeru [Informing Yanagi]. In *Okinawa nippō [Okinawa Daily]* (16 January 1940).
Yoshimi, K. (1889) Bun ni tsuite [On letters]. *Bun [Letters]* 2, 351–353.
Yoshizawa, N. (1955) Kokugogaku [National language study]. In Kokuritsu Kokugo Kenkyūjo (eds) *Kokugo nenkan. Shōwa 30 nenhan [Yearbook of National Language. 1955 Edition]* (pp. 88–94). Tokyo: Dainihon Tosho.

Index

abstand language 85, 94, 140
Ainu kyōiku seido (Ainu Education System) 95
Ainu Mosir 83, 93–95, 98–99, 155
Ainu language 95–98, 140–143, 154
   Hokkaido Ainu 93–94, 141, 153
   Kurile Ainu 93–94, 141
   Sakhalin Ainu 93–94, 141
Allgemeiner Deutscher Sprachverein (General German Language Association) 61
Amami language 85, 139, 146–147
Amane, Nishi 35, 44
Anderson, Benedict 4, 46
Association of Korean Residents in Japan (*Chonryon*) 164–165
ausbau language 85

Baba, Tatsui 32–36, 44

Chamberlain, Basil Hall 60, 86, 134
Chinese language 50, 57, 63–64, 68, 115
Cold War 100
comparative linguistics 60–61
compulsory education 21, 46, 61, 65–67, 69, 72, 88, 95–96, 101, 132–133, 137, 140, 167
conjunctions 45, 50–51, 74, 76, 78, 80
critical linguistics 14–17
cultural liberty 3, 182

dai-hōgen (greater dialect) 86–87, 129, 155
Datong School 164
Dialectology 86
Diglossia 6–7, 24, 29, 41, 108, 132–133, 144
Dojin Kyōikujo (Aboriginal Education Centres) 95

Elementary School Ordinance (*Shōgakkorei*) 67, 72, 75

Empowerment 9–12, 20, 32, 41, 55, 120–121, 131, 148, 170, 178
English 1, 13–14, 20–42, 55, 64, 89, 101–102, 108–112, 114, 143–146, 177
enlightenment 9, 32, 35, 44, 46–47, 52, 114, 119

Fija, Byron 1
Folklorization 142
Fukuzawa, Yukichi 3, 44, 47
Futabatei, Shimei 44, 45, 47, 57

Gabelentz, Georg von der 60, 75
Gaikokujin tōrokurei (Alien Registration Law) 163
Gakkō kyōiku shidō yōryō (Outline for Guidance of School Education) 160
Genbun itchi-kai (Genbun Itchi Club) 45, 71
gabun (elegant writing) 43–44, 51–53, 55–56, 64, 80
gendered particles 74–75, 78–79, 81

Hachijo language 1, 139, 170
Henry, Joseph 23
Herder, Johann Gottfried 5, 35, 63, 117
Higashionna, Kanjun 124–125, 127, 129
hōgen fuda (dialect tag) 90–91, 105, 160
hōgen ronsō (dialect debate) 124–131
Hōgen torishimari-rei (Dialect Regulation Ordinance) 89–90
Hokkaidō kyūdojin hogo-hō (Hokkaido Former Aboriginal Protection Act) 95–96, 152
Honorifics 74–75, 80–81, 108
horobiyuku minzoku (dying people) 96
Hoshina, Kōichi 37, 72

Humboldt, Wilhelm von 5, 35, 61, 117
Hyōjungo reikō undō (Movement for the Enforcement of Standard Language) 90–91, 104, 160

Identity 3, 5, 35, 40, 46, 81, 91, 100, 103, 105–106, 133, 137, 145, 150, 167
Iha, Fuyū 89, 124–126, 128
Inequality 15–16, 22, 56, 83, 96, 134, 136, 178, 180–182

Japanese Sign Language (*nihon shuwa*) 139–140
Japonic 85, 94

Katō, Hiroyuki 60, 70–71
kanji (Chinese characters) 4, 28–29, 37, 44, 47, 67, 72–74, 95, 108
Kayano, Shigeru 97, 142, 152
kikokushijo (repatriate children) 168
Kindaichi, Haruhiko 109, 118–120
Kinjō, Chōei 87
Kojima, Kenkichi 48–54, 56
kokugaku (national philology) 33, 35, 64, 115
Kokugo Chōsa I'inkai (National Language Research Council) 45–46, 58, 62, 66, 69, 70–82
kokugogaku (national linguistics) 35–36, 85–86
kokugo mondai (national language problems) 4, 107–114
Kokugo Kenkyū-shitsu (Seminar for National Language Studies) 66
Kokugo no tame (For the National Language) 63
Kokumin kyōiku (National Citizen Education) 65, 105
Kokumin seishin sōdōin undo (National Spiritual Mobilization Movement) 91
Kokuritsu Kokugo Kenkyūjo (National Institute for Japanese Language) 109
Kokuritsu Kyūdojin Gakkō (National Schools for Former Aborigines) 96
kokusaika (internationalization) 177, 179
Korean language 164–166
Korean Resident Union (*Mindan*) 164
Korean War 99, 101
kotodama (language spirit) 36

Kunigami language 85, 139, 146
Kushi, Fusako 133
Kyōkasho Henshūbu (Textbook Compilation Division) 102–103

linguistic anthropology 14–16
lost decade 107

McArthur, Douglas 101
Mannheim, Karl 10–11, 16–17
Marx, Karl 10, 17
Matsuda, Michiyuki 85
Meiroku zasshi (*Meiji Six Journal*) 44
Migration 93, 97, 138, 143, 147, 150–151, 158, 162–163, 166, 179, 182
Miller, Roy Andrew 110, 119–121
Ministry of Education's Bureau of Higher Education (*Senmon Gakumu-kyoku*) 67
Miyako language 19, 85, 91, 139, 146–148, 157
Miyara, Shinshō 156, 159–160
Mori, Arinori 20, 21–42, 55, 62, 107–108, 110, 112–118
Mother tongue (*Muttersprache*) 40, 62–63, 81, 87
Müller, Max 75

Nakagawa, Hiroshi 143, 153–154
Nakaima, Hirokazu 160
Newspaper 1, 21, 45–46, 48, 125, 132–133, 152, 157
Nihon mingei kyōkai (Folk Craft Society Japan) 124–125, 130
Nikkeijin 150, 162, 166–169

Ogasawara Creole English 143–146, 148
Okinawa henkan undō (Movement for the Return of Okinawa) 104
Okinawa Kyōshokuin-kai (Okinawa Teachers' Association) 104
Okinawa shijun-kai (Okinawan Advisory Council) 102
Okinawa taiwa (*Okinawa Conversation*) 89, 134
Old Japanese 128
Orient 7–8, 115
Ōtsuki, Fumihiko 70–71, 76

Pacific War 99, 111, 144, 145, 162–163
Perry, Matthew 3
personal pronouns 33, 74–75, 77–78, 80

Rōmaji-kai (Roman Letter Club) 48
Russo-Japanese War 62
rusty speaker 137, 142, 147–148
Ryukyu Kingdom 84, 137
Ryūkyū shobun (Ryukyu dispensation) 85, 88, 132

San Francisco Peace Treaty 163
Sayce, Archibald H. 40
semi-speaker 137, 142, 147–148
Shiga, Naoya 107–121
Shimakutuba Kentō I'inkai (Community Language Deliberation Committee) 157
shimkutuba no hi (Community Language Day) 156–157, 159
Shōsetsu shinzui (The Essence of the Novel) 44, 60
Shō, Tai 84–85
Shutsunyūkoku kanri oyobi nanmin ninteihō (Immigration Control and Refugee Recognition Act) 166–167
Sino-Japanese 7, 37, 43, 65, 67
Sino-Japanese War 62, 91, 47
sōgōteki na gakushū (integrated study lessons) 137
Sokoku fukki undō (Movement for a Return to the Fatherland) 104
solidarity 3, 182
Spencer, Herbert 29–30, 98

Taira Tatsuo 100
Taiwa Denshūjo (Conversation Training Centre) 89

Teikoku Kyōiku-kai (Imperial Society for Education) 70–71
Tōjō, Misao 86–87, 124, 126–127, 129
token speakers 142
Tsubouchi, Shōyō 44–45, 60

Uchinaaguchi (Okinawan) 1, 87, 89, 139, 146–148, 156–158, 160
Uchinaaguchi fukyū kyōgikai (Society for Uchinaaguchi Revitalization) 156–157
Ueda, Kazutoshi 37, 46, 58–72, 75, 77, 81–82, 85–86, 110, 116
Ukigumo (Drifting Clouds) 44–45, 47
US Occupation Period 84, 99–100, 102–104, 107, 129, 163

war orphans (zanryū koji) 162
Whitney, Dwight 23–24, 26–29, 31, 34, 37–38, 65
World War II 45, 77, 83–84, 92, 99, 106–107, 109, 111–112, 115–116, 145, 163–164

Yaeyama language 85, 91, 146–148, 157
Yamada, Bimyō 44–45, 48–57
Yanagi, Muneyoshi 124–130
Yanagita, Kunio 124, 127–128
Yokohama Yamate Chinese School 164
Yonaguni language 85, 135–136, 146–147, 157
Yoshida, Shien 124–126, 128–130

zainichi (resident Koreans) 162–165

For Product Safety Concerns and Information please contact our EU Authorised Representative:

Easy Access System Europe

Mustamäe tee 50

10621 Tallinn

Estonia

gpsr.requests@easproject.com

www.ingramcontent.com/pod-product-compliance
Lightning Source LLC
Chambersburg PA
CBHW070608300426
44113CB00010B/1454

9781847696564